FAITH & WORD EDITION
BLEST ARE WE

Faith comes from what is heard,
and what is heard comes through the word of Christ.

Romans 10:17

Series Authors

Rev. Richard N. Fragomeni, Ph.D.
Maureen Gallagher, Ph.D.
Jeannine Goggin, M.P.S.
Michael P. Horan, Ph.D.

Scripture Co-editor and Consultant
Maria Pascuzzi, S.S.L., S.T.D.

Multicultural Consultant
Angela Erevia, M.C.D.P., M.R.E.

The Subcommittee on the Catechism, United States Conference of Catholic Bishops, has found this catechetical series, copyright 2008, to be in conformity with the *Catechism of the Catholic Church*.

Cincinnati, Ohio

FAITH & WORD EDITION

BLEST ARE WE®

Contributing Writers

Theresa Flynn-Nason
Kathleen Whaley, M.A.
Scripture Background: Gloria S. Fuzia
Faith in Action: Kathleen N. Burke
Feasts and Seasons: Marianne K. Lenihan
Our Catholic Heritage: Joyce A. Crider

Advisory Board

William C. Allegri, M.A., Patricia M. Feeley, S.S.J., M.A., Edmund F. Gordon, Patricia A. Hoffmann, Cris V. Villapando, D.Min.

Consultants

Joy Villotti-Biedrzycki, Margaret J. Borders, M.R.S., Kelly O'Lague Dulka, M.S.W., Diane Hardick, M.A., Rev. David C. Hubba, Debra Schurko, Linda S. Tonelli, M.Ed.

Music Advisor

GIA Publications: Michael A. Cymbala, Alec Harris, Robert W. Piercy

Nihil Obstat

M. Kathleen Flanagan, S.C., Ph.D.
Censor Librorum

Imprimatur

✠ Most Reverend Arthur J. Serratelli
Bishop of Paterson

April 28, 2008

The *nihil obstat* and *imprimatur* are official declarations that a book or pamphlet is free of doctrinal and moral error. No implication is contained therein that those who have granted the *nihil obstat* and *imprimatur* agree with the contents, opinions, or statements expressed.

Acknowledgments

Excerpts from the *New American Bible* with Revised New Testament and Psalms Copyright © 1991, 1986, 1970 Confraternity of Christian Doctrine, Inc., Washington, DC. Used with permission. All rights reserved. No portion of the *New American Bible* may be reprinted without permission in writing from the copyright holder.

All adaptations of Scripture are based on the *New American Bible* with Revised New Testament and Psalms Copyright © 1991, 1986, 1970 Confraternity of Christian Doctrine, Inc., Washington, DC.

Excerpts from the English translation of *Rite of Confirmation (Second Edition)* © 1975, International Committee on English in the Liturgy, Inc. (ICEL); excerpts from the English translation of *Rite of Holy Week* © 1970, ICEL; excerpts from the English translation of *Rite of Penance* © 1974, ICEL; excerpts from the English translation of *The Roman Missal* © 2010, ICEL. All rights reserved.

Excerpts from *Catholic Household Blessings and Prayers* (revised edition) © 2007, United States Conference of Catholic Bishops, Washington, D.C.

Music selections copyrighted and/or administered by GIA Publications are used with permission of GIA Publications, Inc., 7404 So. Mason Avenue, Chicago, IL 60638-9927. Please refer to songs for specific copyright dates and information.

Chapter II from *Thoughts in Solitude* by Thomas Merton, p. 79, Copyright © 1956, 1958 by The Abbey of Our Lady of Gethsemani. Reprinted by permission of Farrar, Straus & Giroux, LLC.

Excerpt from Anthony Stern, *Everything Starts from Prayer: Mother Teresa's Meditations on Spiritual Life for People of All Faiths.* Ashland, Oregon: White Cloud Press, 1998, p. 132. Used with permission.

In Appreciation: Blessed Kateri Church, Sparta, NJ; Church of the Assumption, Morristown, NJ; Our Lady of Mercy Church, Whippany, NJ; Our Lady of the Lake Church, Sparta, NJ; Saint Ann's Church, Parsippany, NJ; Saint Joseph's Church, Croton Falls, NY; Saint Peter the Apostle Church, Parsippany, NJ; Saint Thomas More Church, Convent Station, NJ; GIA Publications, Inc., Chicago, IL; WLP Publications, Franklin Park, IL; Rev. George Hafemann

Credits

COVER: Gene Plaisted, The Crosiers

SCRIPTURE ART: Tim Ladwig

ALL OTHER ART: 15, 18–19, 65, 68, 107, 149, 174, 261 Elizabeth Wolf; 17, 26, 28, 38, 46, 48, 56, 58, 70, 88, 90, 100, 110, 112, 120, 130, 132, 140, 142, 152, 154, 162, 176, 182, 184, 196, 204, 214, 216, 224, 226 Tim Ladwig; 30, 125, 249 Martha Doty; 41, 103, 199 Sandy Rabinowitz; 50, 92, 156, 166, 198 Roman Dunets; 57 Charles Shaw; 72 Huy Voun Lee; 79 Claude Martinot; 86, 208 Freddie Levin; 89 Reggie Holladay; 99 Laura Huliska-Beith; 121 Judy Jarrett; 135 Suzanne Muse; 145 Donna Catanese; 157 Shelley Dieterichs; 173 Marcie Hawthorne; 183 Chris Reed; 186-187 Paula Wendland; 219 Deborah Pinkney; 225 Carla Kiwior; 228 Lauren Cryan; 234 David Bathurst; 237, 241, 255 Robin DeWitt; 253 Gershom Griffith; 280 Cindy Rosenheim

PHOTOS: Every effort has been made to secure permission and provide appropriate credit for photographic material. The publisher deeply regrets any omission and pledges to correct errors called to its attention in subsequent editions.

3 ©James L. Shaffer; 4 ©Myrleen Ferguson Cate/PhotoEdit; 5 Gene Plaisted, OSC/The Crosiers; 6 Gene Plaisted, OSC/The Crosiers; 16 ©Réunion des Musées Nationaux/Art Resource, NY; 20 *St. Jerome Reading* (oil on canvas), Georges de la Tour/Louvre, Paris, France/Bridgeman Art Library; 23 ©Steve Maines/Stock Boston; 26 Gene Plaisted, OSC/The Crosiers; 27 ©David Young-Wolff/PhotoEdit; 32 ©F. Pedrick/Image Works; 36 ©James L. Shaffer, Scala/Art Resource, NY; 37 ©David Young-Wolff/Getty Images; 38 ©James L. Shaffer; 40 ©Dennis MacDonald/PhotoEdit; 42 ©Jeff Greenberg/PhotoEdit; 46 Tom McGuire/Cathedral of Valencia; 47 ©Bill Gallery/Stock Boston/Jupiter Images; 50 *The Conversion of St. Paul*, Peter Paul Rubens, Oil on Canvas, Christie's Images/SuperStock; 52 ©Peter Weimann/Animals Animals/Earth Scenes; 56 *Madonna of the Magnificent*, Sandro Botticelli/Summerfield Press/Corbis; 60 ©Lee Snider/Image Works; 65 ©Charles Graham/eStock Photo; 68 National Maritime Museum, London; 69 ©Tony Freeman/PhotoEdit; 74 ©R. Burch/Bruce Coleman Inc.; 78 (T) ©Stephen R. Swan/Canstock Images, Inc./Index Stock Imagery, (B) Saint Maria delle Grazzie, Milan/Canali PhotoBank/SuperStock; 79 (TR) ©Lawrence Migdale/Stock Boston, (Inset) ©Joel S. Fishman/Photo Researchers, Inc.; 80 ©Myrleen Ferguson Cate/PhotoEdit; 82 ©Getty Images; 83 ©Vittoriano Rastelli/Corbis; 89 ©Richard Pasley/Stock Boston; 92 ©Archivo Iconografico, S.A/Corbis; 94 Getty Royalty-Free; 98 (T) ©Bill Aron/PhotoEdit/Jupiter Images, (B) Z. Radovan, Jerusalem; 102 ©Bill Aron/PhotoEdit/Jupiter Images; 103 ©Galen Rowell/Corbis; 104 Francis & Donna Caldwell/Visuals Unlimited; 107 Reprinted from "ABC's of The Bible", ©1991/Used by permission of The Readers Digest Association, Inc., Pleasantville, NY; 114 Courtesy of Franciscan Foundation for the Holy Land; 116 ©Patrick Ward/Corbis; 120 ©LucasFilm LTD/Paramount/Kobal Collection/The Picture Desk; 122 Gene Plaisted, OSC/The Crosiers; 124 ©Jeffrey Jones/The Independent Gallup/AP/Wide World; 126 ©Stephen Studd/Getty Images; 130 ©Warner Bros./Kobal Collection/The Picture Desk; 134 ©Myrleen Ferguson Cate/PhotoEdit; 140 Getty Images; 141 Getty Images; 146 ©Izzet Keribar/Lonely Planet Images/Getty Images; 149 ©Erich Lessing/Art Resource, NY; 152 ©Steve Taylor/Getty Images; 156 *Portrait of St. Francis Xavier* (1506–52), Ernest Monnin/Private Collection/Index/Bridgeman Art Library; 158 ©Frank Whitney/Getty Images; 162 ©Helen King/Corbis; 163 (L) ©David Young-Wolff/PhotoEdit, (TR) ©Mark Richards/PhotoEdit, (BR) ©Michael Newman/PhotoEdit; 164 Gene Plaisted, OSC/The Crosiers; 166 ©Bettmann/Corbis; 167 Max Alexander/©DK Images; 168 Jim Whitmer; 172 (T) ©Erich Lessing/Art Resource, NY, (B) Chris Wozniak/Enchanted Realms; 178 ©Adam Jones/Dembinsky Photo Assoc. Inc.; 182 AP/Wide World Photos; 186 ©Bill Wittman; 188 ©David Matherly/Visuals Unlimited; 191 (Bkgd) ©Sonia Halliday Photographs, (Inset) Scala/Art Resource, NY; 194 (T) Reprinted from "ABC's of The Bible", ©1991/Used by permission of The Readers Digest Association, Inc., Pleasantville, NY, (B) Joel De Grand/Shrine of St. Jude Thaddeus/The Dominicans; 195 ©Ian Shaw/Getty Images; 198 ©Elio Ciol/Corbis; 200 Blimp Photo; 204 Courtesy Subiaco Abbey and Academy; 206 ©Bill Wittman; 209 ©Bill Wittman; 210 (C) ©Jim Strawser/Grant Heilman Photography, (BC, B) ©Larry Lefever/Grant Heilman Photography, (Bkgd) Grant Heilman Photography; 214 Ellen Dooley; 215 ©Celine Amiot/Corbis; 218 Corbis; 220 Gene Plaisted, OSC/The Crosiers; 224 Warner Bros./Kobal Collection/The Picture Desk; 230 (Inset) SuperStock, (Bkgd) ©Gerard Lacz/Animals Animals/Earth Scenes; 233 (T) ©Sepp Seitz/Woodfin Camp & Associates, (B) Gene Plaisted, OSC/The Crosiers; 239 ©Purestock/Alamy; 240 *The Immaculate Conception*, 1627, Guido Reni, Victor Wilbour Memorial Fund, 1959 (59.32)/Metropolitan Museum of Art; 242 Gene Plaisted, OSC/The Crosiers; 243 ©Sepp Seitz/Woodfin Camp & Associates; 244 Scala/Art Resource, NY; 245 ©Michael Newman/PhotoEdit; 246 *Christ in the Wilderness*, Briton Riviere, Guildhall Art Gallery, Corp. of London/Bridgeman Art Library/SuperStock; 247 Jim Whitmer; 250 Getty Royalty-Free; 252 *The Ascension*, 1950–1951, Caserta Bazile, Tempera, Cathedral of St. Trinite, Port-au-Prince, Hait/A & F Pears Ltd., London/SuperStock; 254 Corbis; 255 ©Gabe Palmer/Corbis; 256 Courtesy of the Father Solanus Guild; 258 ©Reuters/Corbis; 263 ©David Lees/Time & Life Pictures/Getty Images; 264 Museo dell'Opera del Duomo, Florence, Italy/Scala/Art Resource, NY; 265 ©W. P. Wittman; 267 Courtesy of Regina McAloney; 271 (T) ©Greg Nikas/Corbis Digital Archive/Corbis, (B) Anne Hamersky; 272 ©David Young-Wolff/PhotoEdit; 275 Skjold Photographs; 276 Corbis; 278 ©Myrleen Ferguson Cate/PhotoEdit; 279 ©David Young-Wolff/PhotoEdit

10th printing. September 2014.

CONTENTS

3

FEASTS AND SEASONS

OUR CATHOLIC HERITAGE

Organized according to the 4 pillars of the Catechism

LET US PRAY

The Sign of the Cross

In the name of the Father,
and of the Son,
and of the Holy Spirit.

> Amen.

Signum Crucis
SIHG-noom KROO-chees

Line 1. In nómine Patris,
> ihn NOH-mee-nay PAH-trees

2. et Fílii,
> et FEE-lee-ee

3. et Spíritus Sancti.
> et SPEE-ree-toos SAHNK-tee.

> Amen.
> AH-men.

The Lord's Prayer

Our Father, who art in heaven,
hallowed be thy name;
thy kingdom come,
thy will be done
on earth as it is in heaven.
Give us this day our daily bread,
and forgive us our trespasses,
as we forgive those who trespass
   against us;
and lead us not into temptation,
but deliver us from evil.

> Amen.

Oratio Dominica
oh-RAHT-see-oh doh-MEE-nee-kah

Lines 1.–2. Pater noster, qui es in caelis:
> PAH-tair NOHS-tair kwee es ihn CHAY-lees:

3. sanctificétur nomen tuum;
> sahnk-tee-fee-CHAY-tor NOH-men TOO-oom;

4. advéniat regnum tuum;
> ahd-VEH-nee-aht REG-noom TOO-oom;

5.–6. fiat volúntas tua, sicut in caelo, et in terra.
> FEE-aht voh-LOON-tahs TOO-ah, SEE-koot ihn CHAY-loh, et ihn TAIR-ah.

7.–8. Panem nostrum cotidiánum da nobis hódie;
> PAH-nem NOH-stroom koh-tee-dee-AH-noom dah NOH-bees HOH-dee-ay;

9.–10. et dimítte nobis débita nostra,
> et dih-MEET-tay NOH-bees DEH-bee-tah NOH-strah,

11.–12. sicut et nos dimíttimus debitóribus nostris;
> SEE-koot et nohs dih-MIHT-ee-moos day-bee-TOR-ee-boos NOH-strees;

13.–14. et ne nos indúcas in tentatiónem;
> et nay nohs ihn-DOO-kahs ihn ten-taht-see-OH-nem;

15. sed líbera nos a malo.
> sed LEE-bair-ah nohs ah MAH-loh.

> Amen.
> AH-men.

* The lines in the Latin prayers are numbered to match the lines in the English prayers.

Glory Be

Glory be to the Father
and to the Son
and to the Holy Spirit,
as it was in the beginning
is now, and ever shall be
world without end.

Amen.

Glória Patri

GLOR-ee-ah PAH-tree

Lines 1.–2. Glória Patri et Fílio
GLOR-ee-ah PAH-tree et FEE-lee-oh

3. et Spirítui Sancto.
et spee-REE-too-ee SAHNK-toh.

4. Sicut erat in princípio,
SEE-koot AIR-aht ihn prihn-CHEE-pee-oh,

5. et nunc et semper
et noonk et SEM-pair

6. et in saécula saeculórum.
et ihn SAY-koo-lah say-koo-LOR-oom.

Amen.

AH-men.

The Hail Mary

Hail, Mary, full of grace,
the Lord is with thee.
Blessed art thou among women
and blessed is the fruit of thy
womb, Jesus.
Holy Mary, Mother of God,
pray for us sinners,
now and at the hour of our death.

Amen.

Ave, María AH-vay, mah-REE-ah

Lines 1.–2. Ave, María, grátia plena, Dóminus tecum.
AH-vay, mah-REE-ah, GRAHT-see-ah PLAY-nah,
DOH-mee-noos TAY-koom.

3. Benedícta tu in muliéribus,
bay-nay-DEEK-tah too ihn moo-lee-AIR-ee-boos,

4.–5. et benedíctus fructus ventris tui, Iesus.
et bay-nay-DEEK-toos FROOK-toos VEN-trees TOO-ee,
YAY-zoos.

6. Sancta María, Mater Dei,
SAHNK-tah mah-REE-ah, MAH-tair DAY-ee,

7. ora pro nobis peccatóribus,
OR-ah proh NOH-bees pek-uh-TOR-ee-boos,

8.–9. nunc et in hora mortis nostrae.
noonk et ihn HOR-ah MOR-tees NOHS-tray.

Amen.

AH-men.

Act of Contrition

My God,
I am sorry for my sins with all my heart.
In choosing to do wrong
and failing to do good,
I have sinned against you
whom I should love above all things.
I firmly intend, with your help,
to do penance,
to sin no more,
and to avoid whatever leads me to sin.
Our Savior Jesus Christ
suffered and died for us.
In his name, my God, have mercy.

Rite of Penance

Hail, Holy Queen

Hail, holy Queen,
Mother of mercy:
Hail, our life, our sweetness, and our hope.
To you do we cry,
poor banished children of Eve.
To you do we send up our sighs,
mourning and weeping
in this valley of tears.
Turn then, most gracious advocate,
your eyes of mercy toward us;
and after this our exile
show unto us
    the blessed fruit of your womb, Jesus.
O clement, O loving, O sweet Virgin Mary.

Amen.

The Apostles' Creed

I believe in God,
the Father almighty,
Creator of heaven and earth,
and in Jesus Christ, his only Son, our Lord,
who was conceived by the Holy Spirit,
born of the Virgin Mary,
suffered under Pontius Pilate,
was crucified, died and was buried;
he descended into hell;
on the third day he rose again from the dead;
he ascended into heaven,
and is seated at the right hand of God
    the Father almighty;
from there he will come to judge the living
    and the dead.

I believe in the Holy Spirit,
the holy catholic Church,
the communion of saints,
the forgiveness of sins,
the resurrection of the body,
and life everlasting.

Amen.

Grace Before Meals

Bless us, O Lord, and these thy gifts,
    which we are about to receive
    from thy bounty,
    through Christ our Lord.

Amen.

The Rosary

The Rosary is a prayer that honors Mary, the Mother of Jesus, and helps us meditate on the life of Christ. We pray the Rosary using a set of beads. A group of ten beads is called a decade. Before each decade, recall one of the mysteries, or important times in the lives of Mary and Jesus. There are twenty mysteries, shown at right. The prayers for the beads are shown below.

The Mysteries of the Rosary

The Joyful Mysteries

1. The Annunciation
2. The Visitation
3. The Nativity
4. The Presentation in the Temple
5. The Finding of the Child Jesus After Three Days in the Temple

The Luminous Mysteries

1. The Baptism at the Jordan
2. The Miracle at Cana
3. The Proclamation of the Kingdom and the Call to Conversion
4. The Transfiguration
5. The Institution of the Eucharist

The Sorrowful Mysteries

1. The Agony in the Garden
2. The Scourging at the Pillar
3. The Crowning with Thorns
4. The Carrying of the Cross
5. The Crucifixion and Death

The Glorious Mysteries

1. The Resurrection
2. The Ascension
3. The Descent of the Holy Spirit at Pentecost
4. The Assumption of Mary
5. The Crowning of the Blessed Virgin as Queen of Heaven and Earth

Fourth Mystery, Lord's Prayer

Ten Hail Marys, Glory Be

Third Mystery, Lord's Prayer

Ten Hail Marys, Glory Be

Ten Hail Marys, Glory Be

Fifth Mystery, Lord's Prayer

Second Mystery, Lord's Prayer

Ten Hail Marys, Glory Be

Three Hail Marys, Glory Be

Ten Hail Marys, Glory Be

Hail, Holy Queen

Sign of the Cross and Apostles' Creed

Lord's Prayer

First Mystery, Lord's Prayer

The Stations of the Cross

1. Jesus is condemned to death.

2. Jesus accepts the cross.

3. Jesus falls the first time.

4. Jesus meets his mother.

5. Simon helps Jesus carry the cross.

6. Veronica wipes the face of Jesus.

7. Jesus falls the second time.

8. Jesus meets the women of Jerusalem.

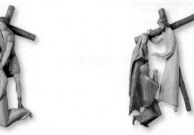

9. Jesus falls the third time.

10. Jesus is stripped of his garments.

11. Jesus is nailed to the cross.

12. Jesus dies on the cross.

13. Jesus is taken down from the cross.

14. Jesus is buried in the tomb.

15. Jesus Christ is risen.

A GREAT BIBLE EXPEDITION

A LOOK INSIDE THE BIBLE

If you were to look at the last page number in the Bible, you would see that the Bible is more than 1,000 pages long! What's inside? There are stories, songs, poems, family histories, letters, wise sayings, parables, prophecies, and many other kinds of writing. Some of the writings date back to about 3,000 years ago. Even the most recently written parts of the Bible are about 2,000 years old. But the Bible is one of the best-selling books of all time, because everything in the Bible has something to reveal about God, human life, and the world.

The Bible is a collection of 73 books. The word *Bible* comes from the Greek word *biblia*, meaning "books." The Bible is also known as *Scripture*, a word that means "word of God" or "sacred writings." This year you will take a great expedition through Scripture.

You will explore the writings in the first part of the Bible, which is called the Old Testament. These writings describe how God revealed to the Hebrews, or Jewish people, knowledge about himself and his ways. As Catholics, we seek to learn about God with an understanding of our link to the Hebrews. They were the first to hear the Word of God and to form a special relationship with God. That is why we sometimes refer to them as "our ancestors in faith." The Old Testament is a collection of 46 books that tell us about the experiences of our ancestors in faith.

You will also study the New Testament, a collection of 27 books that are very important to Catholics and all Christians. These books tell us about the life and teachings of Jesus Christ. He fulfilled the promises God made to our ancestors in faith in the Old Testament.

What Is Your Bible IQ?

10/10

1. The writers of the Bible wrote down stories that were
   (a) completely made up.
   (b) originally passed down by word of mouth.
   (c) all told by Jesus.
   (d) scientifically correct.

2. The first part of the Bible is the
   (a) New Testament.
   (b) Old Testament.

3. What body of water parted so the Israelites could escape Egypt?
   (a) Jordan River
   (b) Red Sea
   (c) Dead Sea
   (d) Mediterranean Sea

4. What animal told Eve to eat the fruit of the Tree of Knowledge?
   (a) a serpent
   (b) a wolf
   (c) a bird
   (d) a mouse

5. What sign did God send to tell Noah there would not be another Great Flood?
   (a) a dove
   (b) a burning bush
   (c) sunshine
   (d) a rainbow

6. According to the Bible, how long did it take God to create the world?
   (a) six days
   (b) five years
   (c) one day
   (d) seven days

7. The man who received the Ten Commandments from God was
   (a) Abraham.
   (b) Jesus.
   (c) Peter.
   (d) Moses.

8. Which angel appeared to Mary to announce to her that she had been chosen to be the Mother of the Savior?
   (a) Michael
   (b) Raphael
   (c) Gabriel
   (d) James

9. Who are the four Gospel writers?
   (a) Mark, Luke, John, James
   (b) Mark, Luke, Matthew, John
   (c) Matthew, Mark, Luke, James
   (d) Mark, Paul, John, Peter

10. When Mary and Joseph lost the boy Jesus, they found him
    (a) talking to John the Baptizer.
    (b) fishing with the Twelve Apostles.
    (c) changing water into wine at Cana.
    (d) talking to teachers in the Temple.

Check your score.

Answer Key:

1) b, 2) b, 3) b, 4) a, 5) d, 6) a, 7) d, 8) c, 9) b, 10) d

Scoring:
Give yourself one point for each correct answer.
8–11 points: You are a Bible Brainiac!
5–7 points: You get a B in the Bible business!
3–4 points: Brush up on the Bible just a bit!
1–2 points: Don't worry. You will improve your Bible IQ this year!

THE HISTORY OF THE BIBLE

1. THE PATRIARCHS (2000–1700 B.C.)

In 1800 B.C. the patriarch Abraham, a nomadic shepherd, left Mesopotamia for a land called Canaan, following the guidance of God. His son Isaac and grandson Jacob were patriarchs who also followed the guidance of God. At this time, the patriarchs' experiences of God were passed down through the generations by word of mouth.

2. THE EXODUS (1700–1200 B.C.)

Jacob's son Joseph was taken to Egypt as a slave but became a great ruler. His father and brothers moved to Egypt. Their descendants thrived there until Pharaoh made them slaves. Moses helped them escape Egypt around 1300 B.C. They journeyed through the desert. God gave them the Ten Commandments. Joshua led them to the promised land, and they conquered Palestine around 1200 B.C. The Bible was not yet written.

3. THE KINGDOM (1200–900 B.C.)

The Israelites (descendants of Jacob's family) settled in Canaan. Leaders called judges helped rule the Israelites between 1200 and 1000 B.C. Around 1000 B.C. David became king of the southern part of the land. Jerusalem was its capital. David's son, Solomon, was king of most of Canaan between 965 and 928 B.C. He built the Temple. Scribes began to write the Bible's histories of the kings, story of the Garden of Eden, and parts of stories about Abraham, Joseph, and Moses.

The Twelve Tribes

A TIMELINE OF BIBLE EVENTS

	1800	1700		1300	1200	1200–1000	1000
IN THE BIBLE	Abraham journeys to Canaan.	Joseph and family live in Egypt.		Moses and Hebrews leave Egypt.	Israelites conquer Palestine.	Judges rule.	King David captures Jerusalem.

THE PATRIARCHS 2000–1700 B.C.		**THE EXODUS** 1700–1200 B.C.		**THE KINGDOM** 1200–900 B.C.

	2000	1600	1350	1200	1150
IN THE WORLD	Stonehenge is built in England.	First Chinese civilizations develop.	Mediterranean peoples migrate to Canaan and Egypt.	Iron Age begins in Middle East.	Olmec civilization in Central America develops.

4. THE PROPHETS AND THE EXILE (900–500 B.C.)

After Solomon's son became king, the empire divided into Judah in the south and Israel in the north. Prophets such as Isaiah and Micah guided people. People added to the stories of Abraham, Joseph, and Moses. In 722 B.C. Assyria destroyed Israel and took its people captive. Hezekiah and Josiah were Israel's kings. Hezekiah made changes to early stories about Abraham, Joseph, and Moses. Josiah's scribes included early versions of stories in new works such as Deuteronomy, Joshua, Judges, 1 and 2 Samuel, and 1 and 2 Kings.

The Babylonians destroyed Jerusalem and the Temple in 587 B.C. Judaens were exiled to Babylon. Joshua, Deuteronomy, Judges, 1 and 2 Samuel, and 1 and 2 Kings were rewritten. In 539 B.C. Cyrus, leader of the Persians, conquered the Babylonians and welcomed the Jews back home. The Jews who returned rebuilt the Temple in 519 B.C.

5. GREEK AND ROMAN RULE (500 B.C.—A.D. 30)

The Jews had peace during Persian rule. Priests copied and rewrote earlier texts. Numbers, Genesis, Exodus, and the prophetic books were written as known today. Leviticus was written. Psalms and Proverbs were rewritten. Deuteronomy was finished. Nehemiah, Jonah, Ezra, Job, and Ruth were written. Alexander the Great conquered the Persian empire in 332 B.C. Greeks ruled the Jews until about 164 B.C. Song of Songs, Sirach, Ecclesiastes, and Wisdom were written. Books were translated into Greek.

Jews called Maccabees defeated the Greeks. Daniel, 1 and 2 Maccabees, and Tobit were written. By this time, all of the Old Testament had been written. Romans began to rule in 63 B.C. Jesus was born around 6 B.C. and died around A.D. 30. The Gospels were written in A.D. 70–100 and the letters of Paul in A.D. 50–60. Paul's followers wrote some letters in A.D. 65–100. The New Testament was completed by A.D. 120.

965–928
Solomon rules and builds Temple.

928
Kingdom divides.

722
Assyrians conquer Israel.

587–537
Jewish exiles live in Babylon.

587
Babylonians destroy Jerusalem.

539
Jewish exiles allowed to return.

63
Roman rule begins.

164
Jews regain independence.

332
Greeks rule Jews.

6
Jesus is born.

A.D. 30
Jesus dies and rises.

THE PROPHETS AND THE EXILE
900–500 B.C.

GREEK AND ROMAN RULE
500 B.C.—A.D. 30

776
First Greek Olympics are held.

753
Rome is founded.

110
Trade opens between Far East and Middle East and Europe.

55
Julius Caesar attacks Britain.

THE PARTS OF THE BIBLE

God inspired the Bible. This means that the Holy Spirit guided the writers of the Bible. Because the Bible is the inspired Word of God, it should be treated with respect and care.

Jesus Christ entrusted the interpretation of God's Word to the leaders of the Church. Through the Holy Spirit, the bishops and the pope lead us to a better understanding of the Bible, and Jesus Christ, the eternal Word of God, opens our minds to understand the Bible.

The Bible read by Catholics contains the books that the Church reveres as inspired by God. About A.D. 400, Saint Jerome, a brilliant priest and scholar, helped the Church decide which books would form the *canon*, or official list, of books of the Bible. He also translated the books of the Bible into Latin for the Latin-speaking Christians. (The books were originally in Greek and Hebrew.) Centuries later, the Bible was divided into chapters and verses. The first translation of the Bible into English was completed in 1384.

Not all religious denominations share the same collections of books. The Protestant Bible contains only 66 books. The Jewish Bible, or Hebrew Scriptures, contains books from the section we call the Old Testment. Here are the books of the Catholic Bible.

Old Testament

Pentateuch
(first five books of the Bible, about Israel's Covenant with God)

Genesis	Numbers
Exodus	Deuteronomy
Leviticus	

(more of the Israelites' story)

Joshua	Ruth
Judges	

Historical Books
(Israel's religious history)

1 Samuel	Nehemiah
2 Samuel	Tobit
1 Kings	Judith
2 Kings	Esther
1 Chronicles	1 Maccabees
2 Chronicles	2 Maccabees
Ezra	

Wisdom Books
(poetry and instruction)

Job	Song of Songs
Psalms	Wisdom
Proverbs	Sirach
Ecclesiastes	

Prophetic Books
(God's Word through the prophets)

Isaiah	Obadiah
Jeremiah	Jonah
Lamentations	Micah
Baruch	Nahum
Ezekiel	Habakkuk
Daniel	Zephaniah
Hosea	Haggai
Joel	Zechariah
Amos	Malachi

New Testament

The Gospels
(life and teachings of Jesus)

Matthew	Luke
Mark	John

Acts of the Apostles
(works of the early Church)

Letters
(letters to early Christians)

Romans	Philippians
1 Corinthians	Colossians
2 Corinthians	1 Thessalonians
Galatians	2 Thessalonians
Ephesians	1 Timothy

2 Timothy	1 Peter	
Titus	2 Peter	
Philemon	1 John	
Hebrews	2 John	
James	3 John	Jude

Book of Revelation
(apocalyptic writing)

HOW TO FIND SCRIPTURE PASSAGES

The Bible is divided into books. The books are divided into chapters.
The chapters are divided into verses. For example, Exodus 19:8–9 means

Verses   Book   Chapter

74	**EXODUS 19**	Appointment of Minor Judges

you, along with your wife and her two sons.''
7 Moses went out to meet his father-in-law, bowed down before him, and kissed him. Having greeted each other, they went into the tent. 8 Moses then told his father-in-law of all that the LORD had done to Pharaoh and the Egyptians for the sake of Israel, and of all the hardships they had had to endure on their journey, and how the LORD had come to their rescue. 9 Jethro rejoiced over all the goodness that the LORD had shown Israel in rescuing them from the hands of the Egyptians. 10 ''Blessed be the ... said, ''who ...

able to stand the strain, and all these people will go home satisfied.'' 24 Moses followed the advice of his father-in-law and did all that he had suggested. 25 He picked out able men from all Israel and put them in charge of the people as officers over groups of thousands, of hundreds, of fifties, and of tens. 26 They rendered decisions for the people in all ordinary cases. The more difficult cases they referred to Moses, but all the lesser cases they settled themselves. 27 Then Moses ... farewell ... his father-in-l ...

To find a Scripture passage, follow these three simple steps. Try to use the steps
to find the passage *Matthew 5:1–12.*

1. Find the name of the book you need on the alphabetical index page at the front of your Bible. (The name *Matthew* can be found under the heading *New Testament.*)

2. In the same list, find the page number of the book you need. This will tell you the page on which the book begins. Turn to that page within your Bible.

3. Now turn the pages until you find the chapter you need. The chapter number is shown either next to the name of the book at the very top of the page or as a large number within paragraphs on the page. When you find the chapter, locate the verses, using the small numbers within the paragraphs.

THE TYPES OF WRITING IN THE BIBLE

The following are some of the types of writing that can be found in the Bible.

Songs: poems or hymns that are often prayers. *Example:* the Book of Psalms

Laws: instructions on how to behave. *Example:* Deuteronomy

Parables: tales that teach a moral lesson. *Example:* the Persistent Widow

Letters: written messages from one person or group to another. *Example:* Romans

Myths: ancient stories written to explain life. *Example:* Adam and Eve

Prophecies: messages from God told through the words of prophets.
Example: Ezekiel

Blest Are We

Words and Music by David Haas
Spanish translation by Ronald F. Krisman

REFRAIN

Blest are we, ho - ly chil - dren of light are we!
¡Ben - de - ci - dos, so - mos san - tos hi - jos de la luz!

Blest are we, cho - sen peo - ple of God!
¡Ben - de - ci - dos y e - le - gi - dos por Dios!

Blest are we, God has plans for you and me!
¡Ben - de - ci - dos, Dios nos quie - re ser cual Je - sús!

Blest are we! We are the chil - dren of God!
¡Ben - de - ci - dos, so - mos los hi - jos de Dios!

Fine

VERSE

1. For our world, each sis - ter and broth - er:
1. Por el mun - do, por to - dos sus pue - blos:

We are called, called to serve!
¡So - mos lla - ma - dos pa - ra ser - vir!

We are here to love one an - oth - er:
Nos a - me - mos los u - nos a los o - tros;

We are called, called to serve!
¡So - mos lla - ma - dos pa - ra ser - vir!

D.C.

2. For the poor, the meek and the lowly:
   We are called, called to serve!
   For the weak, the sick and the hungry:
   We are called, called to serve!

2. Por los pobres, los mansos y humildes:
   ¡Somos llamados para servir!
   Por los enfermos, hambrientos, y débiles:
   ¡Somos llamados para servir!

3. For all those who yearn for freedom:
   We are called, called to serve!
   For the world, to be God's kingdom:
   We are called, called to serve!

3. Por los que sufren y quieren ser librados:
   ¡Somos llamados para servir!
   Venga a nosotros el Reino de los Cielos:
   ¡Somos llamados para servir!

We Answer God's Call

Abraham and Sarah are our ancestors in faith because they were the first to respond to God's call to holiness and fidelity. God calls each of us to be faithful to his Word and to lead others in holiness.

The LORD said to Abram: "Go forth from the land of your kinsfolk and from your father's house to a land that I will show you."

Genesis 12:1

Abraham and
Sarah traveled
across the
desert, just as
these nomads
are doing. The
map shows
their journey.

Abraham
and Sarah's
Journey

MESOPOTAMIA
• Haran

Mediterranean
Sea

• Shechem
Dead
Sea
ARABIA
EGYPT
• Beersheba

I Say "Yes," Lord/ Digo "Sí," Señor

Words and Music by Donna Peña
Arranged by Marty Haugen

VERSE

Cantor

1. To the God who can - not_ die:_
   To the God of the_ op - pressed:_
2. I am a ser - vant of_ the_ Lord:_
   I'm a pris - oner of_ their_ wars:_ I say
3. For the dream I have_ to - day:_ Di - go
   To come to love my en - e - mies:_
4. Like that of Job, un - ceas - ing - ly:_
   Like that of Da - vid in_ a_ song:_

All

Cantor

"Yes," my Lord._ I say "Yes," my Lord._
"Sí," Se - ñor._ Di - go "Sí," Se - ñor._

1. To the
   To the
2. I'm a
   Like a pol - i -
3. To be a
   For your
4. Like that of Ma -
   Like Is - ra -

One who hears_ me_ cry:_
God of all_ jus - tice:_
work - er in_ the_ fields:_
ti - cian, in - ev - i - ta - bly:_ I say
heal - er of_ all_ pain:_ Di - go
peace in all_ the_ world:_
ri - a whole - heart - ed - ly:_
el, for you_ I_ long:_

All

REFRAIN

"Yes," my Lord,_ I say "Yes," my Lord._ I say
"Sí," Se - ñor,_ Di - go "Sí," Se - ñor._ Di - go

"Yes," my Lord,_ in all the good_ times, through all the bad times,
"Sí," Se - ñor,_ en tiem - pos ma - los, en tiem - pos bue - nos.

I say "Yes," my Lord_ to ev' - ry word_ you speak._
Di - go "Sí," Se - ñor a to - do lo_ que ha - blas._

Take Home

FAMILY TIME

Revelation and Response

This chapter introduces the story of our ancestors in faith with the Old Testament figures Abraham and Sarah, who accepted God's plan even though they were unsure of what God had in store for them. Like Abraham and Sarah, we often experience challenges that make us wonder about God's plan for us and how he expects us to respond.

ACTIVITY

A Family Faith Tree Create a colorful family tree showing not only lineage but each person's journey of faith. Include what you know about major events in each person's life, as well as the dates of his or her Baptism, First Communion, Confirmation, and so on.

WEEKLY PLANNER

On Sunday

At Mass, listen to the readings and the homily for stories about people whose faith helped them through major changes.

On the Web

www.blestarewe.com

 Visit our Web site for the Saint of the day and the reflection question of the week.

Saint of the Week

 Saint Joseph, Husband of Mary

Saint Joseph was chosen by God to be the protector of Jesus and Mary. He carried out this calling with fidelity and humility. He is an example for us of trust in God and obedience to his will.

Patron Saint of: the universal Church
Feast Day: March 19

A Prayer for the Week

Lord, may we learn from the example of your faithful servants Abraham and Saint Joseph to trust in your love and surrender to your will. Amen.

Take Home

FAMILY TIME

✝ Scripture Background

Before the Time of Jesus

Abraham A link that binds Christians, Jews, and Muslims is a reverence for Abraham, our common ancestor in faith. Although each religion emphasizes somewhat different qualities in Abraham, at the core of his identity for all three religions is his friendship with God. For Jews, Abraham is honored for his complete obedience to God. Christians honor him as a model of faith in God. And for Muslims, Abraham is a model of one who exhibits *islam*, or unconditional surrender to God's will. Learn more about Abraham's faith in God and obedience to him by reading Genesis 12:1–9 and 22:1–12.

Our Catholic Tradition in the Old Testament

A Common Ancestor God promised Abraham, "I will bless you abundantly and make your descendants as countless as the stars" (Genesis 22:17). Today, thousands of years later, followers of Christianity, Islam, and Judaism consider Abraham part of their religious heritage. Christianity has about 2 billion followers, including Catholics, Protestants, and members of the Eastern Orthodox Church. (An Eastern Orthodox cathedral is shown at right.) Islam is the religion of more than 1 billion people. Followers of Judaism number about 14 million people.

1 Revelation and Response

LET US PRAY

How varied are your works, O LORD!
The earth is full of your creatures.
They all look to you to give them food in due time.

Based on Psalm 104:24, 27

Share

Even though we can't see God with our eyes, he is all around us. God's presence can be found in many ways. Can you remember a time when you felt God's presence with you?

Activity

Complete the following sentences with words that describe ways that God is with us. Some of the letters in the words are already filled in for you.

1. God speaks to us when we read the

   ___ c r ☐ ___ ___ u r ___ s.

2. When we tell God our feelings and thoughts

   in ___ r ☐ y ___ r, God responds to us.

3. We can see God's work in the beauty of

   n ___ ☐ ___ r e.

4. Sometimes we feel closest to God in

   ___ i ___ ___ ___ c e, when everything is quiet.

5. God's love is in the ☐ ___ n ___ s that reach out to us when we share the Sign of Peace.

6. In the Sacrament of Penance and Reconciliation, we celebrate

   God's ☐ ___ r g ___ v ___ n ___ ___ s.

Now unscramble the boxed letters to spell the secret word.
Secret word: ___ ___ ___ ___ ___

How should we respond to God?

Hear & Believe

✝ Scripture Abraham and Sarah

Our story of faith began almost 4,000 years ago with Abram, who was a descendant of Noah. Abram and his wife, Sarai, were nomadic shepherds, or shepherds who moved around in search of new pastures. They had been married for a long time but had no children.

When Abram and Sarai were old and living with relatives in a land called Haran, the LORD spoke to Abram. The LORD told Abram to leave Haran and his relatives for a new land chosen by the LORD. The LORD said, "I will give you many descendants, and they will become a great nation."

Abram and Sarai did as the LORD said. Guided by the LORD, they set off for the new land. At Shechem, a holy place in the land of Canaan in present-day Palestine, the LORD spoke to Abram again. He said, "I will give this land to your descendants." Abram built an altar for the LORD at that place.

Abram and Sarai moved on, worshiping the LORD along the way. They eventually settled in Canaan. Years passed. The LORD again spoke to Abram and said, "Look up at the sky and count the stars, if you can. Your descendants will be as numberless as these." Abram trusted the LORD'S promise.

When Abram and Sarai were very old, the LORD said to Abram, "My promise to you is this: You will have so many descendants that they will become nations. I will be your God and the God of all your descendants." He changed Abram's name to Abraham, which means "father of many nations." The LORD promised that the land of Canaan would belong to Abraham's people. Then he promised that Sarai would have a son and changed her name to Sarah, which means "princess."

The LORD asked that Abraham and his descendants honor him always. The LORD told Abraham, "Walk in my presence and be blameless."

Sarah gave birth to a son, Isaac. Sarah felt blessed to have a son in her old age. She was filled with joy and laughter.

Based on Genesis 12:1–7; 13:1–4; 15:1, 5–6; 17:1–9, 15–16; 21:1–7

Models of Faith

Abraham and Sarah's trust in God and his promises showed their great **faith**. They left for an unknown land, believing in something they could not see or understand. They trusted that God's promises would come true. They lived this definition of faith: "Faith is the assurance of things hoped for, the conviction of things not seen" (based on Hebrews 11:1). Isaac's birth was not only a gift but a sign of the special relationship God had formed with Abraham and Sarah. They would now have many descendants, who would become the nation of Israel.

When God asked Abraham to follow him, he was beginning a special relationship with the Hebrews—the ancestors of Jewish people—whom God called "my people." This relationship eventually embraced all people. God said to Abraham, "All the communities of the earth shall find blessing in you" (Genesis 12:3). Because of Abraham's great faith, God fulfilled this promise and made Abraham the father of countless descendants. Abraham is the **patriarch**, or father, of the Jewish people, he is our own father in faith, and he is honored by Muslims, who also trace their religion back to him.

Our Church Teaches

Catholics believe in **Revelation**, or God's act of revealing himself in words and in deeds. We can know God by reading and learning the Scriptures, which teach God's Word, and by living our faith according to the Tradition of the Church passed down by the Apostles. We can speak with God in prayer. We can see God in creation, the Sacraments, the liturgy, and the good works of our church community. It is because of his love for us that God reveals himself and gave himself to us through his Son, Jesus Christ.

Abraham and Sarah responded to God's Revelation with open hearts. They sought to know God's will, and they obeyed it completely. Saint Paul called this type of response to God "the obedience of faith" (Romans 16:26). In the same way, Mary, the Mother of Jesus, trusted God's promise. When the angel told her she was going to be the Mother of God's Son, Mary did not understand how this could be, yet she answered, "May it be done to me according to your word" (Luke 1:38). Catholics are devoted to Mary and view her as a perfect model of faith.

GO TO page 264 to learn more about Mary's great faith.

We Believe

People with faith in God welcome God's Revelation. They accept God's will and obey it completely.

Faith Words

faith

Faith is the assurance of things hoped for, the conviction of things not seen.

patriarch

A patriarch, a term meaning "father," is a great leader of the Hebrews from early Scripture times. A patriarch is also the male leader of a family or clan.

Revelation

Revelation is God's act of revealing himself and inviting us to respond with faith.

How does God speak to us today?

Respond

Complete Trust

God invites ordinary people—including us—to do his work. We might react with doubt and confusion. Even Abraham, Sarah, and Mary had questions about what God expected of them. Yet they trusted in him completely.

Activities

1. Read the three stories. Complete the third story by writing on the lines how Rosa can respond with faith.

Abraham

Abraham believed in God's promise to make him the father of nations. In the beginning, he showed his devotion to God without words. He built altars to worship God at each stage of his journey to Canaan. Later, Abraham gave the Lord a gentle reminder that he was still waiting for his promise to be fulfilled.

Abraham said, "O Lord GOD, what good will your gifts be, if I keep on being childless?" (Genesis 15:2)

God told Abraham he did not forget his promise, and Abraham believed. Then Abraham and Sarah were blessed with a baby boy.

Mary

An angel told the Blessed Virgin Mary that she would be the mother of the Son of God. Mary asked the angel, "How can this be when I do not have a husband?" In reply the angel assured her that nothing is impossible for God. (Based on Luke 1:34, 37) Mary accepted what the angel told her, saying, "May it be done to me according to your word" (Luke 1:38).

Rosa

Rosa and her religious education class were working hard to organize a sixth-grade penance service. They chose Scripture readings, rehearsed songs, and practiced a candle-lighting ceremony.

Rosa was busy gluing letters onto a banner for the service. Being in the background was fine with Rosa. She stuttered when she was nervous, so she was happy that she didn't have a visible role in the service. Then her catechist approached her.

"Rosa," said her catechist, "you are an excellent reader. Will you do the first reading at the service?"

Rosa couldn't believe what her catechist was asking. How could she stand up and read in front of everyone? Rosa thought for a moment before she responded.

_____

_____

_____

2. Describe a time when God helped you face a challenging situation. Tell how your trust in God helped you overcome your fears. Then tell what this experience taught you about trusting in God.

_____

_____

_____

_____

_____

How might we pray when we are not sure of what God wants?

✞ Prayer Celebration

A Prayer of Trust

Abraham's faithful offerings and prayers to God are important examples of prayer from the Old Testament. Thomas Merton, a well-known monk and writer who lived from 1915 to 1968, wrote the following prayer of trust in God. After each part, repeat:

I trust you always, though I may seem to be lost.

My Lord God,
I have no idea where I am going.
I do not see the road ahead of me.
I cannot know for certain where it will end.
Nor do I really know myself,
and the fact that I think I am following
your will does not mean that I am
actually doing so.

But I believe that the desire to please you
does in fact please you.
And I hope I have that desire in all that I am doing.
I hope that I will never do anything apart
from that desire.

And I know that if I do this
you will lead me by the right road, though I
may know nothing about it.
Therefore I will trust you always though I
may seem to be lost and in the shadow
of death.

I will not fear, for you are ever with me,
and you will never leave me to face my
perils alone. Amen.

A **Match** Column A with Column B by writing the correct number in the space provided.

A	B
1. faith	____ a great leader of the Hebrews from early Scripture times, or the male leader of a family or clan
2. Revelation	____ the assurance of things hoped for, the conviction of things not seen
3. patriarch	____ God's act of revealing who he is and inviting us to respond with faith

B **Write** the name of the person or people described by each clue.

1. We are the ancestors of the Jews; God called us "my people."
_____

2. I am the patriarch of the Jewish people, Christians' father in faith, and a person honored by Muslims. _____

3. I am the son of Abraham and Sarah. _____

4. Catholics are devoted to her and view her as a perfect model of faith. _____

C **Respond** to the following.

1. How did Mary show her trust in God's promise?

_____

_____

_____

2. What are some ways in which you show your trust in God?

_____

_____

Faith in Action

Parish Maintenance Staff Working through the Parish Pastoral Council, maintenance workers serve the parish community in many important ways. Snow removal, for example, makes it possible for parishioners to attend Mass, no matter what the weather. Maintaining electrical equipment helps ensure everyone's safety. A maintenance person's participation in decisions about products, services, and contracts helps parish leaders to be good stewards in making the best use of the parish's financial resources.

In Everyday Life

Activity There are many people who contribute to our lives whom we take for granted. We may never even think of expressing gratitude to these people. Complete this certificate of appreciation for a deserving person to whom you have never said thank you.

Certificate of Appreciation

Presented to

_____

In gratitude for

_____

Presented by _____

In Your Parish

Activity On a scale of 1 to 5, rate your ability to complete each task. A 1 means you are completely unskilled and a 5 means you're an expert. Then circle one task that you can do to help your parish.

___ Rake leaves

___ Make a new friend

___ Plant flowers

___ Fix a computer

___ Write letters

___ Plan a party

___ Shop for a bargain

___ Decorate for a party

___ Create a bulletin board

___ Other: _____

FAMILY TIME

Sacrifice and Promise

Abraham was committed to following God's plan even when God told him to sacrifice his son Isaac. Although Abraham did not understand God's will, he had such strong faith that he was willing to do what God asked. Jesus too showed complete obedience to God, even to the point of sacrificing his own life, so that we might have everlasting life.

ACTIVITY

Weekly Sacrifices Make this "Sacrifice for Others Week." Create a chart listing each family member's name next to a different day of the week. Have each person fill in something he or she will do that day to help another person or another family.

Sacrifice-for-Others Week

Day	Name	Sacrifice	✓
Monday	Judith	Cook meal for neighbors.	
Tuesday	Danielle	Check on Mrs. Sisto's cat.	
Wednesday	Jennifer	Take Joe fishing.	
Thursday	Joe	Mow Grandpa's lawn.	
Friday	Paul	Drive Judith's mom to the airport.	

WEEKLY PLANNER

On Sunday

The Mass celebrates Jesus' sacrifice of his life and the promise of our Salvation. Listen for the words *sacrifice* and *promise* at Mass.

On the Web

www.blestarewe.com

 Visit our Web site for the Saint of the day and the reflection question of the week.

Saint of the Week

Saint Andrew Kim Taegŏn (1821–1846)

Saint Andrew Kim Taegŏn lived in Korea during a time when Christians there were persecuted. In spite of great risk, Andrew Kim lived out his faith. He traveled to Macao, China, to study for the priesthood. When he returned to Korea, he was arrested and executed.

Feast Day: September 20

A Prayer for the Week

Heavenly Father, in your great love for us you sacrificed your only Son. Teach us to respond to your love with the zeal and conviction of Saint Andrew Kim. Amen.

Take Home

FAMILY TIME

✝ Scripture Background

Before the Time of Jesus

The Testing of Abraham   In the Old Testament, we read of Abraham and his near-sacrifice of his son Isaac. It is hard for us to understand Abraham's willingness to sacrifice his own child. Harder still to understand is why God would call upon Abraham to make such a sacrifice. This story shows that Abraham truly believes in God and his plan. Fittingly, the story of Abraham's willingness to sacrifice his son is read at the Easter Vigil liturgy, when we celebrate Jesus' acceptance of his Father's will, and his great sacrifice and Resurrection. Read about the testing of Abraham in Genesis 22.

OUR CATHOLIC TRADITION **in Art**

The Sacrifice of Isaac   The story of Abraham and Isaac represents a profound test of a human's faith in and obedience to God. The Bible account of this story also affords a very dramatic subject for a religious painting. The Italian painter Caravaggio chose this subject matter when he created his masterpiece *The Sacrifice of Isaac* (1603).

In his paintings Caravaggio often emphasized the contrast between light and dark to heighten dramatic impact. This technique is evident in *The Sacrifice of Isaac*. This painting can now be seen in the Uffizi Gallery in Florence, Italy.

2 Sacrifice and Promise

Offer spiritual sacrifices acceptable to God through Jesus Christ.

1 Peter 2:5

Share

A dictionary definition of the word *sacrifice* is "giving up one thing for another thing thought to be more valuable." As Christians, we make sacrifices when we put God and the care of others above other things in our lives. In your own life you make sacrifices when you do good things that might help other people instead of more self-centered things. Each day, you can make "trade-offs" between things you really want and things that are better for other people or yourself.

Activity

Write the letter of each Column B item next to the Column A item for which you could trade it. Number 5 has been done for you. What word do the letters spell when you are done?

Column A

<u>S</u> 1. Talk on the phone.

<u>A</u> 2. Go out with your friends.

<u>C</u> 3. Make friends with only the popular kids at school.

<u>R</u> 4. Use the computer to play games.

<u>I</u> 5. Watch TV until dinner.

<u>F</u> 6. Eat your favorite snack.

<u>I</u> 7. Save up money to buy lots of things for yourself.

<u>C</u> 8. Hide your belongings so that others cannot use them.

<u>E</u> 9. Throw your clothes on the floor of your room.

Column B

C. Make friends with kids who seem lonely.

E. Clean up your room.

I. Donate some money to a good cause.

X. Help set the table for dinner.

S. Talk to God in prayer.

C. Share your belongings.

R. Use your computer for homework.

A. Go to Mass with your family.

F. Give up your favorite snack for Lent.

What great sacrifice was Abraham asked to make?

Worship Easter Vigil Reading

At the Easter Vigil liturgy, we celebrate the great sacrifice and Resurrection of Jesus. The second reading, which is from Genesis 22, is about a great **sacrifice** that proved Abraham's faith in God.

A reading from the Book of Genesis.

God put Abraham to the test. He called to him, "Abraham!" "Here I am!" he replied. Then God said: "Take your son Isaac, your only one, whom you love, and go to the land of Moriah. There you shall offer him up as a holocaust on a height that I will point out to you."

When they came to the place of which God had told him, Abraham built an altar there and arranged the wood on it. Then he reached out and took the knife to slaughter his son. But the LORD's messenger called to him from heaven, "Abraham, Abraham!" "Here I am," he answered. "Do not lay your hand on the boy," said the messenger. "Do not do the least thing to him. I know now how devoted you are to God, since you did not withhold from me your own beloved son." As Abraham looked about, he spied a ram caught by its horns in the thicket. So he went and took the ram and offered it up as a holocaust in place of his son.

Again the Lord's messenger called to Abraham from heaven and said: "I swear by myself, declares the LORD, that because you acted as you did in not withholding from me your beloved son, I will bless you abundantly and make your descendants as countless as the stars of the sky and the sands of the seashore; your descendants shall take possession of the gates of their enemies, and in your descendants all the nations of the earth shall find blessing—all this because you obeyed my command."

Genesis 22:1–2, 9a, 10–13, 15–18

The word of the Lord.
Thanks be to God.

Faith in the Promise

In Abraham's time, people believed that gods controlled their fate. To stay on the gods' "good side" or to ask for special favors, they offered sacrifices of animals, food, or firstborn sons to them. But Abraham offered sacrifices to the one, true God not in exchange for special favors, but as a way to express his feelings toward the Lord. He offered a holocaust, or burnt offering, as a loving gift to God.

Imagine how confused Abraham felt when the Lord asked him to sacrifice his own child, Isaac! Abraham knew that the Lord's promise depended upon Isaac. Isaac needed to grow up and have children of his own if Abraham was to have countless descendants, as God had promised. If Abraham tried to understand God's command without having faith, he might have refused to make the sacrifice.

In our own relationship with God, faith is an essential element. Without faith, we could not accept that to have eternal life, we must participate in Jesus' sacrifice through the Eucharist. In the Gospels, when Jesus explained this to crowds of people who followed him, they questioned him. How were they going to eat his Body and drink his Blood? Jesus answered, "Unless you eat the flesh of the Son of Man and drink his blood, you do not have life within you" (John 6:53). Jesus Christ invites us to receive his Body and Blood so we can share in everlasting life.

Our Church Teaches

An **altar** is a raised place for sacrifice and worship. Abraham built altars for God wherever God spoke to him. At Mass the changing of bread and wine into Christ's Body and Blood takes place on an altar. This altar is also a table, a place where we gather to share a meal and to celebrate that Jesus sacrificed himself for us. At Mass, we commemorate what happened at the Last Supper, when Jesus Christ shared a meal with his friends. He gave them his Body and Blood in the form of bread and wine. Jesus Christ invited all generations to share this meal together. Faithful to the Lord's command at the Last Supper, we continue to gather to share the Eucharistic meal.

We Believe

The Lord calls us to his table to receive his Body and Blood in the Eucharist. When we receive the Eucharist, we receive new life in Christ, who sacrificed his own life for us.

Faith Words

sacrifice

A sacrifice is an act of unselfish giving. It is also a ritual offering made to God by a priest on behalf of the people.

altar

An altar is a raised place where sacrifices are offered. The altar used for the center of worship during the Mass is also a table, where we gather to share the Eucharistic meal.

What sacrifices can we make?

Respond

Giving Blood

A girl named Christina suffered from a rare and serious disease. Her only chance for recovery seemed to be a blood transfusion from her five-year-old brother, Vincent. Vincent's blood had special fighting cells that Christina needed to get better. The doctor explained the situation to Vincent and his parents.

Vincent hesitated for a second, then took a deep breath and said, "I'll give my blood if it will save Christina."

The transfusion, or transfer of blood, from Vincent to Christina began. Vincent smiled when the color started to return to Christina's cheeks. Then his smile faded and his face grew pale. He looked up at the doctor and asked with a trembling voice, "Will I start to die right away?" He had misunderstood the doctor—he thought he was going to have to give his sister all of his blood!

What was Vincent's sacrifice? What did he think he was doing?

He is giving blood to his sister

What does this tell you about Vincent?

He is very brave and unselfish

Activities

1. God kept his promise to Abraham by sparing Isaac's life. Imagine that you are Isaac living in modern-day times. You want to send an e-mail to a friend about what happened that day in Moriah. In the e-mail below, describe what God promised your father, your feelings that day, and how God kept his promise.

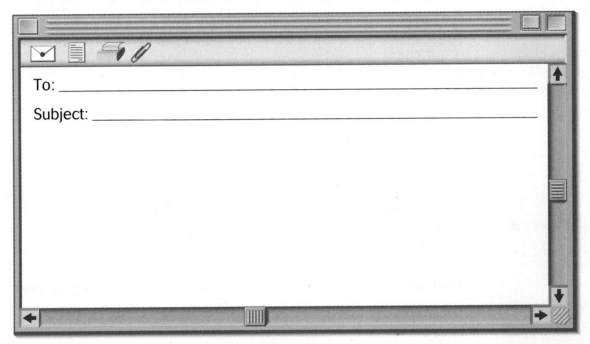

To: _____

Subject: _____

2. Write a journal entry about promises you have made in your own life. At the end of your entry, write one small thing you promise to do this week for someone else.

A Promise Journal

_____

_____

_____

_____

_____

How can we honor Jesus' sacrifice in our prayers?

Prayer Celebration

A Sabbath Blessing

Sunday is our Sabbath. It is a day on which we recollect and celebrate the Resurrection. We celebrate Mass. Jewish families celebrate their Sabbath from sundown on Friday to sundown on Saturday. They end the Sabbath with a ritual called Havdalah. With a braided candle, sweet spices, and a cup of wine, they gather and pray this prayer:

Wine Blessing:	Blessed are you, Lord, God of all creation; you have given us the fruit of the vine.
Spice Blessing:	Blessed are you, Lord, God of all creation, Creator of the spices that bring sweetness and joy to our lives.
Candle Blessing:	Blessed are you, Lord, God of all creation, Creator of the light of fire.
All:	Blessed is the Lord, who separated the Sabbath day from the other days.

Based on the Jewish Havdalah prayers

The family then puts the candle out and wishes each other a good week.

Let us now ask God to bless the food we eat, that it may strengthen us to do his work.

All:	O God, almighty Father, we humbly ask you that the living Bread, which has come down from heaven, may give us strength to relieve our brothers and sisters in their need. Through Christ our Lord. Amen.

Prayer After Communion, Mass in Time of Famine or for Those Suffering Hunger, Roman Missal

2 Chapter Review

A Complete the sentences with words from the box. Not all words will be used.

1. A _____ is an act of unselfish giving, or a ritual offering made to God by a priest on behalf of the people.

2. A raised place where sacrifices are offered is called an _____. It is the center of worship during the Mass.

3. The changing of bread and wine into Christ's _____ takes place on an altar.

4. At Mass we gather to celebrate the fact that _____ sacrificed himself for us.

5. During the Mass we offer our own sacrifice of _____ and thanksgiving to God for his blessings.

> Eucharist
>
> Jesus
>
> sacrifice
>
> praise
>
> Body and Blood
>
> altar

B Fill in the letter of the best answer.

1. Faithful to the Lord's command at the Last Supper, we continue to gather to share _____.
   - a. Penance
   - b. faith
   - c. the Passion play
   - d. the Eucharistic meal

2. _____ said, "Unless you eat the flesh of the Son of Man and drink his blood, you do not have life within you" (John 6:53).
   - a. Mary
   - b. Isaac
   - c. Jesus
   - d. Abraham

3. In Old Testament times, a _____, or burnt offering, was offered as a loving gift to God.
   - a. Havdalah
   - b. ram
   - c. sacrifice
   - d. holocaust

4. In our relationship with God, _____ is an essential element.
   - a. faith
   - b. music
   - c. science
   - d. art

Faith in Action

Altar Servers   Altar servers carry the cross and processional candles at Mass. They hold the Roman Missal, or prayer book, for the priest when he is not at the altar. And they assist in receiving the bread, wine, and water at the Presentation of Gifts. They wash the hands of the priest as he prepares to consecrate the bread and wine. Altar servers participate with the assembly in prayer responses and songs and are encouraged to be models of grace and reverence. Learning responsibility and organization, they serve Jesus in many ways as they grow in their faith and love for God's people.

In Everyday Life

Activity   Choose one of the following settings, and assume the role of authority figure. Describe the three most important rules you want people to follow. As appropriate, include rules about appearance, behavior, and noise levels.

classroom	family meal	Mass
online chat room	soup kitchen	ball field

1. _____

2. _____

3. _____

In Your Parish

Activity   Whether you're participating in Mass as an altar server or as a member of the congregation, being calm and attentive is important. Learn to be more quiet and attentive at Mass by spending more time this week in a quiet way. In the space provided, briefly describe two "quiet and attentive" experiences you can have this week, such as taking a walk or saying a silent prayer.

_____

_____

Take Home

FAMILY TIME

Covenant and Commitment

A covenant is a kind of agreement that was common in Old Testament times. Covenants were sealed in many different ways, such as with a sacred sacrifice, a special blessing, or a ritual meal. This chapter will explore some signs of the Covenant between God and Israel and how this Covenant was renewed in the generations after Abraham. In many ways, the same Covenant has been renewed for us through Jesus.

ACTIVITY

Fidelity Awards Make a list of chores and responsibilities for each family member. Use stars to mark the number of times during the month each person has done his or her chore. Reward the most faithful with a chore-free week.

January

Kevin	Clean the bathroom.	★★
Adam	Fold laundry.	★ ★
Caitlin	Walk Champ.	★★ ★

WEEKLY PLANNER

On Sunday

Think about how attending Mass represents part of our Covenant with God.

On the Web

www.blestarewe.com

Visit our Web site for the Saint of the day and the reflection question of the week.

Saint of the Week

 Saint Paul, Apostle and Martyr

Before Saint Paul was a follower of Christ, he persecuted Christians. His conversion came in a vision he had in which he encountered the Lord. Paul then dedicated his life to teaching people about Jesus. Paul made the ultimate sacrifice for his faith, dying as a martyr.

Feast Day: June 29

 A Prayer for the Week

Lord, in unexpected ways you come into our lives and invite us to share in your plan for Salvation. Help us to respond to your call faithfully. Amen.

Take Home

FAMILY TIME

✠ Scripture Background

Before the Time of Jesus

Rebecca When Rebecca first appears in the Old Testament (Genesis 24) she is innocent and beautiful. When we meet her as Isaac's wife and the mother of their twin sons, Jacob and Esau, she has become hard and calculating. Of her sons, Rebecca favors the younger Jacob. She plots with him to deceive Isaac, so he will receive Isaac's inheritance, which rightfully belongs to Esau. The plot succeeded, but Esau's anger at being cheated out of his birthright grew into a murderous fury. Rebecca sent away her favorite son to save his life, and she never saw him again. Read Genesis 27 to find out more about Jacob's deception.

OUR CATHOLIC TRADITION in Legends

The Holy Grail Since Bible times, Jewish family meals have often begun with blessing wine, the day, and family members. The wine is held in a special cup called a kiddush cup or blessing cup. The cup Jesus raised at the Last Supper was probably such a cup. Tradition says the Apostles saved this cup and Peter used it to celebrate the Eucharist. The cup was handed down through the centuries, and its whereabouts were the subject of many legends. It became known as the Holy Grail. The only cup in existence that might be the true cup is a small agate one, shown in the photograph, located in a cathedral in Valencia, Spain.

3 Covenant and Commitment

May God give to you
    of the dew of the heavens
And of the fertility of the earth.

Genesis 27:28

Share

In Abraham's time, agreements between people were mostly verbal, or spoken. There were no written legal contracts. Only the spoken word was required. Agreements were sealed, or made final, with symbolic rituals. In a custom we still use today, giving a blessing involved laying hands upon the head of the person being blessed. Gestures such as these still seal some of the promises or agreements we make in our everyday lives. Can you think of gestures that you have used to show that your words are truthful?

Activity

Draw a line from the gesture to the promise or thought it expresses.

Hand over one's heart	"I respect your authority."
First two fingers raised in a "V" shape	"In the name of the Father, and of the Son, and of the Holy Spirit."
Three fingers raised	"I'm being honest."
Salute	"We agree."
Shaking hands	"Peace."
Crossing one's heart	"I promise to tell the truth."
Right hand raised	"I will be faithful to my duties in this group."
Sign of the Cross	"I pledge allegiance."

How do God's people show they honor his promise?

Hear & Believe

✝ Scripture Jacob and the Covenant

God had promised Abraham that if he kept the Covenant he would have countless descendants. Isaac honored the Covenant the Lord had made with his father, Abraham. But Isaac's wife, Rebecca, was unable to have children.

Isaac prayed to the LORD, and Rebecca became pregnant with twin boys. Rebecca could feel the babies wrestling in her womb. She asked the LORD why the babies were fighting. The LORD told her, "Two nations are in your womb, but one will be more powerful, and the older shall serve the younger."

Esau was born first. Esau grew up to be burly and hairy, and he enjoyed being outdoors. He was Isaac's favorite. Jacob was the second son. Jacob liked simple things and would rather stay inside. Jacob was Rebecca's favorite, and she tried hard to protect him.

According to custom, Esau was entitled to Isaac's birthright, the right to become the family patriarch and receive a large inheritance when Isaac died. Esau did not care much about his birthright. He even traded it with Jacob for a bowl of stew.

One day, Isaac, who was ill and blind in his old age, called for Esau so he could say a special blessing to give Esau his birthright. Rebecca overheard what Isaac said to Esau, but she wanted Jacob to receive Isaac's blessing. She helped Jacob pretend he was Esau. She dressed him in Esau's clothes and hairy animal skins and sent him to see Isaac.

Isaac fell for the trick. He gave the blessing to Jacob, saying, "May God give to you of the dew of the heavens and of the fertility of the earth abundance of grain and wine. Let peoples serve you, and nations pay you homage."

The blessing could not be taken back, even though Isaac was tricked. Esau was angry with Jacob, so Jacob went away to a safe place. He wandered to a holy place which he later named Bethel, meaning "house of God." One night, he fell asleep with his head on a rock. He dreamed that the LORD promised him many descendants, protection, and land. When Jacob awoke, he took the stone he had slept on and blessed it as a memorial to God. He then vowed to be faithful to the LORD.

Based on Genesis 25:19–34, 27, 28:10–22

Covenant People

It was important for Jacob to receive Isaac's birthright because it meant a special blessing and the right to be the patriarch. Jacob would later have twelve sons whose children would become the Twelve Tribes, or large family groups, of Israel. Jacob's story shows how God renewed his original promise to give Abraham as many descendants as stars in the sky. Rebecca and Jacob's plot to get the birthright was dishonest, but it shows that the fulfillment of God's promises often happens in unexpected ways.

In Jacob's dream at Bethel, God said to him, "I will never leave you until I have done what I promised you" (Genesis 28:15). Jacob trusted God's promises and vowed to be faithful in return. Later on, Jacob would wrestle with a messenger of God. Jacob prevailed against the messenger. Because of this God changed Jacob's name to Israel, which means "one who struggled with God."

Our Church Teaches

God began the everlasting **Covenant** with all living beings when he promised Noah that he would never again destroy the earth by flood. This Covenant was a loving and sacred relationship between God and his people. Noah, Abraham, Isaac, and Jacob honored the Covenant by being faithful to God. We have a part in continuing this relationship. If we try to live as Christ did, honestly, simply, and lovingly, we are Covenant people. The Bible says, "If you belong to Christ, then you are Abraham's descendant, heirs according to the promise" (Galatians 3:29). In Jesus Christ, we have forgiveness of sin and hope of everlasting friendship with God. Believing in Jesus, following his teachings, and participating in the Mass strengthen our commitment to live as God's people.

As Catholics, we have many types of covenants in our lives. In Confirmation, for example, the Holy Spirit strengthens our bond with the Church and our obligation to carry out its mission. Matrimony is a covenant between one man and one woman that requires them to be faithful to each other for their entire lives. We also keep everyday covenants by being loyal to our friends, respecting our parents, and being honest. We strive to keep promises we make and try not to make promises we cannot keep. In the same way, we only take oaths, in which we call on God to be our witness, when absolutely necessary and when the oaths are true.

We Believe

God calls us to bear witness to our faith, in our words and through our actions.

Faith Words

convenant

A covenant is a sacred agreement or relationship, sometimes sealed by a ritual or ceremony. Isaac honored the Covenant the Lord made with his father, Abraham.

How does God's love change people?

Respond

Saint Paul

The early Christians were often persecuted, or punished, sometimes even killed, for their beliefs. If Christians identified themselves publicly as Christ's followers, they put their lives at risk from those who did not believe.

Before Saint Paul was a follower of Christ, he was one of the people who hated the early Christians. His original name was Saul. His mission was to persecute people who called themselves Christians.

One day, while Saul was on his way to Damascus to hunt for more Christians, a great light shone around him. Suddenly, he fell to the ground and was struck blind.

A voice said, "Saul, Saul, why are you persecuting me?"

"Who are you, sir?" Saul asked.

"I am Jesus, the one you are persecuting."

Shaken and confused, Saul asked, "What do you want me to do?" Jesus told him to go on to Damascus, where he would be told what to do. At that moment, through the power of God, Saul received the gift of faith in Jesus. Temporarily blinded, he could see the truth with his heart.

Saul was baptized. He took the name of Paul. After this experience, his mission was to teach people to know and love Jesus. After a life of preaching and imprisonment for his teachings, Paul made the ultimate sacrifice for his faith. He gave up his life for his beliefs, dying as a martyr in Rome. Martyrs were ordinary people whose extraordinary faith enabled them to give their lives for their belief in Christ. This is the greatest sign of commitment to Jesus and the Church. Paul's story shows just how much believing in the Lord can change someone.

Saint Paul's feast day is June 29.

A New Life in the Lord

The stories of Abraham and Sarah, Jacob, and Saint Paul show us how God's Revelation can change people so much that they need new names to identify themselves. Catholics sometimes use new names to mark an important change in themselves. For Confirmation, Catholics may choose the name of a Saint whom they admire and whose characteristics and virtues they want to attain.

Activities

1. Write your full name on the lines provided. Using the letters in your name, create words that describe something special about you, and write them on the lines below.

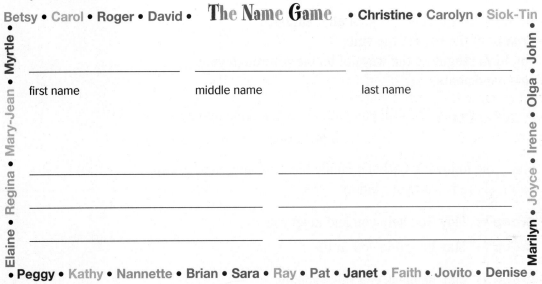

Betsy • Carol • Roger • David • **The Name Game** • **Christine** • Carolyn • Siok-Tin

Elaine • Regina • Mary-Jean • **Myrtle**

Marilyn • Joyce • Irene • Olga • John

_____   _____   _____
first name   middle name   last name

• **Peggy** • Kathy • Nannette • Brian • Sara • Ray • Pat • **Janet** • Faith • Jovito • Denise •

2. Acts of faith are not always as dramatic as Abraham's, Jacob's, or Saint Paul's. Draw or write one thing you can do in your everyday life to show you are committed to following Jesus.

How can we pray as Isaac did?

Prayer Celebration

A Family Blessing

Blessings ask God to make someone or something holy. Before their Sabbath meal, Jewish families pray blessings for the day and one another. They hold a candle-lighting ritual and a ceremony called *kiddush,* which involves blessing wine and bread. The prayers that the priest says over the gifts during Mass are similar.

Blessed are you, Lord, God of all creation,
Creator of the fruit of the vine.
You have taught us the ways of holiness through your commandments.

Blessed are you, O Lord; you make holy the Sabbath day.

Based on the Jewish kiddush blessings

Share the following Catholic family blessing with your group. Later, share it with your family.

Group 1: May God help you and keep you.

Group 2: May he guide you in life.

Group 1: May he bless you this evening.

Group 2: And keep you from harm.

Group 1: May God bless *(make the Sign of the Cross over Group 2)* you *(name the people being blessed).*

Group 2: And God bless *(make the Sign of the Cross over Group 1)* you, too *(name the people being blessed).*

Based on the Parental Blessing of Children,
Canadian Catholic Conference

A **Complete** each sentence below.

1. A _____ is a sacred agreement or relationship, sometimes sealed by a ceremony.

2. Rebecca helped _____ trick Isaac into giving him his _____, which rightfully belonged to Esau.

3. _____ is a covenant between one man and one woman that requires them to be faithful for their whole lives.

4. A(n) _____ is a promise that must be truthful and taken only when necessary.

5. In _____'s dream at Bethel, God said to him, "I will never leave you until I have done what I promised you."

6. _____ is a Sacrament that strengthens our bond with the Church.

7. Before _____ was a follower of Christ, he was one of the people who persecuted the Christians.

8. _____ were ordinary people with extraordinary faith who gave up their lives for their belief in Christ.

9. If we try to live simply, honestly, and lovingly, we are _____ people.

B **Respond** to the following.

1. As Catholics, what are some covenants we have in our lives?

_____

_____

2. Describe some ways in which a person your age can honor the Covenant with God to live as a follower of Christ.

_____

_____

Faith in Action

Legislative Advocacy Groups   Lawmakers spend a lot of time making decisions that affect us all. Influencing lawmakers to make laws that reflect the values of our Catholic faith is the work of parish advocacy groups. As Catholics, we can help shape public policy that respects life and the environment, that promotes peaceful means of resolving conflicts, and that leads to economic justice for all people. Catholic voices speaking out together can be heard loud and clear by lawmakers.

In Everyday Life

Activity   Choose an issue that concerns you, such as pollution, poverty, or an issue affecting your local community, and in the space provided, write what you would want to tell a lawmaker regarding your concerns. Also tell what actions you would like to see lawmakers take.

_____

_____

_____

_____

_____

In Your Parish

Activity   Use your knowledge of Catholic teachings to explain why you would or would not support a motion such as this: *Towns and other communities should have programs that provide food and other assistance to the poor and elderly.*

I agree/disagree (circle one) with this statement because _____

_____

_____

_____.

Take Home

FAMILY TIME

Piety and Prayer

Joseph was one of Jacob's sons and a patriarch, or founding father, of the People Israel. As a boy, Joseph's jealous brothers sold him into slavery in Egypt. Through a series of miraculous events Joseph rose from being a servant to being Pharaoh's chief assistant. Throughout all the ups and downs of his life Joseph was directed by his faith in God. Joseph's trust in God was richly rewarded.

ACTIVITY

Family Callings Have family members draw outlines of themselves and fill them in with clothing, tools, or other objects that illustrate what they would like their lives to be like five or ten years from now. Talk about the work, cooperation, and trust involved in realizing your goals.

WEEKLY PLANNER

On Sunday

When the priest says, "Let us pray," speak to God quietly and listen for God speaking to you.

On the Web

www.blestarewe.com

Visit our Web site for the Saint of the day and the reflection question of the week.

Saint of the Week

 Saint André Bessette (1845–1937)

Saint André Bessette worked as a doorkeeper at Notre Dame College in Montreal for forty years. He had a special ministry to the sick, and many who came to him were healed. Brother André encouraged all who sought intercession to pray to Saint Joseph, to whom he had a special devotion.

Feast Day: January 6

A Prayer for the Week

God, teach us to hear your voice in our hearts and in the presence of those around us. Like Saint André Bessette, may we live a life of prayer and service. Amen.

Take Home

FAMILY TIME

✠ Scripture Background

Before the Time of Jesus

Interpreting Dreams   For many ancient cultures, dreams were accepted as supernatural messages. The dreams of royalty were considered especially significant, and rulers sought advisers who were able to interpret dreams. Those who succeeded were revered, as is evident in Joseph's story. When Pharaoh dreamed of cattle and crops, all the wise men of Egypt were called upon to interpret his dream. None succeeded. When Joseph, a Hebrew, was able to interpret the dream as a warning of seven years of prosperity followed by seven years of famine, Pharaoh made him his chief assistant. Read Genesis 41 to learn about Pharaoh's dream.

OUR CATHOLIC TRADITION in Art

The Madonna of the Magnificat

During the Renaissance, European artists created countless paintings of the Blessed Virgin Mary. One of the most famous is Botticelli's *Madonna of the Magnificat.*

Botticelli created the *Madonna of the Magnificat* in the early 1480s. The painting features nearly life-size figures, and is lavishly covered with gold paint. It depicts Mary being crowned as the Queen of Heaven as she holds the Christ Child and writes the words of the Magnificat.

Today this painting can be seen in the Uffizi Gallery, in Florence, Italy.

4 Piety and Prayer

> The Mighty One has done great things for me,
> and holy is his name.
>
> *Luke 1:49*

Share

Finding and being a loyal friend are wonderful blessings. What do you look for in a good friend? You probably want someone with whom you can share your private feelings. You want a friend you can trust not to judge you or betray you. A good friend will also look out for your safety. Most likely, you will do the same things for your close friend, too. This is what loyal friendship is all about. In the same way, God is loyal and true to his people. God is always there when we need him to listen. God will not betray us, and he protects us always.

Activity

A local newspaper is doing a story on friendships and has chosen you and a good friend as the subjects of the article. Below, write a headline for your article, and draw two pictures about your friendship to go with the story. On the lines under each picture, write a description of what the picture shows.

PAGE 2 • THE COMMUNITY H...

**VOLUME 16
ISSUE 173
50¢**

The COMMUNITY HERALD

Having a fun
time Playinghockey

How does
God respond
to our loyalty?

✝ Scripture Joseph, the Loyal Son

After Jacob left Bethel, God kept him safe. He journeyed to Haran and married a woman named Rachel. Rachel was unable to have children. She prayed to have a child and finally gave birth to a son, Joseph. Jacob and his family settled in Canaan.

Jacob had eleven other sons, but his favorite son was Joseph. Joseph's eleven brothers were jealous of him, especially of a colorful tunic that Jacob had given him. They began to hate him even more when he told them about his dreams. In one dream, Joseph saw eleven stars, the sun, and the moon all bowing down to him. "Are you planning to rule us?" the brothers asked Joseph. They said to each other, "Let us kill Joseph. We can say a wild beast ate him. We shall then see what comes of his dreams!"

The brothers stripped Joseph of his tunic, threw him into a well, and left him out in the desert. Finally, they decided to sell Joseph as a slave, and passing traders took him to Egypt. The brothers dipped Joseph's tunic in goat's blood and gave it to a messenger to bring to their father. "My son's tunic!" Jacob cried. "A wild beast has eaten him!"

But God protected Joseph. Joseph came to live in the home of Potiphar, an assistant of Pharoah, Egypt's ruler. Potiphar liked Joseph and gave him the job of running his household. From then on, the LORD's blessing was upon everything in the home. But then Potiphar's wife began to flirt with Joseph. Joseph ignored her. "How could I commit so great a wrong and offend God?" he said. Potiphar's wife was insulted. To get revenge, she falsely accused Joseph of attacking her, and Joseph was thrown into jail.

Even in jail, the LORD blessed Joseph. The chief jailer put him in charge of the other prisoners. Joseph had a gift for telling other prisoners the meaning of their dreams. Pharaoh was having nightmares, so he sent for Joseph. "In one dream," Pharaoh told Joseph, "I saw seven ears of grain, growing fat and healthy. Behind them sprouted seven ears of grain, shriveled and thin. They swallowed up the seven healthy ears."

Joseph told Pharaoh, "God is telling you that seven years of plentiful food will be followed by seven years of famine." Pharaoh put Joseph in charge of storing food to prepare for the famine. When the famine came, Egypt was ready.

After two years of famine, Jacob and his other sons were running out of food. Jacob sent ten of his sons to Egypt to buy grain. He kept Benjamin, the last child Rachel had before she died, at home with him. Jacob's sons went to see Pharaoh's chief assistant, who was actually Joseph.

Joseph recognized his brothers, but they did not recognize him. Wanting to see his brother Benjamin, Joseph sent his brothers back to get him.

The brothers feared that Jacob, still mourning over Joseph, would never let them take Benjamin. But they did what Joseph asked. When they returned with Benjamin, Joseph told a servant to hide a silver cup in Benjamin's grain bag. Then Joseph accused the brothers of stealing it and ordered Benjamin to be jailed. The brothers panicked.

"If Benjamin is not with us when we go back home, our father will die of grief!" pleaded Judah, one of the brothers.

Joseph was touched by his brothers' concern for their father. "I am your brother Joseph," he revealed, "whom you sold into Egypt." The brothers were shocked. Joseph said he forgave his brothers because he understood God's plan for him. "It was not really you but God who had me come here, for the sake of saving lives," he said. "God has made me a father to Pharaoh, lord of his household, and ruler over Egypt."

The brothers went home and told Jacob the news, and the whole family moved to Egypt. Pharaoh treated the family well. The twelve sons of Jacob had many children and grandchildren. They all became known as the Twelve Tribes of Israel. Each tribe was named after one of Jacob's sons. They waited patiently for the time when they would return to Canaan.

Based on Genesis 29:1–30; 30:1, 22–24; 35:22; 37; 39–47:12; 48:21

An Example of Piety

Joseph brought joy to his father, and reconciliation to his family. His story shows us the rewards of being loyal to God. Joseph remained faithful to God. He never sought revenge for his brothers' actions; instead, he forgave them. When Potiphar's wife tempted him, he resisted. He was patient even when he was jailed unfairly. God rewarded him for this **fidelity** by making him a great ruler in Egypt. Even as a ruler, Joseph was humble. His only concern was how to serve God. Joseph's **piety** is an example for us.

Our Church Teaches

As we see from Joseph's story, there will always be distractions from God. But like Joseph, we can overcome those distractions. Joseph faced many difficulties, but he always remained focused on God's will. Separated from his own father, Joseph relied on God as his father. When we become distracted in our prayers, like Joseph, we should think of God as our caring Father and try to turn our hearts back to him.

Faith Words

fidelity
Fidelity is faithfulness and loyalty to something or someone. Joseph is a model of fidelity to God.

piety
Piety is putting God above everything else.

How did Hebrew prayers address God?

Respond

The Lord Helps the Lowly

Joseph's own brothers had plotted to kill him. They threw him into a ditch, and he ended up a slave. But the Bible tells us that "the LORD was with him and brought success to all he did" (Genesis 39:23). When Joseph became a ruler, he believed that God was responsible for all his blessings. He was a servant of God before anything else.

The Hebrews often prayed to God in hymns and songs that said they were servants of the Lord. They praised God as the protector of all humble servants. Let us sing or pray this traditional hymn, which praises God for the help he gives to faithful people who are powerless or poor.

Alleluia.
Praise the LORD, O my soul;
    I will praise the LORD all my life;
    I will sing praise to my God while
        I live.
Happy he whose help is the God
        of Jacob,
    whose hope is in the LORD,
        his God,
Who made heaven and earth,
    the sea and all that is in them;
Who keeps faith forever,
    secures justice for the oppressed,
    gives food to the hungry.

The LORD sets captives free;
    the LORD gives sight to the blind.
The LORD raises up those that were
        bowed down;
    the LORD loves the just.
The LORD protects strangers;
    the fatherless and the widow
        he sustains,
    but the way of the wicked
        he thwarts.
The LORD shall reign forever;
    your God, O Zion, through all
        generations. Alleluia.

Psalm 146:1–2, 5–10

Activities

1. Reread the lines of the psalm that are in blue. They name things that God does for people who are powerless or in need. Rewrite the blue lines to describe how God helps you.

The Lord _____

The Lord _____

The Lord _____

The Lord _____

The Lord _____

2. Mary, the Mother of Jesus, was a Hebrew woman who may have prayed many traditional hymns such as the one you just prayed. When God asked her to be the Mother of Jesus, she praised the Lord in a *canticle,* a poem or hymn of praise. Her prayer said that the Lord takes care of the poor and lifts them up.

The following song is based on Mary's prayer. Complete Verse 3 by writing two sentences, one that praises God and one that names something wonderful God has done.

Chorus:
Proclaim the greatness of God; rejoice in my God, my Savior!
Rejoice in God, my Savior!

Verse 1:
My soul is filled with joy as I sing to God my Savior:
you have looked upon your servant, you have visited your people.

Chorus

Verse 2:
I am lowly as a child, but I know from this day forward
that my name will be remembered, for all will call me blessed.

Chorus

Verse 3:

_____

_____

What were Mary's own words to God?

Chorus

Chorus: Luke 1:46–55, James Chepponis ©1989 GIA Publications, Inc.
Verses 1 and 2: Luke 1:46–55, David Haas ©1989 GIA Publications, Inc.

✝ Prayer Celebration

The Magnificat

Mary's canticle is called the Magnificat, which means
"praises." The Magnificat is from Luke 1:46–55.
Catholics pray it as an evening prayer.

Leader: Let us pray Mary's canticle of praise.

All:
My soul proclaims the greatness
of the Lord,
  my spirit rejoices in God my
  Savior;
for he has looked with favor on his lowly
  servant.
From this day all generations will
  call me blessed:
The Almighty has done great things for me:
  holy is his Name.
He has mercy on those who fear him
  in every generation.
He has shown the strength of his arm,
  he has scattered the proud in their
    conceit.
He has cast down the mighty from their
    thrones,
  and has lifted up the lowly.
He has filled the hungry with good things,
  and the rich he has sent away empty.
He has come to the help of his servant
    Israel,
  for he has remembered his promise of
    mercy,
the promise he made to our fathers,
  to Abraham and his children forever.
Amen.

A **Match** Column A with Column B by writing the correct number in the space provided.

A

1. Rachel

2. Pharaoh

3. Magnificat

4. fidelity

5. Mary

6. piety

7. Joseph

8. prayer

9. Benjamin

B

_7_ Jacob's favorite son; dreamed of seven years of famine

_3_ Mary's canticle, or song of praise to God

_9_ youngest brother of Joseph

_2_ the title for a ruler of ancient Egypt

_4_ faithfulness and loyalty to something or someone

_8_ requires keeping our minds and hearts focused on God

_6_ putting God above everything else

_1_ wife of Jacob; mother of Joseph

_5_ her prayer said that the Lord lifts up the poor

B **Complete** the sentences, using words from the box. Not all words will be used.

1. God rewarded Joseph for his _____ by making him a great ruler in Egypt.

2. Like Joseph, we should always remain focused on God's __Will__.

3. Joseph and his brothers became known as the __Fidelity__ of Israel.

4. Because we trust God, we pray to him as "__Father__."

5. In the Magnificat, Mary proclaims, "The __Almighty__ has done great things for me: holy is his Name."

| Father |
| fidelity |
| Twelve Tribes |
| Almighty |
| will |
| First Fathers |

Faith in Action

Parish Youth Groups   Parish youth groups are a great place for young people to get to know one another. Youth group members share good times as well as the challenges of growing up as Catholics in a world that doesn't always respect their values. They help with parish fundraisers and participate in service projects. Parish youth groups are where many of us will learn firsthand that Saint Francis was right when he said, "It is in giving that we receive."

In Everyday Life

Activity   In the left-hand column, list some qualities your friends have that make you like them. In the right-hand, list some qualities you have that you think make your friends like you.

What I like about my friends	What my friends like about me
_____	_____
_____	_____
_____	_____
_____	_____
_____	_____

In Your Parish

Activity   List two or three qualities that you feel are essential for a youth minister to have, and that would make this person a good role model. Explain why these are important. Then name someone you know who would be an ideal candidate for this role.

_____

_____

_____

God Saves and Delivers Us

God saved the Hebrew people from slavery in Egypt. Through the life, Death, and Resurrection of Jesus Christ, we are freed from the slavery of sin to live as the new people of God.

Sing to the LORD, for he is gloriously triumphant; horse and chariot he has cast into the sea.

Exodus 15:21

Hebrew slaves may have helped build this statue of the pharaoh Ramses II. The map shows the Hebrew people's journey out of Egypt to the promised land.

Mediterranean Sea

Sea of Galilee

Jordan R.

Jaffa

Promised Land

Gaza

CANAAN

Jerusalem

Jericho

Dead Sea

Goshen

SINAI

Memphis

EXODUS

EGYPT

Gulf of Suez

Mt. Sinai

Red Sea

Journey to the Promised Land

Wade in the Water

African-American spiritual
Arranged by Diana Kodner

REFRAIN
All

Wade in the wa-ter, wade in the wa-ter, chil-dren, wade in the wa-ter, God's a gon-na trou-ble the wa-ter.

VERSE
Cantor

1. See that host all dressed in white,
2. See that band all dressed in red,
3. Look o-ver yon-der, what do I see?
4. If you don't be-lieve I've been re-deemed,

All

God's a gon-na trou-ble the wa-ter;

Cantor

The lead-er looks like the Is-ra-el-ite,
Looks like the band that Mo-ses led,
The Ho-ly Ghost a com-in' on me,
Just fol-low me down to Jor-dan's stream,

All

D.C.

God's a gon-na trou-ble the wa-ter.

Take Home

FAMILY TIME

Slavery and Deliverance

The story of Moses and the Exodus is a key part of the Salvation story of God's people. God spoke to Moses in a burning bush and asked Moses to lead the Israelites out of slavery to their own land. Through escaping slavery in Egypt, the Israelites learned new lessons about themselves as God's special people. We can learn from their story and from our own family journeys.

ACTIVITY

Family Hieroglyphics The ancient Egyptian alphabet, called hieroglyphics, consisted of symbols that represented letters. Create an alphabet of symbols that mean something to your family. For instance, a stick figure of a girl could represent the letter *H* if there is a girl in the family named Hannah.

WEEKLY PLANNER

On Sunday

Listen to the Second Reading at Mass for themes of slavery and freedom.

On the Web

www.blestarewe.com

Visit our Web site for the Saint of the day and the reflection question of the week.

Saint of the Week

Saint Martin de Porres (1579–1639)

Martin de Porres, a Dominican friar, lived near Lima, Peru, during the time of the slave trade. His days were filled with nursing the sick and caring for slaves and the poor of the city. His love for all people, regardless of their color, race, or status, set an example for others of his time.

Patron Saint of: racial harmony
Feast Day: November 3

A Prayer for the Week

Thank you, God, for our freedom to be your followers. Give us the courage to stand firm in our beliefs. Amen.

Take Home

FAMILY TIME

✝ Scripture Background

Before the Time of Jesus

Egypt and the Israelites   The Egyptian civilization developed in the fertile land along the Nile River. From its origins as a distinct state around 3000 B.C. through Roman times, Egypt prospered. The story of the Israelites is often set in Egypt. When famine struck Canaan, Abraham escaped to Egypt (Genesis 12:10). Later, Abraham's great-grandson Joseph rescued his father and brothers and helped them settle in Egypt (Genesis 47:1–12). The book of Exodus recounts the Israelites' enslavement in Egypt and their escape to the promised land under Moses' leadership.

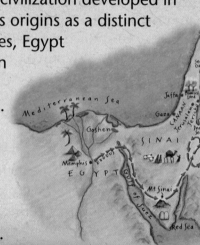

OUR CATHOLIC TRADITION in History

Saint Peter Claver   Saint Peter Claver, a Spanish Jesuit missioner, was sent to Cartagena (part of modern Colombia) in 1610. Cartagena was a port of entry for slave trading ships. Peter soon found himself busy with all the sick and demoralized slaves who had survived the inhumane treatment on the ships. He went into the holds of the ships and gave the slaves food and water. He told them about Jesus and that they were precious in God's eyes. Slave owners believed that slaves only had worth as property, so

Saint Peter Claver's message was a subversive one. He called himself "a slave to the Negroes forever." His feast day is September 9.

5 Slavery and Deliverance

Sing to the Lord, for he is gloriously triumphant;
horse and chariot he has cast into the sea.

Exodus 15:21

Share

When you hear the word *slave*, you probably think of a person who
is completely under the control of another person. But people can
also become enslaved by poverty, prejudice, addiction, violence,
materialism, and other wrongs in society. Many things can take
away a person's freedom to live peacefully and lovingly.

Activity

Complete the sentences under each photograph.

The people in this picture have become

slaves of _____.

They do not have the freedom to _____

_____.

The people in this picture have become

slaves of _____.

They do not have the freedom to _____

_____.

Pick one photograph and write how the people shown might

be delivered, or freed, from slavery. _____

_____

_____

What does
Yahweh
mean?

✝ Scripture The Exodus

God had promised Abraham, Isaac, and Jacob that he would give them land that would be home to their descendants, and he fulfilled his promise.

For many years after Joseph's death, the descendants of Joseph's family prospered in Egypt. They were known as the Hebrews or Israelites.

But then a new Pharoah told the Egyptians, "The Israelites keep growing! Let us stop them before they become powerful." He made the Hebrews slaves, forcing them to build cities and work in fields.

The Hebrew families kept growing. Pharaoh ordered, "Throw every Hebrew baby boy into the river!" Jochebed, a Hebrew woman, gave birth to a son. To keep him from being killed, she hid him. Later, she put him in a basket and placed it in the reeds on the riverbank. Pharaoh's daughter spotted the baby. She adopted him and named him Moses.

A long time passed. The Israelites cried out to God about their slavery. One day, after Moses grew up, he was leading a flock of sheep across the desert. He saw fire coming out of a bush but not burning it.

Moses heard the LORD say, "Come no closer! This is holy ground. I am the God of your father, the God of Abraham, the God of Isaac, the God of Jacob. I have seen my people suffer in Egypt. I will rescue them. I will lead them out of Egypt into a land flowing with milk and honey. Go to Pharaoh to lead my people, the Israelites, out of Egypt."

"But," Moses said, "if I tell the Israelites, 'The God of your fathers sent me to you,' and they ask, 'What is his name?' what should I say?"

God said, "I am who I am. Tell the Israelites: Yahweh sent me to you."

Moses went to Pharaoh and said, "The LORD, the God of Israel, has said, 'Let my people go.'"

But Pharaoh would not obey. Because of this plagues came upon the land. The Nile River turned into blood. Frogs, gnats, flies, animal disease, boils, hail, locusts, and three days of darkness came. Pharaoh still did not give in. Then the LORD commanded the Hebrew families to prepare a special meal and mark their doorways with lamb's blood so that the next plague would "pass over" their homes. It would be a plague of death! That night, all the firstborns in Egypt died, even Pharaoh's son. Pharaoh sent for Moses. "Leave now, you and the Israelites with you!" he cried.

The Israelites marched out of Egypt. But suddenly Pharaoh wished he had not let the Israelites go. He sent out more than 600 chariots with warriors to catch them.

Pharaoh's armies caught up with the Israelites at the Red Sea. The Israelites called out to the LORD in great fright. The LORD told Moses,

"Stretch your hand out over the sea." When Moses did this, the LORD swept the sea with a strong wind, turning the sea into dry land. The Israelites marched in, with a wall of water on their right and left. When the Egyptians chased after them, the water flowed back, drowning Pharaoh's whole army.

The Israelites sang songs thanking the LORD for leading them safely toward the promised land. Moses' sister, Miriam, led the women in dancing and praising the LORD.

Based on Genesis 50:24 and Exodus 1—15:21

God's Love Delivers Us

The story about God's freeing the Israelites from slavery and leading them out of Egypt is called the **Exodus**. Exodus is the second book of the Old Testament. The Israelites in Egypt believed in God's promises to their ancestors, so they cried out to God for help. God chose Moses to teach the Israelites his word and to lead them to freedom.

At the burning bush, God revealed an important mystery he had not revealed to the patriarchs Abraham, Isaac, Jacob, and Joseph. God told Moses his sacred name, **Yahweh**, which means "I am who I am." This means God is the only God, who exists forever. No one created God; he created everything and everyone and only he has this power to create. God creates our souls with the plan to reward us with everlasting life with him. All creation is destined for God's glory. God delivered the Israelites from their suffering in Egypt and led them to the **promised land**. In the same way, he delivers us from sin and leads us to everlasting life. This is the greatest deliverance of all.

Our Church Teaches

The Book of Exodus describes one of the most important saving acts of God. The Old Testament is filled with signs of God's love and faithfulness. But the New Testament tells of God's greatest act of love: sending his Son, Jesus, into the world to save all people. Jesus suffered and died for our sins. Because of Jesus, the Church can forgive any sin, no matter how great. Jesus Christ rose from the dead and ascended into Heaven. With him we can share in the promised land of Heaven. Because of Jesus' Death and Resurrection, people do not have to be afraid of death. If we love God and others as Jesus taught, death leads to everlasting happiness with God.

Faith Words

Exodus
The Exodus is the Old Testament story of how God freed the Hebrews in Egypt. Exodus is the second book of the Old Testament.

Yahweh
Yahweh is the most sacred name of God, spoken to Moses. It means "I am who I am."

promised land
The promised land is Canaan, the sacred place God promised to Abraham, Isaac, Jacob, and the Israelites in Egypt.

How do God's people express their need to be free?

Bound by Faith

In the eighteenth and nineteenth centuries, African people were forced to come to America as slaves. African slaves were robbed of their freedom and self-esteem. They suffered in many of the same ways as the Hebrews did in Egypt.

To help them survive, African slaves sang songs called *spirituals*, which expressed their faith in God. The slaves sang about a journey to spiritual as well as physical freedom and asked Jesus to set them free on the inside. They called on the heroes of the Old Testament as friends who could help them in their struggles. One person began the spiritual by singing about his or her sadness or joy. A group would sing a response. The following spiritual is called "Go Down, Moses."

Solo: When Israel was in Egypt's land

Group: Let my people go!

Solo: Oppressed so hard they could not stand

All (refrain):
Let my people go!
Go down, Moses,
'way down in Egypt's land.
Tell ol' Pharaoh to
let my people go!

Solo: The Lord told Moses what to do

Group: Let my people go!

Solo: To lead the children of Israel through
Refrain

Solo: As Israel stood by the water side

Group: Let my people go!

Solo: At God's command it did divide
Refrain

Solo: When they had reached the other shore

Group: Let my people go!

Solo: They sang a song of triumph o'er
Refrain

Solo: Oh, let us all from bondage flee

Group: Let my people go!

Solo: And let us all in Christ be free
Refrain

Did You Know...

...African slaves used their songs as secret codes? The song "Steal Away to Jesus" was used to call secret meetings. Frederick Douglass, a slave liberator, used the line "I am bound for Canaan" to signal that he was going North.

Activity

The ancient Egyptian alphabet was made of pictures instead of letters. The pictures are called *hieroglyphics*. The key shows hieroglyphics for the letters in our alphabet. Use it to translate the song Miriam sang when the Hebrews crossed the Red Sea.

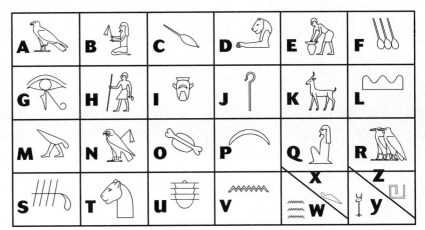

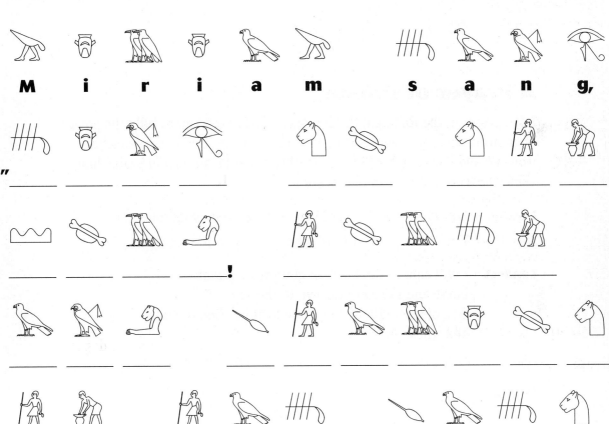

M i r i a m   s a n g,

"_____

_____ !

_____

_____

_____ ."

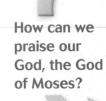

How can we praise our God, the God of Moses?

 ## Prayer Celebration

A Prayer of Praise

After crossing the Red Sea, the Israelites understood more fully the power of Yahweh. Their praises went up to God in a song. God has freed us all from sin and death by his Son, Jesus Christ. Let us stand and praise him, using the words of the Israelites' song.

Leader: Let us sing to the Lord who is covered in wondrous glory.

All: Let us sing to the Lord who is covered in wondrous glory.

Leader: I will sing to the Lord, in glory triumphant;
horse and rider are thrown to the sea.
God of strength, of song, of salvation, God of mine,
hear these praises.

All: Let us sing to the Lord who is covered in wondrous glory.

Leader: My God is a warrior whose name is "The Lord."
Pharaoh's army is thrown to the sea.
Your right hand is magnificent in pow'r,
your right hand has crushed the enemy.

All: Let us sing to the Lord who is covered in wondrous glory.

Leader: In your mercy you led the people you redeemed.
You brought them to your sacred home.
There you will plant them on the mountain that is yours.
The Lord shall reign forever!

All: Let us sing to the Lord who is covered in wondrous glory.

A **Identify** who or what is described by each clue, using words from the box.

1. Called Canaan, this is the sacred place God promised to Abraham, Isaac, Jacob, and the Israelites. _____

2. The story of how God freed the Hebrews in Egypt; the second book of the Old Testament. _____

3. He conquered death for us; at Baptism he gives new life to our souls and will give new life to our bodies in the Kingdom of Heaven. _____

4. The most sacred name of God, spoken to Moses. It means "I am who I am." _____

5. This part of the Bible is filled with signs of God's love and faithfulness.

   _____

6. This part of the Bible tells of God's greatest act of love.

   _____

7. Just as God led his people to the promised land, he leads us to this.

   _____

8. When he and the Israelites reached the Red Sea, the Lord turned it into dry land. _____

spiritual
Moses
Exodus
Old Testament
everlasting life
promised land
Yahweh
New Testament
Jesus

B **Respond** to the following.

1. What is God's greatest act of love? _____

   _____

2. How did Jesus make it possible for us to share in the promised land of Heaven? _____

   _____

Faith in Action

Parish Support Groups Most of us know someone who has had difficulties in life. It might be a friend whose parents are divorced. Maybe it's a neighbor who survived cancer. Or it could be a best friend's uncle fighting alcoholism. More and more, parishes are hosting or organizing groups for people who share similar problems to come together to encourage one another. These groups help many people overcome difficult situations and learn and grow from them.

In Everyday Life

Activity In the space below, write three or more words or phrases that tell people why they can count on you for support.

"You can count on me because..."

_____

_____

_____

_____

In Your Parish

Activity Praying for one another is sometimes the best thing we can do to help in difficult times. Think about someone you know who needs your prayers right now. Without writing the person's name, write a prayer asking God to protect and help that person.

_____

_____

_____

_____

Take Home

FAMILY TIME

Passover and the Eucharist Celebration

This chapter recalls the Old Testament story of the Passover, when God delivered his people from the plague of death in Egypt and Pharaoh let the Israelites go. We remember that Jesus' Passover gave us the freedom of Salvation. We celebrate this deliverance in the liturgy and in our feast days, especially Easter.

ACTIVITY

Family Identity   The Israelites were bound together as God's people. To symbolize your family's unity, have everyone dress in the same colors one day this week. Or create a family crest, make photocopies of it, cut them out, and give one to each family member to wear.

WEEKLY PLANNER

On Sunday

Thank God for his blessings after you receive the Eucharist.

On the Web

www.blestarewe.com

 Visit our Web site for the Saint of the day and the reflection question of the week.

Saint of the Week

Saint Sharbel Makhlouf (1828–1898)

Saint Sharbel was a Maronite Catholic monk in the Monastery of St. Maron in Lebanon. Sharbel lived as a hermit from 1875 until his death. He followed a strict fast and was very devoted to the Blessed Sacrament. His only travel was to nearby villages to administer Holy Communion.

Feast Day: July 24

A Prayer for the Week

Dear Lord, you lead us to Salvation in the celebration of the Eucharist. Make us worthy to receive your Body and Blood that we may share in your heavenly kingdom. Amen.

Take Home

FAMILY TIME

✝ Scripture Background

In the Time of Jesus

The Paschal Lamb   During the Exodus, when the plague of death was about to strike Egypt, Moses commanded all Hebrew families to slaughter a lamb and sprinkle its blood on the doorpost of their home (Exodus 12:21–22). This slaughtered lamb was called the paschal lamb. Just as on Passover Jews recall the events of their being saved from death and suffering during the Exodus, on Holy Thursday we commemorate the Last Supper, when Jesus offered himself as the new Paschal Lamb, saving us from eternal death. Read about the Last Supper in Luke 22:14–20.

OUR CATHOLIC TRADITION in Art

The Last Supper   The Last Supper is the subject of one of the world's most famous paintings: Leonardo da Vinci's *The Last Supper*. The masterpiece is a fresco, or wall painting, located in the church of Santa Maria delle Grazie in Milan, Italy. It miraculously survived bombings in World War II only to be threatened with deterioration from climatic conditions in the church. Fortunately, a vast restoration project has saved da Vinci's painting from destruction.

6 Passover and the Eucharist Celebration

 Blessed are you, Lord, God of all creation.

Roman Missal

Share

Many celebrations have unique symbols. The Jewish feast of the Exodus, called Passover, is held around Easter time, and lasts for seven or eight days. On the first night, Jewish families have a meal called the Seder. They share foods eaten by the Hebrews on the night that the plague of death passed over their homes. The Seder foods are symbols. Bitter herbs represent the Hebrews' bitter slavery. Lamb represents the lamb's blood on the Hebrews' doorways. Unleavened bread—bread baked without yeast—represents the hurry to flee Egypt. (There was no time for bread to rise.)

Activity

Under each symbol write the celebration or holiday it represents.

         cake

_____   _____   _____   _____

Choose one of the events above, and name items that are part of your family's celebration of it.

_____

_____

_____

How do Catholics celebrate Jesus' sacrifice?

🕯 Worship   Mass of the Lord's Supper

Holy Thursday is a very important day in the Church's calendar of celebrations, known as the **liturgical year**. Holy Thursday honors the night on which Jesus shared the Last Supper with the Twelve Apostles. He washed their feet to teach them about serving others. On that night, the Apostle Judas handed Jesus over to be arrested. Jesus was crucified the next day, Good Friday. His followers kept vigil outside his tomb on the following day, Holy Saturday. The period from Holy Thursday evening until the evening prayer on Easter Sunday is the *Easter Triduum*.

During the Holy Thursday Evening Mass of the Lord's Supper, we remember the Last Supper and prepare for the remembrance of Jesus' Crucifixion. Priests and parishioners act out the Gospel reading about Jesus' washing of the Apostles' feet. The first reading is about how the Israelites were passed over when God brought the final plague upon Egypt: death to the firstborns. God told Moses how the Israelites should prepare for, and remember, this event.

A reading from the Book of Exodus.

THE LORD said to Moses and Aaron in the land of Egypt, "…Tell the whole community of Israel: On the tenth of this month every one of your families must procure for itself a lamb, one apiece for each household.… You shall keep it until the fourteenth day of this month, and then, with the whole assembly of Israel present, it shall be slaughtered during the evening twilight. They shall take some of its blood and apply it to the two doorposts and the lintel of every house in which they partake of the lamb. That same night they shall eat its roasted flesh with unleavened bread and bitter herbs.

"This is how you are to eat it: with your loins girt, sandals on your feet and your staff in hand, you shall eat like those who are in flight. It is the Passover of the LORD. For on this same night I will go through Egypt, striking down every firstborn of the land, both man and beast, and executing judgment on all the gods of Egypt—I, the LORD! But the blood will mark the houses where you are. Seeing the blood, I will pass over you; thus, when I strike the land of Egypt, no destructive blow will come upon you."

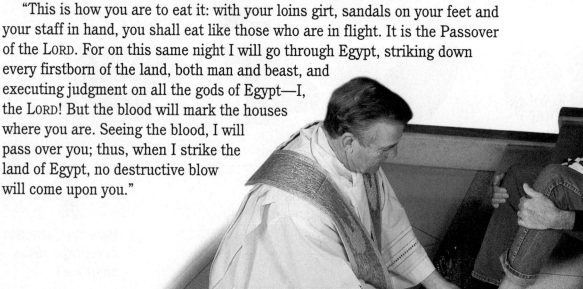

"This day shall be a memorial feast for you, which all your generations shall celebrate with pilgrimage to the LORD, as a perpetual institution."

Exodus 12:1, 3, 6–8, 11–14

The word of the Lord.
Thanks be to God.

The Passover of the Lord

Jesus' Death and Resurrection took place during the Jewish feast of **Passover**. The Last Supper may have been a Passover meal. But Jesus gave Passover a whole new meaning. At the Last Supper, Jesus blessed the bread and wine, then distributed them as his Body and Blood. He said, "Do this in memory of me" (Luke 22:19). The Eucharist is a memorial of Jesus' Passover—his work of Salvation through his suffering, Death, Resurrection, and Ascension. His Body and Blood would enable his followers to be redeemed from sin and find eternal happiness in God's kingdom.

Our liturgies celebrate the great mystery that gave us the chance for happiness in God's kingdom: the Passion (suffering), Death, Resurrection, and Ascension of Jesus. This is the **Paschal Mystery**. We honor it at Mass in communion, songs, prayers, and readings. The seasons of the liturgical year also celebrate parts of the Paschal Mystery. Easter celebrates Jesus' Resurrection. Lent is a season of sacrifice and preparation for Easter. The Triduum honors the events of Jesus' Death and Resurrection. Jesus' Ascension is celebrated forty days after Easter. Our liturgies also honor people already in heaven—Mary and the Saints.

 page 234 for more information about the liturgical year.

Faith Words

liturgical year
The liturgical year is the Church's yearly calendar of celebrations and seasons.

Passover
Passover is the Jewish celebration of the Israelites' exodus from Egypt.

Paschal Mystery
The Paschal Mystery is the way that Jesus' Passion, Death, Resurrection, and Ascension saved us from sin and gave us life after death.

Our Church Teaches

Passover was a sign of the sacrifice of Jesus Christ. Just as a lamb was sacrificed to save the Israelites, Jesus sacrificed his life on the Cross to save all people. The Church also teaches that Jesus' miracle of feeding 5,000 followers with five loaves of bread (Matthew 14:13–21) was a sign of the special food he would give the whole world: the Eucharist. We celebrate the Eucharist with confidence that we will one day be able to enjoy the glory of Heaven.

Who teaches us about God's love today?

Respond

The Election of Pope Francis

The election of a new pope is an important event in the life of the Church. All of the cardinals meet in Rome and stay at the Vatican, where the pope lives. They do not read newspapers or watch TV while there, and no one tells them how they should vote.

The cardinals pray for the guidance of the Holy Spirit. Catholics from throughout the world gather outside in Saint Peter's Square to pray for the cardinals, and Catholics throughout the world join them in prayer and wait for news regarding the election of the new pope.

The voting process begins when each cardinal writes his vote on a piece of paper. The votes are tallied, and if no one has enough votes to be named the new pope, the papers are burned with chemicals that make black smoke. The black smoke that is seen coming from the chimney means that the cardinals have not yet made a decision.

The voting process continues until a cardinal receives enough votes to be named pope. When a new pope is finally elected, the papers are burned with a different chemical so that white smoke is seen coming from the chimney. This signals to all that we have a pope!

In March of 2013, Cardinal Jorge Bergoglio was elected pope. Pope John Paul II named Cardinal Bergoglio, a Jesuit, a cardinal in 2001. He grew up in Argentina, and is the first pope to come from Latin America.

Cardinal Bergoglio chose the name Francis after he was elected pope, in honor of Saint Francis of Assisi. As pope, he is the leader of the Church all over the world. He follows in the footsteps of Saint Peter, who was chosen by Jesus to be the very first leader of the Church on Earth.

Together with the bishops and the College of Cardinals, the pope leads and serves the Church, helping it to grow in holiness and helping us to live as faithful disciples of Jesus.

Activities

1. Imagine that you have the opportunity to meet with Pope Francis and interview him. What questions would you ask him? In the space provided, write three questions that you would ask, including one question about his life as a young Catholic.

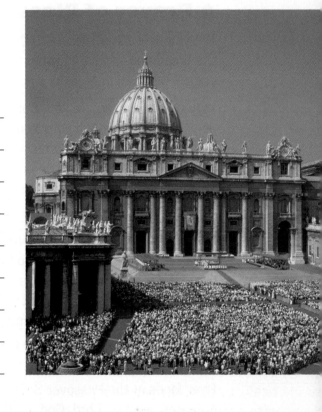

_____

_____

_____

_____

_____

_____

_____

_____

2. When he was elected pope, Jorge Mario Bergoglio, now Pope Francis, chose the motto "Lowly but Chosen." Tell some ways that you are chosen to be one who is an example to others of what it truly means to live as a Catholic.

_____

_____

_____

_____

_____

_____

_____

What do Catholics believe?

Prayer Celebration

A Prayer of Blessing

Did you ever listen closely to the offering prayers the priest says after the bread and wine are brought to the altar during Mass? The prayers come from blessings Jesus said at the Last Supper.

Priest: Blessed are you, Lord God of all creation,
for through your goodness we have received
the bread we offer you:
fruit of the earth and work of human hands,
it will become for us the bread of life.

Congregation: Blessed be God forever.

Priest: Blessed are you, Lord God of all creation,
for through your goodness we have received
the wine we offer you:
fruit of the vine and work of human hands,
it will become our spiritual drink.

Congregation: Blessed be God forever.

Roman Missal

Over foods at the Passover Seder, Jewish families say prayers such as "Blessed are you, Lord, God of all creation, because you . . ." Later, they may pray, "On this day of liberation, make us a blessing." Let us thank God for our own liberation and ask him to make us a blessing.

Leader: Blessed are you, Lord, God of all creation, because you have made us free to *(complete the prayer)*.

All: Blessed be God forever.

Leader: On this day, make us a blessing by helping us to *(complete the prayer)*.

All: Blessed be God forever.
Amen.

*Based on prayers from
the Passover Haggadah*

6 Chapter Review

A **Complete** the sentences, using words from the box.

1. _____ is the Jewish celebration of the Israelites' exodus from Egypt.

2. The Church's yearly calendar of celebrations and seasons is called the _____.

3. The period from Holy Thursday evening until Evening Prayer on Easter Sunday is the _____.

4. When Cardinal Jorge Bergoglio became Pope, he chose the name _____.

5. _____ honors the night on which Jesus shared the Last Supper with the Twelve Apostles.

6. The _____ is a memorial of Jesus' work of Salvation through his suffering, Death, _____, and Ascension.

7. Our liturgies celebrate the _____, the way that Jesus' Passion, Death, Resurrection, and Ascension saved us from _____.

> liturgical year
>
> Passover
>
> Resurrection
>
> sin
>
> Holy Thursday
>
> Francis
>
> Eucharist
>
> Easter Triduum
>
> Paschal Mystery

B **Respond** to the following.

1. Tell how Jesus is like the lamb that was sacrificed by the Israelites on Passover. _____

_____

_____

_____

2. How can a person your age share in Jesus' mission by making sacrifices for others? _____

_____

_____

Faith in Action

Extraordinary Ministers of Holy Communion Those who participate in this ministry help distribute Communion at Mass. They also bring the Eucharist to people who are sick and homebound. The people they visit are often elderly and lonely. They look forward to seeing these parish ministers who bring them Communion. They know that through Holy Communion, they are being touched by God's love in a very special way.

In Everyday Life

Activity In the left-hand column, describe a time when you helped or cared for someone. In the right-hand column, describe something extraordinary you could have done to walk the extra mile for that person.

A time when I helped someone...	Something extraordinary I could have done...

In Your Parish

Activity An extraordinary minister of Holy Communion brings the Eucharist to those who are ill or homebound. In what ways can you help people you encounter know of God's love?

_____

_____

_____

_____

Take Home

FAMILY TIME

Commandment and Fulfillment

The Israelites traveling in the desert toward what would become their homeland were hungry, thirsty, and angry at Moses. Their complaints were met with miracles from God that filled their needs: food falling to the ground each morning and water bursting from a rock. In addition to meeting the Israelites' physical needs, God also tended to their spiritual needs by giving them the Ten Commandments. The Commandments helped the Israelites remain in a faithful, rewarding relationship with God.

ACTIVITY

House Rules What are your family rules? Such rules might be enforced each day without anyone thinking about it. Post your family rules. Have everyone contribute to the list.

House Rules

1. Stereos off by 10 p.m.
2. No TV-watching during dinner.
3. Put all dirty clothes in hampers.
4. Don't waste water.
5. Keep the front door locked.
6. Wipe your feet when you come in the door.
7. Wash your hands before you eat.

WEEKLY PLANNER

On Sunday

During the First Reading, listen for Yahweh's promises. During the Second Reading and Gospel, listen for ways God fulfilled those promises.

On the Web

www.blestarewe.com

Visit our Web site for the Saint of the day and the reflection question of the week.

Saint of the Week

 Saint Teresa of Ávila (Teresa of Jesus)

(1515–1582)

Saint Teresa was born in Spain, the daughter of nobles. Although her father strongly objected, Teresa joined the Carmelite order. Teresa spent much of her life writing about prayer, including how she overcame her difficulties with praying.

Patron Saint of: Spain
Feast Day: October 15

A Prayer for the Week

Lord, through the ages you have sent us holy people to teach us how to live. Open our hearts and minds to their guidance that we may share their joy in eternity with you. Amen.

Take Home

FAMILY TIME

✝ Scripture Background

In the Time of Jesus

Teaching from the Mountaintop   When the Israelites left Egypt, on their journey to the promised land, God revealed to them the Ten Commandments, which Moses received on Mount Sinai (Exodus 19—20). In the New Testament, when Jesus delivered the Sermon on the Mount (Matthew 5—7), where he taught his followers the Beatitudes and the Golden Rule, he too taught from a mountain. At Mount Sinai, God gave his people laws to guide their relationship with him and with others. In the Sermon on the Mount, Jesus explained more fully how to apply those laws to everyday living.

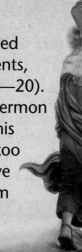

OUR CATHOLIC TRADITION in Sacramentals

Eternal Light   The Israelites regularly refreshed oil lamps that burned outside the Ark of the Covenant, the sacred box containing the stone tablets of the Ten Commandments. In the Temple in Jerusalem, the ritual continued in the sacred space where the ark was kept. When their Temple was destroyed, the Israelites began to worship in synagogues, where a continuously burning light called *Ner Tamid* ("eternal light") shines above the Ark, now holding the Torah. The light represents God's eternal Covenant.

In our churches, at least one oil lamp or candle continually shines near the tabernacle holding the Blessed Sacrament. The light signifies the purity and divinity of Christ, the Light of the world.

This is a tabernacle holding the Blessed Sacrament.

7 Commandment and Fulfillment

LET US PRAY

I will place my law within them, and write it upon their hearts, . . . says the LORD.

Jeremiah 31:33–34

Share

You follow rules every day—in school, clubs, sports, and your home. These rules usually keep things running smoothly. Many rules help keep people safe. Try to think of some rules you follow each day that keep people from physical or emotional harm.

Activity

What do you remember about the rules called the Ten Commandments? In the first column, list everything you already know about the Commandments. In the second column, write a few questions you have about them. Complete the third column at the end of class.

BEACH
RULES AND REGULATIONS
NO: Disorderly Conduct
Dogs
Glass Containers
Fires - Grills
Littering
Motor Vehicles
Soliciting
Throwing missiles
or Objects

BEACH CLOSED 1 AM - 5 AM
CITY OF TREASURE ISLAND
ORDINANCE CHAPTER 20

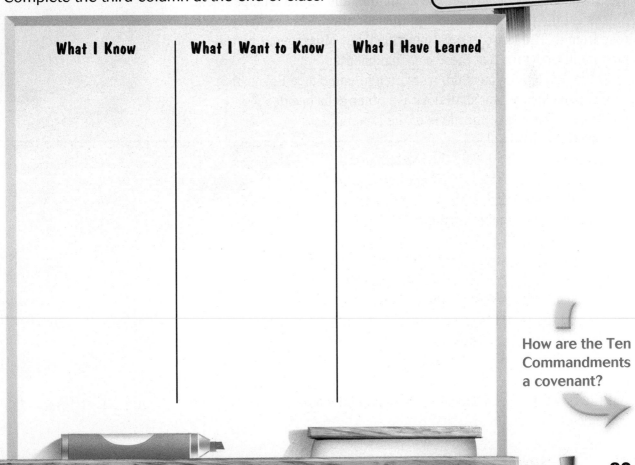

What I Know	What I Want to Know	What I Have Learned

How are the Ten Commandments a covenant?

Hear & Believe
✝ Scripture The Covenant at Sinai

After the Israelites left Egypt, God led them through the desert. The journey was rough, and the Israelites grumbled against Moses. But God protected the Israelites and eased their hardships.

The Israelites complained to Moses that they were starving. The next morning, breadlike flakes covered the desert. The Israelites asked, "What is this?" Moses told them, "This is the bread which the Lord has given you to eat." The Israelites called this food manna. It was white and tasted like wafers made with honey. The people complained that they were thirsty. At the LORD's command, Moses struck a rock with his staff, and water flowed out for the people to drink.

About three months after they left Egypt, the Israelites came to the desert of Sinai. They camped at the foot of Mount Sinai. Moses went up the mountain to speak to God.

The LORD said, "Tell the Israelites: You have seen for yourselves how I brought you here safely to me. Therefore, if you listen to me and keep my covenant, you shall be dearer to me than all other people. You shall be to me a holy nation."

Then the LORD told Moses to have the people prepare to meet the LORD in three days. On the third day, there were peals of thunder and lightning, a heavy cloud over the mountain, and a loud trumpet blast. Moses led the people to the foot of the mountain. Flames and smoke rose from it. The Israelites were terrified, but Moses went up the mountain. God gave him these commandments:

"I, the LORD, am your God, who brought you out of Egypt, that place of slavery. You shall not have other gods besides me.

"You shall not take the name of the LORD, your God, in vain.

"Remember to keep holy the sabbath day.

"Honor your father and your mother.

"You shall not kill.

"You shall not commit adultery.

"You shall not steal.

"You shall not bear false witness against your neighbor.

"You shall not covet your neighbor's wife.

"You shall not covet anything that belongs to your neighbor."

Moses told the Israelites God's commandments. They offered sacrifices to the LORD. Then Moses went up the mountain again. When Moses came down the mountain, he was carrying stone tablets upon which God had written the Ten Commandments. But the Israelites were dancing, drinking, and worshiping a golden calf.

Moses angrily threw the tablets and broke them. He went back to the Lord to ask the Lord to forgive the Israelites. The Lord commanded Moses to cut two new stone tablets.

"Here is the covenant I will make," said the Lord. "Before your people's eyes I will work wonders that have never been seen in any nation on earth. People will see the power of the Lord. But you must keep my commandments. Write down these words, for with them I have made a covenant with you and Israel."

Moses wrote the commandments on the tablets. Then skillful Israelites created a gold and wood box and a special tent. Moses brought the tablets down the mountain and placed them in the box, called the **ark of the covenant**. After that, the Israelites carried the ark of the covenant in the tent wherever they traveled.

Based on Exodus 16:13–15, 31; 17:5–6; 19–20; 32; 34:1–4, 10–11, 27–29; 35; 40

God's Love and Laws

The covenant God made with Abraham and his descendants was a two-way relationship. God loved his people, and he would work wonders before their eyes, just as he had done when he fed them **manna** from Heaven. The people loved God and would keep his Commandments, which he revealed through Moses. The Ten Commandments express the way we all want to live: without offending God or harming other people and ourselves. Because we are created in God's image, we have a natural desire for goodness. We also have a special dignity as well as rights and duties, such as the right to practice our faith and the duty to love and care for one another.

Our Church Teaches

God is the ultimate authority for our society. God revealed the Ten Commandments. By following them, we show love for God and choose good over evil. Jesus taught us how important it is to keep God's Commandments. He also said, "You shall love the Lord, your God, with all your heart, with all your soul, and with all your mind. This is the greatest and the first Commandment. The second is like it: You shall love your neighbor as yourself" (Matthew 22:37–39).

How do you show that you love God and others?

Saint Teresa of Ávila (Saint Teresa of Jesus)

As a teenager in Spain in the 1500s, Teresa of Ávila shared many of the concerns of modern teenagers. She worried about her appearance and what boys thought of her, and she liked to flirt. The last thing on her mind was spending her life in a convent! But Teresa's strict father was worried about his daughter's behavior. When she was sixteen he sent her to a convent.

Teresa soon wanted to spend the rest of her life in service to the Lord. She became a Carmelite nun. Teresa tried to keep Jesus present within her through prayer, which she described as a mental sharing between friends. She believed that prayer should be time spent alone, reflecting only on God. When Teresa prayed, she felt God's presence overwhelm her. People who watched her pray said that her whole body would lift off the ground.

But there was a time in Teresa's life when praying was a struggle. She found it very hard to concentrate. She worked hard to overcome this difficulty. Teresa realized that there were others who also had trouble praying. She wanted to help them experience the beauty of prayer. So she spent much of her life writing and teaching others how to pray.

As an adult, Teresa founded a religious order called the Discalced Carmelites. Members of this order show their love for God by living a simple life of poverty, devoted to prayer. Teresa helped others discover that one finds inner peace through prayer. The Church recognized Teresa for her life of holiness and her contributions to the Church. She was canonized in 1622. In 1970, Saint Teresa of Ávila was named a Doctor of the Church. Her feast day is October 15.

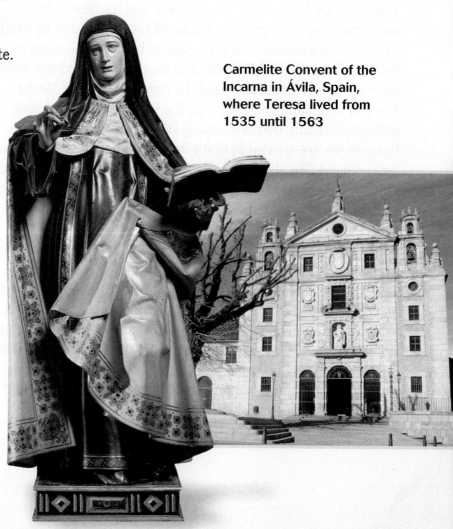

Carmelite Convent of the Incarna in Ávila, Spain, where Teresa lived from 1535 until 1563

Activity

For each of the Ten Commandments, tell the meaning of the Commandment for today. Four have been done for you.

BIBLE

I, the LORD, am your God. You shall not have other gods besides me.

You shall not take the name of the Lord, your God, in vain.

Remember to keep holy the sabbath day.

Honor your father and your mother.

You shall not kill.

You shall not commit adultery.

You shall not steal.

You shall not bear false witness against your neighbor.

You shall not covet your neighbor's wife.

You shall not covet anything that belongs to your neighbor.

Based on Exodus 20:2–17

MEANING FOR TODAY

_____

_____

_____

_____

_____

_____

_____

Respect life. Take care of your health. Work to protect unborn children, the sick, and the elderly.

Avoid situations that might lead to sexual sins.

Keep promises and agreements. Do not purposely keep things that you have borrowed or people have lost.

_____

_____

Keep your heart pure and thoughts focused on God. Respect people's marriage vows.

_____

_____

GO TO page 274 for more information about the Ten Commandments

✝ Prayer Celebration

Praying with Scripture

Saint Teresa of Ávila (Saint Teresa of Jesus) said that she often started praying by reading Scripture and reflecting upon it. Try her method of prayer. Silently read the following Scripture passage. (In it, Moses is speaking to the Israelites.)

> "Hear, O Israel! The LORD is our God, the LORD alone! Therefore, you shall love the LORD, your God, with all your heart, and with all your soul, and with all your strength. Take to heart these words which I enjoin on you today. Drill them into your children. Speak of them at home and abroad, whether you are busy or at rest."
>
> *Deuteronomy 6:4–9*

Quietly reflect on what these words mean for you today. Then write a prayer telling God how you will love him "with all your heart, with all your soul, and with all your strength."

_____

_____

_____

_____

_____

_____

_____

7 Chapter Review

A **Circle** the letter of the correct answer.

1. _____ revealed the ultimate meaning of the Ten Commandments and taught us to keep God's Laws in the spirit of love.
   a. Moses
   b. Abraham
   c. Jesus
   d. Miriam

2. _____ is the ultimate authority in our society.
   a. Moses
   b. God
   c. the President
   d. the Supreme Court

3. The _____ express the way we all want to live: without offending God or hurting others or ourselves.
   a. Ten Commandments
   b. Israelites
   c. Carmelites
   d. First and Third Commandments

4. Saint Teresa of Ávila often began her prayers by reading _____ and reflecting upon it.
   a. Saint Augustine's *Confessions*
   b. Scripture
   c. her journal
   d. the words to a hymn

B **Match** Column A with Column B by writing the correct number in the space provided.

A	B
1. Ark of the Covenant	____ laws that guide our moral lives
2. Ten Commandments	____ "You shall love the Lord, your God, with all your heart, with all your soul, and with all your mind."
3. Sinai	____ the breadlike food that God gave the Israelites
4. manna	____ the desert through which the Israelites passed on their journey from Egypt
5. the Great Commandment	____ a special box that held the stone tablets of the Ten Commandments

Faith in Action

Employment Assistance Programs   People turn to their parishes for all kinds of needs. Sometimes they look to the parish for assistance in finding work. Some people cannot find work because they lack sufficient education. Some are afraid because they are new immigrants and are looking for jobs for the first time. Some parishes offer literacy programs as well as job skills and job placement seminars. Employment assistance ministries help people take responsibility in their search for jobs that they can perform with dignity.

In Everyday Life

Activity   Julie wants to audition for the school play. Her older sister Angela is helping her prepare for the audition, saying, "Make sure you speak loudly and clearly." What other advice might Angela give Julia?

_____

_____

_____

_____

In Your Parish

Activity   In the space provided, write an announcement for your parish bulletin describing the parish's employment assistance program. Be sure your message will clearly tell parishioners how this program will be helpful to them if they are searching for a job.

_____

_____

_____

_____

Take Home

FAMILY TIME

Our Journey and God's Presence

We are a pilgrim people with roots in the wanderings of the nomadic Israelites. We seek a "promised land" just as they did. Their promised land was Canaan, which they reached after forty years in the desert, led by God. Our promised land is a land of happiness for our souls, reached by being faithful followers of Christ throughout our lives.

ACTIVITY

Signs of God Joshua and the Israelites had to pay careful attention to God's directions when storming the promised land. Have each family member draw a symbol of something that keeps him or her in touch with God. Swap symbols, and try to experience another person's way of hearing God's voice this week.

WEEKLY PLANNER

On Sunday

Think of your trip to church as a journey. Identify what makes your destination special.

On the Web

www.blestarewe.com

 Visit our Web site for the Saint of the day and the reflection question of the week.

Saint of the Week

 Saint Frances Xavier Cabrini (1850–1917)

From her early childhood in Italy, Frances Xavier Cabrini had wanted to be a missionary to China. As a Missionary Sister of the Sacred Heart, she traveled to America instead, where she founded sixty-seven institutions dedicated to the care of the poor.

Patron Saint of: hospitals and orphans

Feast Day: November 13

 A Prayer for the Week

Lord, with your help we can achieve great things. Help us to rely on your love and to see your goodness in the world around us. Amen.

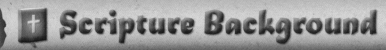

Take Home

FAMILY TIME

✠ Scripture Background

Before the Time of Jesus

The Ram's Horn   The ram's horn *(shofar)* is a powerful image throughout Scripture. Joshua and his soldiers were able to topple Jericho's city walls by blowing horns and shouting (Joshua 6:1–21). The deep mournful sound of the horn called Israel to arms and launched battle. Horns were used to call assemblies, to announce a new year, and to warn of danger. They were also used in anointings, as when Samuel anointed David as king (1 Samuel 16:13). Shofars are still used today. A shofar is sounded at the Jewish new year (Rosh Hashanah) and to signal the end of fasting on the Jewish day of atonement (Yom Kippur).

OUR CATHOLIC TRADITION in Sacramentals

The Jordan River   Joshua crossed the Jordan River, which was also the river where Jesus was baptized. Blessing rivers or fountains is a custom of Eastern countries. In Africa the Nile is blessed on the Feast of the Epiphany and in commemoration of the Baptism of the Lord. Christians traditionally would dip themselves in the blessed water three times, and even animals would be herded into the water to receive its blessing.

8 Our Journey and God's Presence

In the tender compassion of our God,
the dawn will break upon us,
to shine on those who dwell in darkness.

Based on Luke 1:78–79

Share

The natural world is filled with reminders of God's power and goodness, such as a colorful rainbow that follows a storm, a tiny, detailed snowflake, or a perfect looking rose. What other events in the natural world remind you of God's love for people?

Activity

Inside each natural wonder below write adjectives that describe what it tells you about God.

How did God show his goodness when the Israelites reached the promised land?

✝ Scripture   Conquest of the Promised Land

The Israelites had wandered in the desert for forty years. After Moses died, the LORD appointed Joshua to lead the Israelites to the promised land, Canaan.

The LORD said to Joshua, "Prepare to cross the Jordan River here, with all the people, into the land I will give the Israelites. Do not fear. The LORD, your God, is with you wherever you go."

Joshua secretly sent two of his men to spy on the land. The spies took shelter in the city of Jericho, in the house of a woman named Rahab. The king of Jericho heard about the spies and sent Rahab the order, "Put out the visitors who have entered your house, for they have come to spy on my land." Instead, Rahab hid the men. She told the king's messengers, "The men you speak of came to me, but I did not know where they came from. They left at dark, and I do not know where they went."

After the king's messengers went in search of the spies, Rahab said to the spies, "I know that the LORD has given your people our land. All the people here are afraid. We heard how the LORD dried up the waters of the Red Sea when you came out of Egypt. Since I am showing kindness to you, I want you to spare my family and save us from death."

She helped the spies down through the window with a rope. "Go up into the hill country," she said, "so that your pursuers may not find you. Hide there for three days. Then you may go on your way."

The men told Rahab, "Hang a red cord from this window. Gather your family. When we return," they promised, "everyone inside this house will be spared."

Early the next day, Joshua led the Israelites to the banks of the river. They camped out for three days. Then Joshua said to the people, "Tomorrow the LORD will perform wonders among you."

The next day, the LORD told Joshua, "Command the priests carrying the ark of the covenant to stop in the waters at the edge of the Jordan." When the priests entered the Jordan River, the river stopped flowing. The priests stood there until the Israelites had crossed the Jordan safely. Then they carried the ark out and the river flowed back.

The LORD said to Joshua, "Have all the soldiers circle the city, marching once around it. Do this for six days, with seven priests carrying rams' horns ahead of the ark. On the seventh day, march around the city seven times and have the priests blow the horns."

The Israelites followed the LORD's directions. As the horns blew on the seventh day, the people raised a tremendous shout. The walls of Jericho collapsed, and the Israelites stormed the city and conquered it. Rahab and her family were spared.

City by city, the Israelites took the land the LORD had promised. Years later, Joshua called the people together. He reminded them of all that the LORD had done for them. "Acknowledge with your whole heart and soul that every one of the promises the LORD has made to you has been fulfilled. Therefore, love the LORD completely and sincerely, and obey his commandments."

The Israelites agreed to serve the LORD alone.

Based on Exodus 16:35; Joshua 1—6; 18: 24

Listening for God's Voice

The Israelites reached the promised land, but they could not have succeeded without God's help. Joshua led the Israelites into Canaan by listening to God's instructions. God told Joshua how the Israelites should cross the Jordan, and it worked. God told Joshua how the Israelites should get inside the city, and they did. Because they talked to and listened to God, Joshua and the Israelites successfully conquered and settled the promised land. With Joshua's guidance, the Israelites promised to continue to listen to God. They wanted to continue to be God's **chosen people**. God had chosen to reveal his love and fidelity to them so many times. God *is* love and fidelity.

Our Church Teaches

Prayer is talking to and listening to God. We can pray in words, thoughts, gestures, or song. Our Church has certain prayers for each day of the week, for the morning, the middle of the day, and the evening. Praying every day can help us become people who pray continually. Praying continually—during every event of our lives—will help us hear God's instructions for our lives and to discover his will for us. Praying as much as we can—every day—will make it easier to discover God's will. This discovery process is called **discernment**. It also happens through seeking God's will in the Scriptures and reflecting on the teachings of the Church.

Faith Words
chosen people
In the Old Testament the chosen people were Abraham and his descendants, whom God had selected to receive his Word. People who choose to follow God's will today are also chosen people.

discernment
Discernment is discovering, with God's help, God's will for our lives.

How do you show that you are one of God's chosen people?

Respond

Celebrating the Lord's Wonders

The Scripture story of the Israelites' conquest of the promised land
tells how God fulfilled his promise to the Israelites. The following
prayer is called "The Lord's Wonders at the Exodus." Pray it
aloud, and think about how God showed his power and
goodness to the Israelites.

When Israel came forth from Egypt,
   the house of Jacob from a people of alien tongue,
Judah became his sanctuary,
   Israel his domain.
The sea beheld and fled;
   Jordan turned back.
The mountains skipped like rams,
   the hills like the lambs of the flock.
Why is it, O sea, that you flee?
   O Jordan, that you turn back?
You mountains, that you skip like rams?
   You hills, like the lambs of the flock?
Before the face of the Lord, tremble, O earth,
   before the face of the God of Jacob,
Who turned the rock into pools of water,
   the flint into flowing springs.

Psalm 114

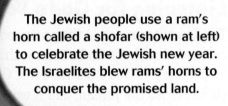

**The Jewish people use a ram's
horn called a shofar (shown at left)
to celebrate the Jewish new year.
The Israelites blew rams' horns to
conquer the promised land.**

Activity

What everyday events, such as seeing a full moon, remind you of the
power and goodness of the Lord? List or draw two of these events below.

Constant Prayer

Berahot are short blessing prayers that Jewish people may say throughout the day to praise the power and goodness of the Lord. They pray them upon everyday events, such as noticing a blossoming tree. Here are some examples you can pray.

Upon opening the eyes:

Blessed are you, Lord, God of all creation, for you open the eyes of the blind.

Upon going to breakfast:

Blessed are you, Lord, God of all creation, for you provide for all my needs.

Based on berahot blessings

Activities

1. Choose one of your items from the activity on page 102. Write a berahot prayer for this event.

   _____

   _____

   _____

   _____

   _____

2. Create a berahot prayer for an event or activity that is always a part of your religious education session. You may work with your group to create this prayer, then pray it together during every session.

Religion Group Berahot

How can you make daily prayer a part of your life?

Prayer Celebration

The Canticle of Zechariah

Catholics have certain prayers for the morning, evening, and middle of the day, which are treasured as sources of constant prayer. The following prayer, the Canticle of Zechariah, is a morning prayer of the Church. Zechariah was the father of John the Baptist. This was his prayer after his wife, Elizabeth, gave birth to John. Pray it in the morning, and think about how it makes you feel.

Blessed be the Lord, the God of Israel;
    he has come to his people and set them free.
He has raised up for us a mighty savior,
    born of the house of his servant David.
Through his holy prophets he promised of old
    that he would save us from our enemies,
    from the hands of all who hate us.
He promised to show mercy to our fathers
    and to remember his holy covenant.
This was the oath he swore to Abraham:
    to set us free from the hands of our enemies;
free to worship him without fear,
    holy and righteous in his sight
        all the days of our life.
You, my child, shall be called the prophet of the Most High,
    for you will go before the Lord to prepare his way,
to give his people knowledge of salvation
    by forgiveness of their sins.
In the tender compassion of our God
    the dawn from on high shall break upon us,
to shine on those who dwell in darkness
        and the shadow of death,
    and to guide our feet on the road to peace.

Based on Luke 1:68–79

8 Chapter Review

A **Match** Column A with Column B by writing the correct number in the space provided.

A

1. prayer
2. discernment
3. chosen people
4. berahot

B

____ short blessing prayers

____ helps us know God's will

____ discovering God's will for our lives

____ Abraham and his descendants; all people who choose to follow God's will

B **Number** the following events from the story of Joshua in the order in which they occurred.

____ When the priest carrying the Ark of the Covenant entered the Jordan River, its waters stopped flowing so the men could cross safely.

____ City by city the Israelites took the land the Lord had promised.

____ The Lord appointed Joshua to lead the Israelites to the promised land.

____ As the horns blew, the people raised a tremendous shout and the walls of Jericho collapsed.

____ Joshua's spies took shelter in the home of a woman named Rahab.

C **Respond** to the following.

1. How and when can Catholics pray?

_____

_____

2. When do you pray most frequently? During what other times or occasions can you also pray?

_____

_____

Faith in Action

RCIA Catechists   Adults and older children who want to learn more about the Catholic faith and are interested in joining the Church participate in the Rite of Christian Initiation for Adults (RCIA). RCIA catechists, along with priests and deacons, help catechumens and candidates to discern where God is leading them in the RCIA process. As they study and pray together, they listen for God's voice to guide them to the next step. With each new step, the catechumen or candidate comes closer to his or her full initiation into the Church.

In Everyday Life

Activity   Those in the RCIA process are preparing to receive the Sacraments of Initiation—Baptism, Eucharist, and Confirmation. Which of these Sacraments have you received? When did you receive them? Which other Sacraments have you received?

In Your Parish

Activity   Inquirers in the RCIA process get to ask a lot of questions about what it means to be a Catholic. Write three questions you have about the Church, the Bible, or about living as a committed Catholic.

1. _____

2. _____

3. _____

God Invites Us into His Kingdom

The people of Israel were called to build up a kingdom that would be a tribute to God's love. Jesus taught us about the Kingdom of Heaven, where God's love will be evident in justice and peace.

> *It is he who shall build a house for my name.*
> *And I will make his royal throne firm forever.*
> 2 Samuel 7:13

Ark of the Covenant

Main Hall

Porch

Holy of Holies

Solomon's Temple

Brass Pillars

The Israelites wanted a permanent holy place to worship God, so they built the Temple on Mount Zion in Jerusalem.

Let Us Go Rejoicing

Psalm 122, Adapted by Michael Joncas

Music by Michael Joncas

REFRAIN

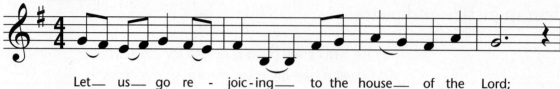

Let us go re - joic-ing to the house of the Lord;

Let us go re - joic-ing to the house of the Lord.

VERSE

1. I rejoiced when I heard them say:
   "Let us go to the house of the Lord,"
   and now our feet are standing
   within your gates, O Jerusalem.
   Refrain

2. Jerusalem is a city built
   with unity and strength.
   It is there, it is there that the tribes go up,
   the tribes of the Lord.
   Refrain

3. For Israel's law is to praise God's name
   and there to give God thanks.
   There are set the judgment thrones
   for all of David's house.
   Refrain

4. Pray for the peace of Jerusalem!
   "May those who love you prosper;
   May peace ever reign within your walls,
   and wealth within your buildings!"
   Refrain

5. For love of my fam'ly and love of my friends,
   I pray that peace be yours.
   For love of the house of the Lord our God
   I pray for your good.
   Refrain

Take Home

Our Land and God's Kingdom

The Jewish people in the promised land were guided by the wisdom of several leaders called judges. But some Israelites wanted a king to represent all the tribes of Israel. The judge and prophet Samuel asked God for guidance in choosing a king. God revealed how the people could follow a king and remain loyal to the Covenant. A family can function well under different styles of leadership, as long as God is behind all its decisions.

ACTIVITY

Your Kingdom Is Your Castle Think of your home as your family's kingdom. Have family members draw or paint a sign expressing what this kingdom is all about. The sign may show a popular expression or your last name with symbols of things you value, such as a cross. Hang the sign in a prominent place.

Everyone in this family is a special sign of God's love.

WEEKLY PLANNER

On Sunday

Think of fellow parishioners as travelers on the journey to God's kingdom. Ask God to bless them.

On the Web

www.blestarewe.com

 Visit our Web site for the Saint of the day and the reflection question of the week.

Saint of the Week

 Saint Francis of Assisi (1181–1226)

As a young man Francis enjoyed a rich and easy life. After a conversion experience, he gave up all his wealth to follow Jesus. He began living as a mendicant, begging for his daily needs. He spent his time preaching and caring for the poor and sick. He is the founder of the Franciscan order of religious.

Feast Day: October 4

A Prayer for the Week

Lord, help us to build your kingdom on Earth as the Saints have done, that we may enjoy everlasting happiness with you in Heaven. Amen.

Take Home

FAMILY TIME

✝ Scripture Background

Before the Time of Jesus

From Judges to Kings   During Samuel's rule as a judge, Israel was invaded by its neighbors, the Philistines. Samuel was a man of power and influence, and many looked to him for help in selecting a leader who would protect them. Although Samuel wrestled with the idea of an earthly king, he ultimately selected Saul as the first king of Israel. Samuel realized that it was God's will that the country have a human ruler to unite it against its enemies. Read 1 Samuel 8—10 to learn how the monarchy was established in ancient Israel, uniting all Israelites under a single ruler.

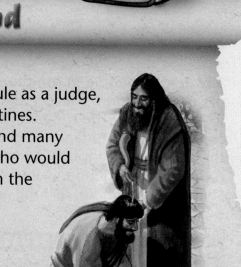

OUR CATHOLIC TRADITION in the Holy Land

St. Catherine's Church   Next door to the Church of the Nativity in Bethlehem is the Roman Catholic church of St. Catherine. Built by the Franciscans in 1881, the church is situated over a cave where, according to tradition, Saint Jerome lived when he was translating the Scriptures from Greek to the Latin Vulgate in the fourth century. A statue of Saint Jerome stands in the church's courtyard, which was once part of a Crusader cloistered convent.

9 Our Land and God's Kingdom

Do you not know that your bodies are members of Christ?

1 Corinthians 6:15

Share

God made each of us unique, but we were not meant to live alone. We are part of families, neighborhoods, cities or towns, states, and countries. In many of these communities, people are appointed to lead us.

We are also part of parish communities. What is the name of your parish? Your parish is part of a bigger community, the Catholic Church. Through the leadership of the Pope and the bishops of each diocese, the Church guides Catholic parish communities all over the world. We call the Church our mother because she gives birth to the faithful at Baptism and nurtures them in faith. The Church spreads and protects the truth God has revealed. We also call the Church the Bride of Christ because of Christ's sacrifice and love for her.

Activity

What groups or communities do you belong to? Draw yourself participating in one of these groups or communities.

What makes a good leader?

✝ Scripture The First Leaders of Israel

After Joshua died, judges helped the Israelites stay faithful to the Covenant. Judges were leaders gifted with good judgment. Under their guidance the Israelites enjoyed peace for forty years.

The Israelites had an especially wise judge named Samuel. Samuel was the son of Hannah, a faithful Israelite woman. She could not have children at first. One day she prayed hard for a son. "Lord," she promised, "if you give me a son, I will give him to you as a servant for as long as he lives." God heard Hannah's prayer, and Samuel was born. Hannah brought Samuel to the Temple to live with the priest, Eli. "This child shall be dedicated to the Lord as long as he lives," she told Eli.

Eli taught the boy about serving God. One day, something remarkable happened. As Samuel was sleeping in the Temple, he heard, "Samuel!"

Samuel woke up and ran to Eli. "Here I am. You called me."

"I did not call you," Eli said. "Go back to sleep."

Samuel went back to sleep. Again, a voice called him. He got up and went back to Eli. "Here I am," he said. "You called me."

Eli answered, "I did not call you, my son. Go back to sleep."

The voice called Samuel a third time. Samuel went to Eli again. Eli then understood that the Lord was calling Samuel. He told the boy, "Go to sleep. If you are called, reply, 'Speak, Lord, for your servant is listening.'"

After Samuel fell asleep, the Lord called again. Samuel answered, "Speak, for your servant is listening." The Lord told Samuel about events that would happen later. Samuel told Eli, and Eli knew Samuel would be a great prophet.

God watched over Samuel as he grew up. All of Israel came to know Samuel as a leader and a prophet of the Lord. When the people wanted him to choose a king to lead them, Samuel asked God for help.

One day, a man named Saul came to the city looking for lost donkeys. Saul was a descendant of Benjamin, one of Jacob's sons. The Lord told Samuel that Saul would be king. Samuel anointed Saul with oil and declared him king in the name of God. The Israelites praised God and said, "Long live the king!"

Samuel reminded them, "The Lord made you his people. Now you have the king you want, a king the Lord has given you. But you must obey the Lord."

As king of Israel, Saul bravely fought Israel's enemies and delivered Israel from its invaders. But then he disobeyed the Lord. Samuel told Saul, "Because you have rejected the Lord's command, the Lord has rejected you as king."

Based on Judges 2:16, 18; 5:31; 1 Samuel 1–15

Kingdoms on the Earth

The Israelites in the promised land sometimes failed to keep their Covenant with God. Samuel and the judges helped keep them on the right path. When the Israelites decided they wanted a king, Samuel knew that the king had to be someone who made decisions based on what God wanted. Samuel asked for God's help. God chose Saul to be king. But when Saul failed to obey the Lord, he could no longer lead the people.

God gave the Israelites the promised land, and leaders who would help them remain faithful to him. In the same way, God promises us that we will share in his heavenly kingdom and gives us the Church to guide us. Like the Israelites in Canaan, we experience sin and suffering in our world. The Church helps keep us on the path of Jesus. The Church also spreads the saving message of Jesus throughout the world.

Like Samuel, we are called by God to carry out the Church's mission and give witness to the kingdom through a **ministry**, or way of serving. We may care for the poor or sick, teach about Christ, help with the liturgy, pray for others, or work for the parish office. We may serve as religious brothers or sisters (members of communities who take vows of poverty, chastity, and obedience), as clergy (ordained ministers of the Church, such as bishops, priests, or deacons), or as **laity** (all other people who serve in the Church). Many different ministries accomplish the Church's one mission.

Our Church Teaches

The Church is the beginning of God's kingdom on Earth. The kingdom will reach fulfillment at the end of time when Christ comes again. The Catholic Church welcomes and brings together people of all lands, languages, backgrounds, and races. It is a symbol of the unity of the whole human race. That is why we say the Church is **catholic**, or universal. We also believe that the Church is one (united in faith, worship, and authority), holy (in communion with God), and apostolic (following the tradition and teachings of the Apostles). Jesus gave the Apostle Peter a special authority over the Church that continues with the Pope today.

GO TO page 263 to learn more about the Church.

We Believe

Our mission as Catholics is to prepare the world for the coming of God's heavenly kingdom. We do this by serving others and teaching the saving message of Christ.

Faith Words

ministry
A ministry is a way of serving and caring for others in Christ's name.

laity
The laity are people who are part of the Church and are not clergy or religious brothers or sisters.

catholic
The word *catholic* means "universal." With a capital C, it describes the Church founded by Christ's Apostles.

What are some ways we can serve others as Christ did?

The Franciscans in the Holy Land

In the spirit of Saint Francis, members of the Franciscan order minister to those in need in all parts of the world. In the Holy Land—the place where Jesus lived—Franciscans minister to the needs of Palestinian Christians.

Because of the religious and political disputes between Israelis and Muslim Arabs, Palestinian Christians living in the Holy Land often find themselves caught up in a conflict that forces them to live in war-zone conditions. They are deprived of many basic needs, such as jobs and schooling, and even suffer the confiscation of their homes and land. Because of this, many Christians have emigrated to other countries in search of a better life.

The Franciscans, through such organizations as the Franciscan Foundation for the Holy Land, work to ease some of the suffering of Palestinian Catholics and other Christians, as well as non-Christians, in the region. They assist families in finding and paying for housing that is safe and livable, in cities such as Bethlehem, Jericho, and Nazareth. The Franciscans also help families overcome financial hardship by offering unemployed adults job training, and by hiring them to work in their schools, parish centers, and medical facilities. In addition, they run boys' and girls' schools, and offer university scholarships to Christian Palestinian students in need so they can complete their schooling.

In addition to their humanitarian work in the region, the Franciscans care for and maintain many of the holy sites and shrines, including the Holy Sepulchre and the Church of the Nativity. They also serve pilgrims who visit the Holy Land, providing housing and other services.

The Franciscans have worked in the Holy Land for 800 years, since the Order of Friars Minor was founded by Saint Francis. Through their work, Christians can continue to live in the land sacred to all Christians, and the holy sites that are so important to our faith will continue to be cared for and available to all Christian pilgrims.

Activities

1. Like Samuel, we may have trouble telling when God is calling us. But as God's children, we all have a mission. The Franciscans in the Holy Land carry out their mission by helping Christians and others in their community, by caring for holy sites and shrines, and by their prayers. How can you work for God's kingdom? In each finger of the hand, write one thing you might do to carry out your mission as a member of the Church.

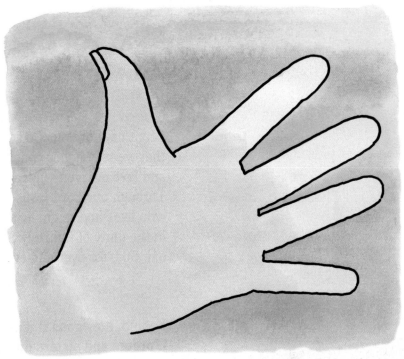

2. Complete the crossword puzzle with words you learned in this chapter.

Across

1. universal

6. _____ of God, or Heaven

7. following the Apostles

8. united in faith, worship, and authority

9. in communion with God

Down

1. a group of people united in some way

2. a leader with good judgment

3. to put oil on a person who has been chosen

4. a way of serving

5. people who serve in the church community

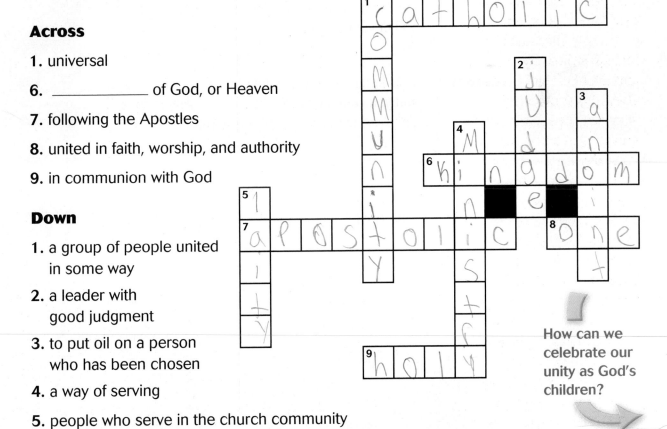

How can we celebrate our unity as God's children?

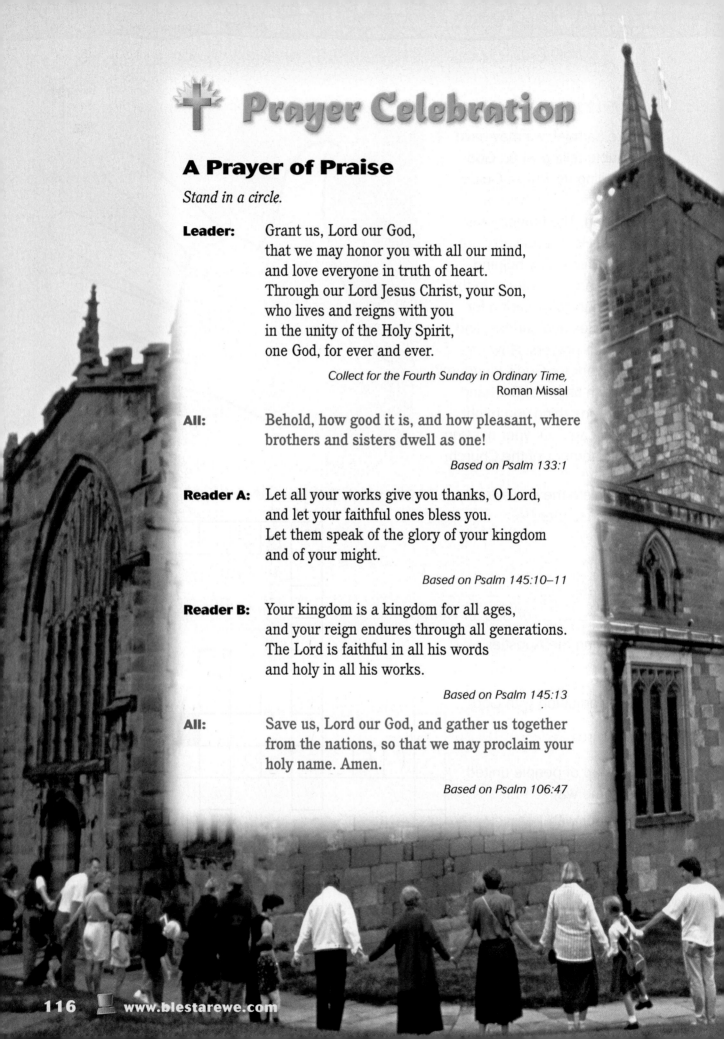

✝ Prayer Celebration

A Prayer of Praise

Stand in a circle.

Leader:
Grant us, Lord our God,
that we may honor you with all our mind,
and love everyone in truth of heart.
Through our Lord Jesus Christ, your Son,
who lives and reigns with you
in the unity of the Holy Spirit,
one God, for ever and ever.

Collect for the Fourth Sunday in Ordinary Time,
Roman Missal

All:
Behold, how good it is, and how pleasant, where
brothers and sisters dwell as one!

Based on Psalm 133:1

Reader A:
Let all your works give you thanks, O Lord,
and let your faithful ones bless you.
Let them speak of the glory of your kingdom
and of your might.

Based on Psalm 145:10–11

Reader B:
Your kingdom is a kingdom for all ages,
and your reign endures through all generations.
The Lord is faithful in all his words
and holy in all his works.

Based on Psalm 145:13

All:
Save us, Lord our God, and gather us together
from the nations, so that we may proclaim your
holy name. Amen.

Based on Psalm 106:47

9 Chapter Review

A **Match** Column A with Column B by writing the correct number in the space provided.

A

1. ministry
2. catholic
3. holy
4. apostolic
5. laity
6. Catholic
7. one

B

_5_ people who are part of the Church but are not clergy or religious brothers or sisters

_3_ in communion with God

_1_ a way of serving others in Christ's name

_7_ united in faith, worship, and authority

_6_ the Church founded by Christ

_4_ following the teachings of the Apostles

_2_ universal

B **Complete** the paragraph, using words from the box.

Covenant	judges	God
promised land	heavenly kingdom	

Many of the first leaders of the Israelites were ___judges___. They helped the Hebrew people remain faithful to their ___Covenant___ with God. Samuel was an especially wise judge. He knew that a leader had to make decisions based on what ___God___ wanted. Just as God gave the Israelites the ___Promised land___, he promises us that we will share in his ___heavenly kingdom___.

C **Describe** some ways in which members of the Church contribute to its mission.

___They volunteer at the mass to help. They volunteer to teach religous ed.___

Faith in Action

Social Service Ministries Catholic social service ministries serve neighbors in need both near and far. They offer relief and hope wherever people need food, clothing, housing, medical care, and the kindness of caring people. Social service ministries change the lives of people every day. Through the ministries of local parishes, priests and laypeople alike put their faith into action as they serve people in need.

In Everyday Life

Activity Describe two actions that might go along with the statement below, one that will show the statement is true (Action A) and one that might make others doubt its truth (Action B).

I care about people who are suffering in any way, such as from poverty or loneliness.

Action A _____

_____

Action B _____

_____

In Your Parish

Activity Choose a parish ministry that you are interested in, such as a parish pantry or outreach to new immigrants, and tell how you can be helpful as a member in the group.

_____

_____

_____

_____

Take Home

FAMILY TIME

The Ark and the Temple

To the Israelites, worship before the Ark of the Covenant in the tent was a treasured way to present oneself before God. Washing one's hands and feet before entering and continually burning lamps outside were rituals that showed respect for God's holy presence. Many of the Israelites' rituals found new meaning in Christ and became the basis for Catholic ways of coming to the Holy Spirit through Jesus, such as Baptism.

ACTIVITY

Baptism Anniversaries Mark the dates of your baptisms on a household calendar. Celebrate your Baptism anniversaries by reflecting on your mission in spreading God's love. Also have a small celebration on each person's special day.

WEEKLY PLANNER

On Sunday

Meditate upon the tabernacle, in which the Blessed Sacrament is kept. Thank God for his presence among us.

On the Web

www.blestarewe.com

Visit our Web site for the Saint of the day and the reflection question of the week.

Saint of the Week

Saint John Vianney
(1786–1859)

John Vianney was parish priest at Ars, a remote French hamlet. His life was one of extreme simplicity and self-deprivation. He was loved by everyone who knew him. He heard confessions for sixteen hours each day, and dedicated his life to bringing people to God.

Patron Saint of: priests
Feast Day: August 4

A Prayer for the Week

Lord, through the intercession of John Vianney, strengthen our faith and enrich your Church through those you have called to the priesthood. Amen.

Take Home

FAMILY TIME

✝ Scripture Background

In the Early Church

Baptism Among the Early Christians   In the Easter Vigil reading we hear Jesus instruct his disciples to "make disciples of all nations, baptizing them in the name of the Father, and the Son, and the holy Spirit" (Matthew 28:19). Jesus' followers accepted this call. The Acts of the Apostles contains numerous accounts of Baptisms carried out by the Apostles, often of large crowds of people. Peter baptized a crowd of 3,000 (Acts 2:38–41). Paul preached in Corinth and led many to believe in Jesus and be baptized (Acts 18:1–8). Philip preached the Good News, and many came to him to be baptized (Acts 8:12–16).

OUR CATHOLIC TRADITION in Film

Raiders of the Lost Ark   In *Raiders of the Lost Ark*, several people are looking for the ark that held the original stone tablets of the Ten Commandments given to Moses on Mount Sinai. Harrison Ford plays Indiana Jones, leader of the "good guys" seeking the ark. Archaeologists and fortune seekers are interested in the ark for its historical significance on one hand and its enormous worth on the other. One "bad guy" is particularly interested in the prospect of possessing an object known to have great power. Although this action-adventure flick presents an unlikely story, it does highlight the importance of the ark to present-day and ancient people.

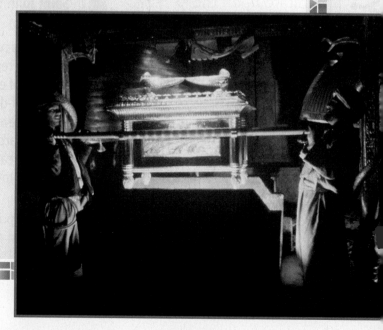

10 The Ark and the Temple

Springs of Baptismal Water, bless the Lord;
praise and exalt him above all for ever.

Easter Vigil Blessing of Water acclamation, Roman Missal

Share

Your school day usually begins with the Pledge of Allegiance. You stand, face the flag, and place your hand over your heart. Sports events usually begin with the singing of our national anthem. These are rituals, or ceremonial practices. They remind us of and honor our unity and freedom as Americans.

In the Church, rituals help us honor and prepare for God's presence. Special actions and objects remind us of Jesus Christ and prepare us for God's life in us.

Activity

The words below relate to things that remind us of Jesus Christ and prepare us for God's life in us. Find the words in the flame and circle them. You may find them across, up, down, diagonally, or backwards.

anoint
bless
candle
crucifix

genuflect
holy water
oil
palms

rosary
Sign of the Cross
Stations of the Cross

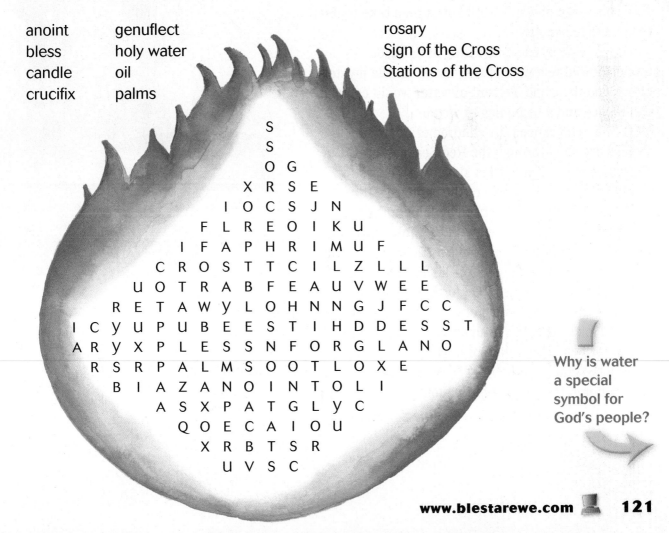

Why is water a special symbol for God's people?

Worship   The Blessing of Water

In the Old Testament, water is a sign of God's power. The first Creation story from Genesis says God's spirit moved over the oceans. Genesis also describes the Great Flood, sent to destroy evil on Earth. In the Exodus, God parted the Red Sea to help the Israelites escape Egypt, and he gave them water in the desert. God also calmed the Jordan River so the Israelites could cross over to the promised land.

In the Sacrament of Baptism, through water blessed with the Holy Spirit, we are cleansed of Original Sin and given new life in Christ. During the Easter Vigil, a priest blesses water that is to be used to baptize people who have been preparing to become Catholics. In the blessing, the priest celebrates Old Testament events as signs of the saving power of the water of Baptism. He sings,

O God, who by invisible power accomplish a wondrous effect through sacramental signs and who in many ways have prepared water, your creation, to show forth the grace of Baptism;

O God, whose Spirit in the first moments of the world's creation hovered over the waters, so that the very substance of water would even then take to itself the power to sanctify;

O God, who by the outpouring of the flood foreshadowed regeneration, so that from the mystery of one and the same element of water would come an end to vice and a beginning of virtue;

O God, who caused the children of Abaraham to pass dry-shod through the Red Sea, so that the chosen people, set free from slavery to Pharaoh, would prefigure the people of the baptized;

O God, whose Son, baptized by John in the waters of the Jordan, was anointed with the Holy Spirit, and, as he hung upon the Cross, gave forth water from his side along with blood, and after his Resurrection, commanded his disciples: "Go forth, teach all natioons, baptizing them in the name of the Father and of the Son and of the Holy Spirit," look now, we pray, upon the face of your Church and graciously unseal for her the fountain of Baptism.

May the power of the Holy Spirit, O Lord, we pray, come down through your Son into the fullness of this font . . ."

Blessing of Baptismal Water, The Easter Vigil, **Roman Missal**

Signs of God

The Israelites in the Old Testament saw God work wonders through water. They saw water's power to bring purity and goodness. In order to be pure in God's presence, they washed their hands and feet before worshiping God in the tent that held the Ark of the Covenant. Many Jewish people still practice ritual washings for special occasions. Through such rituals, the Israelites and their modern descendants have celebrated God's goodness throughout their history.

The Israelites felt God's presence when they were near the Ark of the Covenant. To honor God, they continually burned oil lamps outside it. When the Israelites settled in Canaan, they needed a permanent holy place to keep the ark and worship God together. Israel's first two kings, Saul and David, wanted to build a magnificent place to gather for worship. During the rule of King Solomon, the son of David, the **Temple** was finally built on Mount Zion, a hill in Jerusalem. The ark was kept in the Temple in a sacred space called the Holy of Holies. A continual light shone there, to remind worshipers of the eternal covenant with God.

Our Church Teaches

Early Christians adapted some of the rituals used by the Israelites to celebrate the presence of God. For example, Baptism and blessing ourselves with holy water may have grown out of Jewish ritual washings. However, Jewish rituals received new meaning from Jesus Christ. Through Jesus Christ, God could truly be present within us. Baptism and the other **Sacraments** fill us with God's very life and presence, or grace. They are more than symbolic. They help us participate in God's kingdom on Earth as well as prepare us for everlasting life with God. The holy water used in Baptism and for blessings is a **sacramental**, something that reminds us of Jesus Christ and prepares us for God's life in us. The sacramentals of the Church change us spiritually, but they do not give grace the way Sacraments do.

In the same way the Israelites went to the Temple to worship and be close to God, Catholics go to church. But we also attend church to be filled with Christ. In our churches, blessed candles (which are also sacramentals) are placed upon the altar. At least one lamp continually shines near the tabernacle holding the Blessed Sacrament, Christ's Body. The light reminds us that Christ is there and that he is the eternal Light of the world.

Faith Words

Temple
The Temple was the Jewish place of worship in Jerusalem that contained the Ark of the Covenant.

Sacrament
A Sacrament is a sacred sign and cause of grace instituted by Christ in the Church to continue his saving action through the Holy Spirit.

sacramental
A sacramental is a symbolic prayer, blessing, object, or action instituted by the Church that can lead us to a fuller participation in the grace of the Sacraments.

What sacramentals are used in the Sacrament of Holy Orders?

Respond

The Rite of Holy Orders

Hector, James, and Nick are in the cafeteria, discussing the weekend.

Hector: My uncle Rodrigo was ordained a priest on Saturday.

Nick: What was that like?

Hector: First, the bishop asked my uncle and the other men if they truly wanted to be priests. They said, "I do." They promised to follow the bishop's guidance.

James: Did your uncle and the others just stand there?

Hector: Well, when they were blessed the first time, they were kneeling. Then they lay on the floor while everyone sang the Litany of the Saints, asking Saints to pray for the new priests.

Nick: Why were they on the floor?

Hector: My uncle says it shows their surrender to God. My uncle and the others became priests when the bishop laid his hands on their heads and prayed over them. Then they received the vestments they'll wear for Mass. Their hands were also anointed with oil called *Chrism*. Once they became priests, they all joined in the celebration of the Mass.

Sacraments at the Service of Communion

Holy Orders is a Sacrament at the Service of Communion. The other Sacrament at the Service of Communion is Matrimony. Those who receive these Sacraments have a special mission to serve the Church and work for the Salvation of others. Men who receive Holy Orders can serve the Church as bishops, priests, or deacons. A bishop receives the fullness of the Sacrament of Holy Orders. Under the authority of the Pope, he is in charge of a group of church communities. Bishops succeed the Apostles. Priests assist the bishop in ministering to the community by presiding at Eucharistic celebrations and administering the other Sacraments. They also proclaim God's Word and lead the parish community. Deacons assist with the work of the parish. They can lead the celebrations of Baptism and Matrimony. They can also read the Gospel and give the homily at Sunday Mass.

page 267 to learn more about the Sacraments at the Service of Communion and page 278 to learn more about priests.

Activities

1. Using the clues, unscramble the words.

MHICRS _____

Clue: oil used to anoint

TRENCSAAMLA _____

Clue: something symbolic that reminds us of Christ's presence

EEMTLP _____

Clue: the Israelites' center of worship

MASTCRANE _____

Clue: a sacred sign and cause of grace

OHYL DRORSE _____

Clue: the Sacrament at the Service of Communion by which priests are ordained

2. In Old Testament times, people filled clay jars with water for their ritual washings. In each jar below, write something for which you are sorry—a failure you would like to wash away.

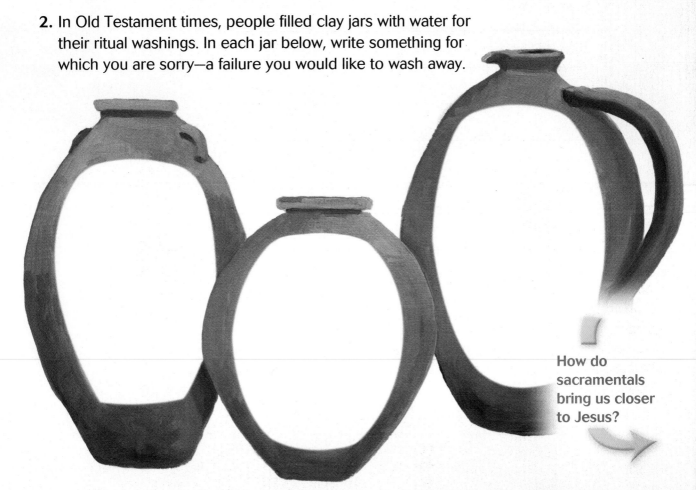

How do sacramentals bring us closer to Jesus?

 **Prayer Celebration**

A Prayer for Guidance

Some of the sacramentals used by Catholics include holy water and candles. Candles are often used in the liturgy as a reminder that Jesus is the light for our lives. He leads us out of the darkness of sin and onto the path of Salvation. In the space below, write a prayer asking Jesus to be your light and to guide you. Be specific in the ways in which you need Jesus' guidance.

_____

_____

_____

_____

_____

_____

_____

_____

The Sign of the Cross is the sacramental that Catholics use to start their prayers. Beginning with the Sign of the Cross, quietly and reflectively say your prayer to Jesus.

Make the Sign of the Cross again.

10 Chapter Review

A **Complete** the sentences, using words from the box.

1. Through the _____, which were instituted by Christ and entrusted to the _____, God's grace is given to us.

2. In the Sacrament of _____, we are cleansed of Original Sin and given new life in Christ.

3. The Sacraments at the Service of Communion are

   _____ and _____.

4. _____ succeed the Apostles.

5. At the _____, a priest blesses water that is to be used to baptize people who are going to become Catholic.

Matrimony
Baptism
Church
bishops
Holy Orders
Easter Vigil
Sacraments

B **Match** Column A with Column B by writing the correct number in the space provided.

A

1. sacramental

2. Holy Orders

3. Sacrament

4. Temple

5. Holy of Holies

B

____ the Sacrament by which men are ordained to the priesthood or to become deacons

____ the Jewish place of worship in Jerusalem

____ a sacred sign and cause of grace instituted by Christ to continue his saving action

____ a sacred space that contained the Ark of the Covenant

____ a symbolic prayer, blessing, object, or action instituted by the Church

C **Circle** the rituals that the early Christians adapted from the Israelites to celebrate the presence of God.

blessing the water

continually burning a lamp

going to a holy place to worship

exchanging the Sign of Peace

Faith in Action

Catechetical Ministry   To help young people grow in their faith and become fully participating member of the Catholic community, parishes instruct young people in the catechism of the Catholic Church. A parish's catechetical program also prepares young people to receive the Sacraments of Penance and Reconciliation and Eucharist, as well as Confirmation. Under the direction of the pastor and a director of religious education, parishioner volunteers prepare young members of the community to receive these Sacraments for the first time and teach them about the Catholic faith.

In Everyday Life

Activity   List three ways in which your own experience with the parish catechetical ministry helps you live as a good Catholic.

1. _____

2. _____

3. _____

In Your Parish

Activity   All the people gathered as an assembly to celebrate a liturgy are considered "ministers" to one another in a parish. Describe some ways members of a parish minister to one another. Here are some ideas to get you started.

✝ Celebrating Catholic beliefs together
✝ Proclaiming God's Word as lectors

✝ _____

✝ _____

✝ _____

✝ _____

Take Home

FAMILY TIME

David's Sin and the Story of the Fall

The happiness of many people can be lost by just one person's choosing personal satisfaction over virtue. The Bible story about David and what he did to marry Bathsheba is a prime example. Even though David was forgiven, he could not undo the consequences of his actions. The story of the Fall of Man in Genesis also explains the disobedience of humans and its consequences. But Jesus Christ brought Salvation from sin, and God is always there to help us resist temptation.

ACTIVITY

Valuable Tears A tradition holds that Jewish women's tears were collected in jars and later used for special rituals. Have each family member write a one-line prayer for forgiveness on a teardrop-shaped piece of paper, fold it, and drop it into a glass jar. Imagine these prayers are tears poured out to Jesus.

WEEKLY PLANNER

On Sunday

During Mass, pay attention to teachings about forgiveness or mercy.

On the Web

www.blestarewe.com

 Visit our Web site for the Saint of the day and the reflection question of the week.

Saint of the Week

 Blessed Laura Vicuña (1891–1904)

From a young age, Laura Vicuña was troubled by the life her mother led. She continually prayed for her mother. When Laura was twelve years old, she was ill and dying. She comforted her mother, saying she was happy to give up her life for her mother's Salvation. Upon Laura's death, her mother repented and returned to the Church.

Feast Day: January 22

 A Prayer for the Week

Merciful Father, help us recognize all our sins and failings, lead us to your mercy, and guide us to your eternal kingdom. Amen.

Take Home

✚ Scripture Background

Before the Time of Jesus

King David The Bible contains more stories about David than about any other person apart from Jesus. David is honored in Scripture for his accomplishments. As a warrior, David defeated Goliath. After Saul's death, David was crowned king of the tribe of Judah. Seven years later he became leader of the unified tribes and established Jerusalem as his capital. But David's human weaknesses are also presented in Scripture. A chief example is his adultery with Bathsheba. Read about David's sin in 2 Samuel 11, and about his repentance in 2 Samuel 12.

OUR CATHOLIC TRADITION in Legend

King Arthur and King David

The flaw in Camelot in the story of King Arthur was the same as the flaw that brought down David's kingship. The musical *Camelot* tells this story in great detail. Arthur's father had Lady Igraine's husband killed in battle so he could marry the widow. Then Lancelot and Guinevere betrayed Arthur and destroyed the virtue of Camelot. Similarly, David's pursuit of another man's wife damaged his capacity for leading Israel.

11 David's Sin and the Story of the Fall

The Lord is kind and faithful to those
who keep the covenant and the laws.

Based on Psalm 25:10

Share

Making decisions is not always easy. God gave us free will, the freedom to decide how we are going to act. Think of a time when you had to choose what you knew was right over something that seemed easier to do. Since the beginning of time, people have had to make such choices. Sometimes our choices lead to uncomfortable consequences for us or for others. Sometimes it is hard to admit we have made a mistake.

Activity

Have you ever been in a situation when you knew the right choice was going to be difficult? What choice did you make? Draw yourself doing what you decided, then answer the questions.

What situation led you to have to make the choice?

The situation that led me to disíon was to help so we could finish faster.

Did you make the right choice? Why or why not?

I made the right choice because we worked together so we each had a equal share for the project.

What happens when people do not choose goodness?

✝ Scripture King David and the Sin of Humanity

God was unhappy with Saul's leadership. God told Samuel to anoint a shepherd boy named David to be the new king of the Israelites. David was the youngest son of Jesse, a man from Bethlehem.

Saul was sad that he had lost favor with the LORD. He said to his servant, "Find a talented harpist to cheer me up."

"The youngest son of Jesse is a good musician," said the servant. "He is also a good soldier. Besides, the LORD is with him."

David was brought to Saul. Saul's spirits were lifted in David's company. David became a loyal friend and soldier to Saul. Saul soon realized that God had chosen David to be the next king of Israel.

When David became king, he was a powerful leader. The LORD was with him, and he ruled honorably and fairly for many years. He made Jerusalem the capital of Israel.

But there was a beautiful married woman, Bathsheba, whom David coveted. David sent her husband, Uriah, into battle, and Uriah was killed. David and Bathsheba married and had a son. The baby died soon after it was born. God was not pleased with David's actions.

David asked for forgiveness. "I have sinned against the LORD," he said. The LORD forgave David. A new baby, called Solomon, was born.

David's sin might remind us of the story of Adam and Eve, written around David's time. It explains the human weakness for disobeying God.

Out of the soil, God created the first humans, Adam and Eve, to enjoy the beauty of the earth. God gave them a peaceful garden so that they could experience God's love every day. God also made them partners in charge of caring for the other things he had created. In return, God told Adam and Eve to not eat fruit from a certain tree in the garden, the tree of knowledge of good and evil, or they would die.

One day, a serpent tempted Eve to eat the fruit of the tree. The creature said that the fruit would make Adam and Eve smarter. Adam and Eve knew God forbade it, but they tried the fruit. Their choice made God very angry. When he asked what they had done, they were ashamed.

God said, "The humans have become like us, knowing what is good and bad!" God said to Adam, "By the sweat of your face shall you get bread to eat, until you return to the ground from which you were taken. For you are dirt, and to dirt you shall return."

God banished Adam and Eve from the happiness of the garden. The original sin of the first humans would hurt all generations after them.

Based on 1 Samuel 16:14–23; 2 Samuel 1–12; Genesis 2:4–3:23

True Freedom

The story about Adam and Eve is sometimes called "the fall of humans." It helps explain the origins and effects of sin. The author tried to help people understand how sin affects everyone and why humans struggle. Because of their human weakness, the Israelites had trouble obeying God's Laws and finding true happiness. Even God's anointed, Saul and David, were not free from temptation and its consequences. David gave in to his envy of another man. As we see from his story, envy is a serious sin that can lead to many other sins. David's envy resulted in Uriah's death and damaged David's relationship with God and the kingdom. Like Adam, Eve, and David, people sometimes use their free will to make choices that separate them from God. But David's story shows God's great ability to forgive.

Our Church Teaches

Along with free will, each of us has a **conscience**, an ability to know what is right and what is wrong. We must examine our conscience often to correctly identify what God wants. This means thinking about our choices, whether they reflect God's love, and what their results might be. A good, moral act is more than something that turns out all right in the end. It is something that we start, continue, and finish with good intentions toward ourselves, others, and God. If our conscience tells us that something is wrong, we must not do it, even if it will bring about something good. If we are sure something is right and good, we should choose it. Although our conscience is not always correct, this may not be our fault. To help us develop our conscience God gives us **guidance**. We are obligated to listen to the guidance of the Church, the Scriptures, and parents or other adults, and to be open to the guidance of the Holy Spirit.

Through the Sacraments God gives us grace, which also helps us make good decisions. **Sacramental grace** is the unique gift of God's love that we receive in each Sacrament. Grace strengthens us to be more holy and to avoid sin. But God's love is always with us, even when we sin. We accept that love in the Sacrament of Penance and Reconciliation. When we repent and accept God's love in Reconciliation, God forgives us, frees us from our sins, and gives us grace so we can truly be free.

Faith Words

conscience
Our conscience is our ability to judge what is right and what is wrong.

guidance
Guidance is help in making the right choices. God gives us guidance to help us develop our conscience.

sacramental grace
Sacramental grace is the unique gift of God's love that we receive in each Sacrament.

How do we decide what is right?

Respond

Making Choices

One Friday, Carlos's teacher, Mrs. Meyer, showed a video about the book his class was reading for English.

"Don't forget—Tuesday is your test," she said. "There will be a bonus question based on the movie we just watched. I hope you were paying attention."

Now I am, thought Carlos. *If only she had told us before. I would have stayed awake and taken notes!* Carlos hadn't read the book, and his grades in English weren't great. Any bonus points would help.

"May I borrow the tape to watch at home?" asked Carlos.

"I'm sorry, Carlos, but it wouldn't be fair to the rest of the class," Mrs. Meyer said.

The bell rang, and the class was dismissed. As Carlos walked by the teacher's desk, he grabbed the tape and slipped it into his backpack. He would return it to the teacher before she knew it was missing.

That weekend, Carlos watched the tape twice. He was sure he would be able to answer the bonus question and get the extra points.

On Monday morning, Mrs. Meyer made an announcement. "I had planned on showing the tape again today, but I can't seem to find it. Does anyone know where it might be?"

The students looked at each other. Carlos, of course, knew where it was: on his desk at home. He forgot to bring it back to school!

"Well," said Mrs. Meyer, "I have no choice but to base the test only on the book. If you read the book, you won't have any problem doing well."

Carlos panicked. The class groaned.

"This doesn't seem fair," said Theresa.

Carlos got a sinking feeling in his stomach. Maybe he hadn't made such a good choice.

Activities

1. Help Carlos decide the right thing to do. Fill in answers to his questions. Then discuss what you would do if you were Carlos.

What would Jesus say about this?

What should I do now?

What would my parents think?

2. Think back to the situation you drew on page 131. How did you feel after you followed through on your decision? Choose the words below that describe the way you felt. Write them inside the cardboard box where you think they belong.

relieved	happy	nervous	faithful	loved
guilty	proud	unsure	afraid	alone
lonely	ashamed	confident	free	sad

3. Prayer and the Sacraments strengthen us to avoid sin. During the Sacrament of Penance, we say a prayer called the Act of Contrition, or Prayer of Sorrow. In this prayer, we express our sadness about sinning and our desire to do better. We also pray that God will have mercy. Write your own act of contrition.

Dear God,

How do we ask God for forgiveness during the liturgy?

Prayer Celebration

The Confiteor

During the Mass, Catholics perform the Penitential Act. The priest asks us to call to mind our sins. Then we pray the Confiteor, a prayer of sorrow for ourselves and for our community. A Catholic tradition is to hit our chests lightly as a sign of regret while praying this prayer.

As you pray the Confiteor, think about your actions during the past week. Did you purposely do or say something that hurt someone else? Did you neglect an opportunity to show kindness to someone who needed it? If you had the chance, would you act differently?

The Confiteor

All: I confess to almighty God
and to you, my brothers and sisters,
that I have greatly sinned,
in my thoughts and in my words,
in what I have done and in what I have failed to do,
through my fault, through my fault,
through my most grievous fault;
therefore I ask blessed Mary ever-Virgin,
all the Angels and Saints,
and you, my brothers and sisters,
to pray for me to the Lord our God.

Roman Missal

11 Chapter Review

A. Circle the letter of the best answer.

1. _____ is the unique gift of God's love that we receive in the Sacraments.
   - **a.** Conscience
   - **b.** Knowledge
   - **c.** Sacramental grace
   - **d.** Guidance

2. The Church, the Scriptures, our parents and other adults, and the Holy Spirit can give us _____ to help us make good decisions.
   - **a.** guidance
   - **b.** free will
   - **c.** permission
   - **d.** happiness

3. Our _____ is our ability to know what is right and what is wrong.
   - **a.** free will
   - **b.** conscience
   - **c.** strength
   - **d.** consequence

4. The story of Adam and Eve helps explain _____.
   - **a.** envy as a sin
   - **b.** the origin and effects of sin
   - **c.** the importance of prayer
   - **d.** the bounty of nature

5. During Mass we pray the _____, a prayer of sorrow for our sins.
   - **a.** Confiteor
   - **b.** Nicene Creed
   - **c.** Hail Mary
   - **d.** Act of Contrition

B. Respond to the following.

1. Describe ways in which the Church's teaching and Scriptures guide you in living a moral life.

   _____

   _____

2. Describe a situation that may lead a young person to sin. Then tell how conscience can affect the choices the young person makes.

   _____

   _____

Faith in Action

Parish Pastoral Council   Like the Christian communities of the first century, Catholics today need help in living out the message of Jesus. Members of your parish pastoral council meet regularly to talk about ways parish leaders can provide this help through ministries of worship, education, service, and stewardship. Their most important job is to help us all become more like Jesus in the ways we live, learn, celebrate, and serve together.

In Everyday Life

Activity   Choose two of the qualities below that you think are most important in a good leader. Then explain your choices.

has good ideas	communicates openly
is a hard worker	is a good listener
is generous	is respectful
prays regularly	is caring

_____

_____

_____

In Your Parish

Activity   Describe one event or issue you would like to see your parish involved in.

_____

Do you think Jesus would support this? Why or why not?

_____

_____

_____

Take Home

FAMILY TIME

Psalms of Praise and Works of Wonder

Music gives us a different way to experience prayer. The tone of the music can bring joy, consolation, or hope to prayer. Poetry, too, conveys messages of faith in more emotional ways than normal speech. Psalms are prayers, poems, and songs all wrapped up into one. They are a powerful part of the Church's prayer life, with a rich Old Testament history.

ACTIVITY

Prayer Gear To show that prayer time is special and sacred, choose a holy item—the Bible, a crucifix, a rosary—that people in your family can keep close by during prayer time.

WEEKLY PLANNER

On Sunday

During the Responsorial Psalm, try to experience the calm that Saul felt when David sang and played the harp.

On the Web

www.blestarewe.com

Visit our Web site for the Saint of the day and the reflection question of the week.

Saint of the Week

Saint Gregory the Great, Pope and Doctor of the Church (540–604)

As Pope, Gregory the Great worked to reform the Church by removing unfit clergy and abolishing clerical fees for burial and ordinations. He was responsible for bringing Christianity to England and is credited with initiating Gregorian chant, which is still popular in liturgies today.

Feast Day: September 3

A Prayer for the Week

We praise you, Lord, for your wonderful ways. You have given us many gifts. We especially thank you for the gifts of music and poetry. Amen.

Take Home

FAMILY TIME

✝ Scripture Background

Before the Time of Jesus

The Psalms   The Book of Psalms contains hymns and laments of ancient Israel—150 altogether. Many psalms are attributed to David. The Psalms date from the tenth century B.C. through the third century B.C. Because they were written over such a long period of time, the Psalms present varying ways of addressing God. Some speak of the God of a single people and place, while others speak of a God of all people. The Psalms describe virtually every aspect of everyday life. Psalms is truly the common book of prayer of Christians and Jews. Choose a favorite Psalm to read.

OUR CATHOLIC TRADITION in Poetry

Gerard Manley Hopkins

Gerard Manley Hopkins was a Jesuit priest who lived in the nineteenth century. He was the brilliant son of a wealthy English couple, whom he shocked by becoming Catholic and then a priest. He had a unique way of expressing his thoughts and a deep appreciation for God in nature. He ended the poem "Pied Beauty" by reminding the reader to praise God. Hopkins lived only forty-five years and was not published until thirty years after his death.

12 Psalms of Praise and Works of Wonder

LET US PRAY

You are God: we praise you;
you are God: we acclaim you;
you are the eternal Father:
all creation worships you.

Te Deum, Catholic Household Blessings and Prayers

Share

How do you feel when someone compliments you?
We all feel special when we are noticed for
something good. We like it when people see
what we have done and say, "Wow!"

What makes you say "Wow!" about God? a sunrise
or sunset? a forest? the mountains? another person?
Everything around you shows that God is great and
loves you. The world is full of things that remind us
of God and make us say "Wow!"

Activity

Fill in the following song of praise for God,
using the clues for parts of speech to help you.

Every day I will _____ you, and
                        (verb)

I will bless your _____ forever and ever.
                        (noun)

I will _____ the fame of your goodness and sing
                (verb)

_____ of your _____.
        (adverb)   (noun)

The Lord is _____ to all his people, and holy
                (adjective)

in all his _____.
                (noun)

May my _____ speak of the praise of the
                (noun)

Lord, and may all _____ bless his
                        (noun)

_____ name.
        (adjective)

Based on Psalm 145

When do we
sing songs of
praise for God?

 Scripture David's Songs

King David had great faith in the Lord. David used his musical talent to praise God and thank him for coming to his aid in battle.

David had to defend Israel in battle many times. After one victory, he sang the following song to thank God for his protection, power, and faithfulness.

"O LORD, my rock, my fortress, my deliverer,
    my God, my rock of refuge!
'Praised be the LORD,' I exclaim,
    and I am safe from my enemies.
In my distress I called upon the LORD
    and cried out to my God;
From his temple he heard my voice,
    and my cry reached his ears.
The LORD thundered from heaven;
    the Most High gave forth his voice.
He sent arrows to put my enemy to flight;
    he flashed lightning and routed them.
He rescued me from my mighty enemy."

Later, when David was too old to rule over Israel, God chose Solomon, the son of David and Bathsheba, to be the next king. David knew Solomon would fulfill his dream of building a magnificent temple in Jerusalem.

"Bless the LORD your God!" David told the people when God had chosen Solomon. David reminded Solomon to honor the LORD's covenant and to be faithful always. David said, "O LORD, God of our fathers Abraham, Isaac, and Israel, direct the hearts of your people toward you. Give my son Solomon a wholehearted desire to keep your commandments."

Solomon was anointed king. David soon ended his forty-year rule over Israel. He died a faithful follower of the LORD.

*Based on 2 Samuel 22:1–18; 1 Kings 1–2;
1 Chronicles 28:1–21, 29:18–28*

Singing Praise

For centuries David was believed to have been the author of the **Psalms** from the Book of Psalms in the Old Testament. However, several people may actually have written them from David's time until about 400 B.C. The Book of Psalms is a collection of 150 religious songs and prayers. The song of David you just read is found in the Book of Psalms as Psalm 18.

The name *psalm* comes from the Greek word *psalterion*, which was a stringed musical instrument. Often, a psalm's purpose was to express praise, thanksgiving, or sorrow. We believe that the psalms were composed for use during religious ceremonies. The singing was often accompanied by stringed or wind instruments.

Psalms tell of God's great actions and people's response to God. The words and themes of the psalms are still fitting today. They may be prayed alone or with a congregation.

Our Church Teaches

Many psalms begin and end with the exclamation *"Hallelujah!"* This word— which means "Praise the Lord!"—is a combination of a Hebrew word for praise (*hallelu*) and the beginning of the word *Yahweh*. Today, we say "Alleluia!" when we want to express our joy and praise for God. Another important part of our prayers is the word **amen**, also from the Hebrew tradition of prayer. *Amen* means "I believe" or "So it is."

The Catholic Church has adapted many psalms for our liturgical celebrations. In the Liturgy of the Word, we pray a responsorial psalm. A leader sings or reads a psalm, and the congregation sings or reads a response after each verse. During the Mass, we may also sing several songs that are based on psalms. Psalms are simple and loving ways for us to express our **reverence** for God.

Faith Words

Psalms

Psalms are religious songs and prayers from the Old Testament. Psalms often express praise, thanksgiving, or sorrow.

amen

Amen is a word we usually say at the end of our prayers. It means "I believe" or "So it is."

reverence

Reverence is honor and respect. We can show reverence for God by praying the Psalms.

What are some ways that God is worthy of praise?

Respond

"Little Less Than the Angels"

Read the verses from Psalm 8 below. What does the psalm writer say about people's place in the universe? How do humans measure up to the rest of creation?

Psalm 8	My Psalm

O LORD, our LORD,
    how glorious is your name over all the earth!
When I behold your heavens, the work of
    your fingers,
    the moon and the stars that you
    set in place—
What are people that you should be mindful
    of them?
You have made them little less than
    the angels
and crowned them with glory and honor.
You have given them rule over the works
    of your hands, putting all things under
    their feet:
All sheep and oxen,
    yes, and the beasts of the field,
The birds of the air, the fishes of the sea.
O LORD, our LORD,
    how glorious is your name over all the earth!
	_____
	_____
	_____
	_____
	_____
	_____
	_____
	_____
	_____
	_____
	_____
	_____
	_____
	_____

Based on Psalm 8:2, 4–9

Activities

1. In the second column, rewrite Psalm 8 in your own words, or write your own psalm, using Psalm 8 as a model. Address God with reverence and identify the blessings God has given you.

2. You have been asked to film some of the events that are described in the psalm below. The film is called *You Are at My Side*. In the frames, draw scenes to show how God loves his people.

The Lord, Shepherd and Host

The LORD is my shepherd, I shall not want.
In verdant pastures he gives me repose;
Beside restful waters he leads me;
he refreshes my soul.
He guides me in right paths
for his name's sake.
Even though I walk in the dark valley
I fear no evil; for you are at my side
With your rod and your staff
that give me courage.

Psalm 23:1–4

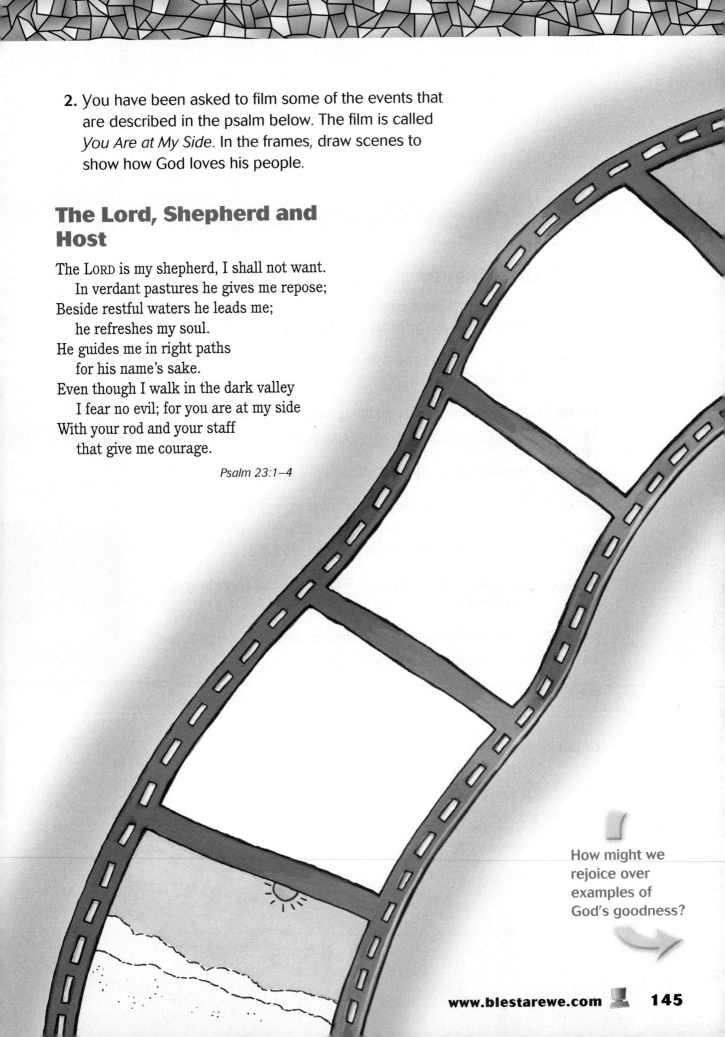

How might we rejoice over examples of God's goodness?

Prayer Celebration

A Psalm Prayer

This is a church song that we might sing at Mass. It is based on Psalm 122. The actual music and lyrics are on page 92.

Group 1: I rejoiced when I heard them say: "Let us go to the house of the Lord."

Group 2: And now our feet are standing within your gates, O Jerusalem.

All: Let us go rejoicing to the house of the Lord.

Group 1: Jerusalem is a city built with unity and strength,

Group 2: It is there, it is there that the tribes go up, the tribes of the Lord.

All: Let us go rejoicing to the house of the Lord.

Group 1: For Israel's law is to praise God's name and there to give God thanks.

Group 2: There are set the judgment thrones for all of David's house.

All: Let us go rejoicing to the house of the Lord.

Group 1: Pray for the peace of Jerusalem! "May those who love you prosper;

Group 2: May peace ever reign within your walls, and wealth within your buildings!"

All: Let us go rejoicing to the house of the Lord.

Text: Psalm 122; Michael Joncas, © 1987, GIA Publications, Inc.; refrain trans. © 1969, ICEL Music: Michael Joncas, © 1987, GIA Publications, Inc.

12 Chapter Review

A **Complete** the following sentences.

1. When David was too old to rule, God chose _____ to rule Israel.

2. In our prayers, we say "_____" to express our praise for God.

3. The _____ is a collection of 150 religious songs and prayers.

4. _____ often express praise, thanksgiving, or sorrow.

B **Fill in** the letter of the best answer.

1. Through songs and prayers of praise, we express our ____ for God as our Creator.
   - **a.** adoration
   - **b.** humility
   - **c.** talent
   - **d.** sincerity

2. *Amen* means "____."
   - **a.** Praise God
   - **b.** I believe
   - **c.** Alleluia
   - **d.** Peace be with you

3. The Catholic Church has adopted many psalms for our ____ celebrations.
   - **a.** Old Testament
   - **b.** Christmas
   - **c.** Lenten
   - **d.** liturgical

4. Psalms are simple and loving ways for us to express our ____, or respect, for God.
   - **a.** reverence
   - **b.** humility
   - **c.** enthusiasm
   - **d.** unity

C **Complete** the following prayer to praise God for something special he has done for you.

Praised be the Lord,

for he has _____

_____

_____.

Faith in Action

Music Ministry   It may seem that participating in a parish's music ministry is all fun. But don't be fooled! Music ministers work hard. The music you hear at Mass is the result of lots of practicing and a great deal of planning. Each song needs to be appropriate for its place in the liturgy and for the season of the liturgical year. The talents and traditions of the local parish also need to be taken into consideration. Many music ministers work with a worship or liturgy committee to plan ways to help everyone at Mass participate as fully as possible in the music.

In Everyday Life

Activity   Write the title of a song or poem that you especially like. Describe the feelings it evokes or the memory it helps you recall.

Title: _____

Feelings/memory: _____

_____

_____

In Your Parish

Activity   Choose a special season of the liturgical year and describe a church tradition for the season. Then describe some of the musical and liturgical traditions that your parish honors during this time.

Season: _____

Church traditions: _____

Parish traditions: _____

_____

_____

God Reminds Us to Do His Will

The faith of the Israelites was tested through exile and persecution. We are called to live our faith, even in a world that challenges our Christian values.

For the LORD of hosts will have his day
against all that is proud and arrogant,
all that is high, and it will be brought low.

Isaiah 2:12

Exile of the Israelites

Haran
Nineveh
ASSYRIA
BABYLONIA
Mediterranean Sea
Damascus
Babylon
Samaria
Jerusalem
ARABIA
EGYPT

Exile from Israel to Assyria →
Exile from Judah to Babylon →

Forced into exile, the Israelites carried their possessions on their backs, as they traveled to Assyria and Babylon. The map shows their journeys.

We Are Climbing Jacob's Ladder

African-American spiritual

1. We are climb - ing Ja - cob's lad - der,
2. Ev - 'ry round goes high - er, high - er,
3. Sin - ner, do you love my Je - sus?
4. If you love him, why not serve him?
5. We are climb - ing high - er, high - er,

We are climb - ing Ja - cob's lad - der,
Ev - 'ry round goes high - er, high - er,
Sin - ner, do you love my Je - sus?
If you love him, why not serve him?
We are climb - ing high - er, high - er,

We are climb - ing Ja - cob's lad - der,
Ev - 'ry round goes high - er, high - er,
Sin - ner, do you love my Je - sus?
If you love him, why not serve him?
We are climb - ing high - er, high - er,

Sol - diers of the cross.

Take Home

FAMILY TIME

Disobedience and Guidance

This chapter explores what happens when people feel that they no longer need God, concentrating on the period of King Solomon's rule of Israel. Israel enjoyed a time of renown and riches when Solomon ruled. Good fortune began to cloud the people's ability to focus on God. Prophets stepped in and tried to remind the Israelites of their Covenant with God. Who plays the role of prophet in your family's life of faith?

ACTIVITY

There's an Old Saying . . .
Solomon gained fame for his wise sayings, or proverbs. Work together on a poster listing some proverbs that are popular in your home. Contact grandparents or great-grandparents for their input.

WEEKLY PLANNER

On Sunday
At the Sunday liturgy, listen for wise sayings in the readings that can provide guidance for particular areas of your life.

On the Web
www.blestarewe.com

 Visit our Web site for the Saint of the day and the reflection question of the week.

Saint of the Week

 Saint Francis Xavier
(1506–1552)

Saint Francis Xavier is known as the "Apostle of the Indies and Japan" because of his missionary work in India and Japan. As a young man studying at the University of Paris around 1530, Francis met Ignatius of Loyola and became one of the first seven Jesuits.

Patron Saint of: Catholic missionaries
Feast Day: December 3

A Prayer for the Week

Lord, give us the wisdom and courage to follow your will for our lives and to lead others to you. Amen.

Take Home

FAMILY TIME

✝ Scripture Background

Before the Time of Jesus

King Solomon's Wisdom Solomon was the son of King David and Bathsheba. After David's death, Solomon inherited the throne. Early in his reign, God asked Solomon in a dream to name a gift he wanted. Solomon asked for wisdom (1 Kings 3:5–15). Solomon built the First Temple and played an important part in Israel's development, but his reputation as a man of wisdom surpassed all his other accomplishments. Solomon became the patron of wisdom literature, inspiring a long tradition of scholars who wrote books such as Proverbs, the Song of Songs, Ecclesiastes, and Wisdom. Read about Solomon's wise judgment in 1 Kings 3:16–28.

OUR CATHOLIC TRADITION in Language

The Origin of Everyday Words
Many everyday sayings come from the Bible or from Catholic tradition. Have you ever said that someone "got off Scot free"? This used to refer to being exempt from a tax to support the clergy, paid with a coin called a *sceat*. Do you call important days "red letter days"? This referred to Saints' feast days and holidays, traditionally printed in red on calendars. The word *tawdry* is a corruption of the name of Saint Audrey, at whose annual festivals showy, low quality jewelry once could be seen. When you say, "Leopards never change their spots," you echo the feelings of Jeremiah about the sinfulness of Jerusalem (Jeremiah 13:23).

The filbert nut is named after Saint Philibert because it is ripe by his feast day.

13 Disobedience and Guidance

**When you look for me, you will find me.
Yes, when you seek me with all your heart.**

Share

Sometimes when things are going well for us, we forget to thank God. We might even forget about God altogether. We can be so caught up in the good things that are happening and the fun we are having that we forget to take time out for God. It sometimes takes another person to remind us to pray, to worship, and to do good things for other people.

Activity

Place a check mark next to each person who reminds you to stay faithful to God.

- ❏ parent
- ❏ grandparent
- ❏ coach
- ❏ friend
- ❏ brother or sister
- ❏ priest

- ❏ religious sister
- ❏ teacher
- ❏ neighbor
- ❏ mentor
- ❏ other: _____

How did God remind his people to be faithful?

Hear & Believe

✝ Scripture The Rule of King Solomon

When Solomon became king of Israel, he thanked God for allowing him to become king. He asked God for wisdom to lead his people.

God told Solomon, "You have not asked for riches, treasures, or glory. Instead, you have asked for wisdom and knowledge to rule my people. So, I will give you wisdom and knowledge. I will also give you riches, treasures, and glory." The LORD kept his promise. He blessed Solomon, giving him a glorious reign no other king of Israel had enjoyed.

Other kings came to hear the wisdom God had put in Solomon's heart. Solomon had many wise sayings, called proverbs. People brought treasures to Solomon. His nation soon had thousands of horses, chariots, gold and silver items, and garments. Israel became a rich and powerful nation. Solomon decided to build a great temple in Jerusalem to honor the LORD. When it was finished, priests carried the ark of the covenant into the Temple. The community of Israel gathered in the Temple. They sang and offered sacrifices to the LORD.

Solomon ruled Israel for forty years. When he died, his son Rehoboam became king. Rehoboam ignored advice from elders who had helped Solomon rule. Seeing that the king would not listen to them, some Israelites revolted. The kingdom divided into Judah in the south and Israel in the north. Many of the people, spoiled by their riches, began to forget their covenant with the LORD. They did not keep God's laws. They worshiped false gods. Rich people mistreated the poor.

The LORD was displeased. He sent people to remind the Jews of Israel and Judah of their covenant with him. One prophet, Elijah, called the people together and said, "The God who answers with fire is God." The people prepared a sacrifice. Then Elijah asked the LORD to bring his people back to their senses. Suddenly, the LORD's fire came and consumed the sacrifice. The people fell to the ground and said, "The LORD is God!" But they did not change.

The LORD sent the prophet Hosea, who told the people that their behavior was similar to that of an unfaithful wife. He said that even though they had broken their covenant with the LORD, the LORD still loved them and waited for their return as a loving husband would.

The prophet Micah urged the people to act justly and love others. He saw that if the people did not change their ways they would be scattered among their enemies.

Finally, the prophet Isaiah warned, "This land is full of treasures and idols. Get behind the rocks and hide from the terror of the LORD. For the LORD will have his day against all that is proud and arrogant. All that is high will be brought low."

Based on 1 Chronicles 29:25; 2 Chronicles 1:8–15; 5; 9:23–31; 10:1–19; 36:14–16; Hosea 3–4; 1 Kings 15:22–24; 18:21–39; Micah 2–6; Isaiah 2:6–19

Guidance from the Lord

When the Israelites were suffering, it was easy for them to remain faithful to God. They needed God's help, so they prayed and worshiped him. After they settled into the kingdom of Israel, they enjoyed great wealth under Solomon's rule. Many of the Israelites stopped praying and worshiping the Lord. Because of this, they were open to distractions from God. They eventually began to worship other gods.

God was not about to let his people abandon him. He intended to save them from their sinful ways. The Old Testament **prophets**, such as Hosea and Micah, served God's plan by preaching to the people that God would forgive them, free them from sin, and welcome them back into their covenant relationship with him. Through the prophets, God helped the people begin to hope for **Salvation**.

Our Church Teaches

God made the world good and created people to be faithful to him. But as the Bible tells us, the sin of the first humans, Adam and Eve, brought disobedience of God into the world. Sin and death resulted for everyone, and all humans now disobey God's Law at times. But Jesus Christ came to save us. He gave us the gift of Baptism, which washes away **Original Sin**, the sin of the first man and woman that was passed on to all human beings.

Jesus' obedience to God brought new life to the world. Jesus is the "new Adam" and the son of Mary, the "new Eve." *Christ* means "anointed one." God anointed Jesus Christ with the Holy Spirit and made him our Priest, our King, and the Prophet who would always guide us back to God. We can find his guidance in the Scriptures, in the Eucharist, in the Sacraments, in forgiveness, in faithful Christians, and in prayer.

We Believe

Jesus Christ is our Priest, Prophet, and King.

Faith Words

prophet
A prophet is a person sent by God to speak out against behavior that does not follow God's will.

Salvation
Salvation is freedom from the pain of sin.

Original Sin
Original Sin is the sin of the first man and woman, passed on to all human beings. Because of it, we are weakened in our ability to resist sin and do good.

What can we do to call others back to God?

Saint Francis Xavier

Francis Xavier was born in his family's castle in Spain in 1506. He studied philosophy at the University of Paris. Francis was a bright student who enjoyed discussing the great thinkers of his time. When Francis graduated, he was hired to teach as a university professor in Paris.

At the university, Francis met Ignatius Loyola, a man who would change Francis' life forever. Ignatius saw in Francis an ability to spread the good news to those who had never heard of Jesus. It took Ignatius a while to convince Francis that this was what God wanted him to do, but eventually Francis agreed. Together with a few other interested men, Francis Xavier and Ignatius Loyola began the Society of Jesus, also known as the Jesuits.

In Venice, Italy, in 1537, Francis and Ignatius were ordained to the priesthood. The two men went to Rome and worked at building up their new order of priests. In 1540, the king of Portugal invited Francis to join his delegation on a sailing trip to Goa, on the west coast of India. This trip became Francis Xavier's first journey as a missionary for the Society of Jesus.

Father Francis traveled farther into India, and then on to Japan and other lands in the Far East. Throughout his missionary travels, Francis introduced thousands of people to Jesus. It is said that he baptized so many people in one day that he could no longer hold up his arms!

There was nothing Francis wouldn't do to help people live better lives. He washed the wounds of people with skin diseases and taught religion classes to children. He endured extreme heat and extreme cold without complaining in order to work with the poor he met on his travels. Francis even fought off invaders with only his prayers and his crucifix.

It was Francis' dream to preach the Gospel to the people of China. At that time, however, foreigners were not permitted to enter the country. Finally, with the help of the Portuguese government, Francis was given permission to enter China. But he never made it. At the age of forty-six, Francis died of a severe fever on a small island off the coast of China.

Francis Xavier was made a saint in 1602. We celebrate his feast day on December 3. He is the patron Saint of sailors and missioners.

Portrait of St. Francis Xavier **by Ernest Monnin**
Private Collection/Index/Bridgeman Art Library

Send Me, Lord!

Throughout history, God has sent special messengers to lead people to him. In Old Testament times, when the Israelites turned away from God, God sent prophets such as Hosea to lead them back to him. Throughout Church history, many holy people have worked to lead people to God and to Salvation. One of these people was Saint Francis Xavier, who traveled to many parts of the world to bring people the Good News of Salvation.

Activities

1. Who do you know who has done extraordinary work in bringing other people closer to God? Tell what this person has done and which of his or her qualities you would like to develop.

   _____

   _____

2. It's often difficult to tell other people that we don't approve of their moral choices. What do you do when you see a friend doing something sinful, such as cheating or mistreating someone? Do you speak out or do you pretend it doesn't matter? Write a diary entry about a time when you observed a friend doing something sinful and what you did (or should have done) in response.

What kinds of prayer can keep us focused on God?

Prayer Celebration

A Litany Prayer

A litany is a prayer in which we call upon Jesus, God, Mary or other Saints, or holy people and repeat a response. The repetition gives the prayer rhythm and helps us concentrate on the prayer. Praying litanies helps us focus on God. Litanies are popular in several religions. At a Jewish Day of Atonement service, worshipers may pray this litany.

Leader: Our Father, our King, we have sinned before you.

Response: Our Father, our King.

Our Father, our King, grant us a year of happiness.

Our Father, our King.

Our Father, our King, pardon all our sins.

Our Father, our King.

Based on the Jewish "Our Father, Our King" litany

Our Church has many litanies. The Litany of the Most Holy Name of Jesus is one example. As the leader prays each line about Jesus, pray the response with your eyes closed. Focus on the idea that Jesus is in the center of your being. Whenever you are distracted, return to Jesus by focusing on the repetition.

Leader: Jesus, Son of the living God:

All: Have mercy on us.

Jesus, our God: Have mercy on us.

Jesus, king of glory: Have mercy on us.

Jesus, father of the poor: Have mercy on us.

Jesus, our way and our life: Have mercy on us.

Jesus, most powerful: Have mercy on us.

Jesus, king of patriarchs: Have mercy on us.

Jesus, God of peace: Have mercy on us.

Based on the Litany of the Most Holy Name of Jesus

Think about the presence of Jesus around and within you.
Slowly and quietly pray the Lord's Prayer.

A **Complete** the sentences, using words from the box.

1. A _____ is a person sent by God to speak out against behavior that does not follow God's will.

2. A _____ is a prayer in which we call upon Jesus, God, Mary or others Saints or holy people and repeat a response.

3. Because of Adam and Eve's _____, sin and death came into the world.

4. _____ is freedom from the pain of sin.

5. Jesus' _____ to God brought new life into the world.

6. Jesus Christ is our _____, Prophet, and _____.

7. Solomon had many wise sayings, called _____.

8. Hosea told the Israelites that even though they had broken the _____ with God, God still loved them.

9. Because of _____, we are weakened in our ability to resist sin and do good.

King
proverbs
Prophet
disobedience
Covenant
Original Sin
obedience
litany
Priest
Salvation

B **Respond** to the following.

1. What was the Israelites' relationship with God when they were suffering? How did it change when they prospered?

_____

_____

_____

2. What should your own relationship with God be like, regardless of what is happening in your life?

_____

_____

Faith in Action

Poverty Relief Ministries The poverty relief ministries of your parish help people in need learn about diocesan and community resources that can help them. For example, the working poor have low-paying jobs and cannot support their families. Some have no medical benefits. The parish's poverty relief ministry can help such people obtain help from local agencies that can provide food, clothing, shelter, and medical care in emergencies. But poverty relief ministries also help people take responsible steps toward overcoming poverty.

In Everyday Life

Activity Think about a time when someone suggested something for you to do better at, such as getting a better grade or being more forgiving. Describe the advice that you were given, and how it was given to you (with kindness, with anger, and so forth). Then tell how this made you feel and whether you followed through on the advice.

_____

_____

_____

In Your Parish

Activity Discuss with classmates how you would spend $100 from your parish's Poverty Relief Committee to help an individual or family in your parish. Be sure to consider both the needs and the feelings of the people you will help. Fill in your budget on the lines provided.

Amount	Purpose
_____	_____
_____	_____
_____	_____

Total: $100.00

Take Home

FAMILY TIME

Exile and Remembrance

As time went by, the chosen people lost sight of their Covenant and turned away from God. Then they were forced into exile, and they thought that God had abandoned them. They found that God was still there for them, however, when he sent prophets to guide them back to him. God is always there for us, even though we sometimes turn away from him.

ACTIVITY

Exile Your family or ancestors may have left their homeland to come to America. With your family, explore the feelings of sadness, loss, and hope that such a change would bring.

WEEKLY PLANNER

On Sunday

For the Sign of Peace, make an effort to grasp people's hands warmly, look them in the eyes, and smile.

On the Web

www.blestarewe.com

 Visit our Web site for the Saint of the day and the reflection question of the week.

Saint of the Week

 Saint Maximilian Kolbe (1894–1941)

Father Maximilian Kolbe was arrested and sent to Auschwitz when Poland was taken over by the Nazis. When ten prisoners at the camp were to be executed, Father Maximilian offered his life in exchange for that of a man in the group who had a family. The man whose life was spared lived to tell the story.

Feast Day: August 14

A Prayer for the Week

Lord, whatever difficulties our lives bring, help us always be near to you and to follow your guidance. Amen.

Take Home

FAMILY TIME

✠ Scripture Background

In the Early Church

The Call to Repentance When the Pharisees complained that Jesus sat with sinners, he said, "Those who are not sick do not need a physician, but the sick do" (based on Luke 5:31–32). Jesus is the physician who cures souls and who has come to call sinners to repentance. In the early Church, the Sacrament of Penance was viewed as a second baptism. In his first letter to the early Christians, John tells them that if they acknowledge their sins to God, he will forgive them and cleanse them of every wrongdoing. Read all of John's message about confession in 1 John 1:5—2:2.

Our Catholic Tradition in Liturgy

The Language of Prayer
Synagogues are Jewish places of worship. Synagogue prayer and study may have begun while the Israelites were in exile in Babylon. Prayers and traditions in the synagogue and the home came to replace rituals and sacrifices that had been held in the Temple.

Many elements of Christian prayer and worship have their origins in Judaism. Although Latin was the language of the Catholic liturgy for much of the Church's history, a few Hebrew words are part of the Christian liturgy (*amen*, *hosanna*, and *alleluia*). Christian and Jewish services also share many of the same prayers and acclamations.

14 Exile and Remembrance

LET US PRAY

O Lord, [you] willed that your Son should lay down his life to gather into one your scattered children...

Based on the prayer over the gifts,
Mass for Refugees and Exiles, Roman Missal

Share

Activity

The people shown in the photographs are all lost in some way. On the lines under each photograph, explain what the person in the picture might be looking for and what might have caused the person to become lost.

_____

_____

_____

_____

_____

_____

How does God help those who are lost?

Worship Celebration of the Lord's Passion

The chosen people had forgotten their Covenant with God. When the Lord sent prophets to remind them to keep the Commandments, they rejected the prophets. In 722 B.C., Assyria invaded Israel, the northern kingdom. The Assyrians captured some Israelites and took them to Assyria. Forced into **exile**, the Israelites felt lost. But God sent more prophets to guide them. One of these prophets was Second Isaiah, a disciple of the prophet Isaiah.

In church on Good Friday, we gather to remember the Lord's Passion, or suffering, and recall his Death on the Cross. We also *venerate*, or adore, the Cross, often by bowing, kissing it, or genuflecting. The first reading on Good Friday is from Isaiah 53, a prophecy of Second Isaiah. Second Isaiah explains that the suffering and death of a **messiah** will save the Israelites from their sins. His prophecy gave the Israelites hope and was fulfilled by Jesus Christ.

A reading from the Book of the Prophet Isaiah.

We had all gone astray like sheep,
    each following his own way;
But the LORD laid upon him
    the guilt of us all.

Though he was harshly treated, he submitted
    and opened not his mouth;
Like a lamb led to the slaughter
    or a sheep before the shearers,
    he was silent and opened
        not his mouth.
Oppressed and condemned,
    he was taken away,
and who would have
    thought any more of
      his destiny?
A grave was assigned him
    among the wicked
and burial place
    with evildoers,
Though he had done
    no wrong
nor spoken any
    falsehood....

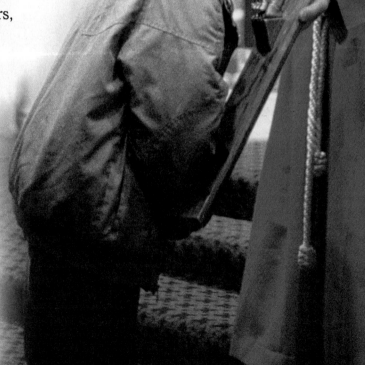

If he gives his life as an offering for sin,
    he shall see his descendants in a long life,
    and the will of the LORD shall be accomplished through him.

Because of his affliction
    he shall see the light in fullness of days;
Through his suffering, my servant shall justify many,
    and their guilt he shall bear.

Isaiah 53:6–11

The word of the Lord.
Thanks be to God.

Saving Grace

The Israelites in exile knew they could not rise above their failures on their own. They needed the Lord's help. Even before Second Isaiah, prophets had told the people that their loving God would send a messiah who would conquer their sins and weaknesses.

The prophets Ezekiel and Micah told the people that their exile would end with the coming of a messiah. Ezekiel told the people that God would look after them as a shepherd looks after his sheep. The Lord had told him, "I will appoint one shepherd over them to pasture them" (Ezekiel 34:23). Micah said, "From you, Bethlehem, shall come forth one who is to be ruler in Israel. He shall shepherd his flock. He shall be peace" (based on Micah 5:1–4). The prophet Jeremiah told God's people: "Behold, the days are coming, says the LORD, when I will raise up a righteous descendant of David. As king he shall reign and govern wisely. He shall do what is just and right in the land. In his days Judah shall be saved" (based on Jeremiah 23:5–6).

Our Church Teaches

Jesus Christ is the Messiah described by the prophets. He was the shepherd God sent to gather the lost sheep of Israel and of all nations. Christ is always there to bring us back from our own "exile"—our separation from God because of sin. During our life on Earth, we are in exile from Heaven. In the Sacraments, especially the celebration of the liturgy, we meet Christ and receive grace to continue our journey to our heavenly home. All the members of the Church—those here on Earth and those already in Heaven—form one Body of Christ. The example of those in Heaven encourages us. We celebrate their memory throughout the liturgical year. We join them in praise and thanksgiving for God's goodness.

> ## We Believe
> God's love for his people is everlasting. Even if we suffer "exile" because of our sins, God is with us and loves us.

> ## Faith Words
> **exile**
> Exile is the forced removal of people from their homeland to another land. The Israelites captured by the Assyrians were living in exile.
>
> **messiah**
> A messiah is a person chosen to save people from a particular fate. The word means "savior." Jesus Christ is our Messiah, chosen by God to free us from sin and death.

How can you show that God is with you?

Respond

Saint Maximilian Kolbe

Raymond Kolbe was born in Poland in 1894. He came from a devout Catholic family. When he was twelve, Mary appeared to him in a dream. She held out two crowns: one white, the other red. The white crown meant that he should keep himself pure, the red one meant that he would be a martyr. In the dream, Raymond accepted both crowns.

Raymond entered a Franciscan seminary at age thirteen. In 1918, he was ordained a priest and took the name Maximilian Mary.

Soon after his ordination, Father Maximilian discovered he had tuberculosis, a disease of the lungs. In spite of his poor health, Maximilian worked hard to promote devotion to the Blessed Mother. He began to publish *Knight of the Immaculata*, a monthly magazine dedicated to Mary, and started a Franciscan friary dedicated to her.

When the Nazis invaded Poland in 1939, they killed many people and drove others out of their homes. The Nazis were taking "undesirables"—Jews, Roma (gypsies), and Catholic priests and nuns, among others—to concentration camps. Maximilian's community became a haven for refugees. As many as 1,500 refugees were housed there at a time, cared for by the Franciscan friars. Father Maximilian wondered how long it would be before the Nazis came for him and his brothers.

In May 1941, Father Maximilian and four other priests at the friary were sent to Auschwitz. At Auschwitz, Maximilian secretly heard confessions and offered Communion from his daily ration of bread. Later in 1941, some prisoners tried to escape from Auschwitz. In order to discourage others from doing the same thing, the guards decided to kill ten men. One of the ten men cried in despair. He would never see his family again. Father Maximilian stepped forward and said, "I am a Catholic priest from Poland. I would like to take his place because he has a wife and children."

Witnesses say Father Maximilian prayed, sang hymns, and recited the Rosary while waiting to die by starvation. After two weeks, when the guards saw that he was still alive and encouraging others, they killed him by lethal injection.

We celebrate the feast of Saint Maximilian Kolbe on August 14, the date of his martyrdom.

Activities

1. While waiting to die by starvation, Maximilian Kolbe said prayers, sang hymns, and recited the Rosary. How might his actions have provided encouragement to the other prisoners?

   _____

   _____

   _____

   _____

   _____

   _____

2. Saint Maximilian Kolbe gave up his own life to save another person from death. Describe at least three everyday sacrifices you can make for others.

   _____

   _____

   _____

   _____

   _____

3. His faith in Mary was a source of inspiration and strength for Maximilian. In the space provided, write a short prayer to the Blessed Mother, asking her to help you grow spiritually.

   _____

   _____

   _____

   _____

How can our prayer express our trust in God?

Prayer Celebration

Praying in Jesus' Words

According to the Scriptures, as Jesus died, he called out to God in the words of Psalm 22. We pray these words in the Good Friday liturgy.

Leader: Jesus took all our sins upon himself and asked forgiveness for our offenses, placing his trust in God. According to the Scriptures, as Jesus died, he called out to God in the words of Psalm 22. We pray these words in the Good Friday liturgy.

Reader 1: My God, my God, why have you forsaken me,
far from my prayer, from the words of my cry?
O my God, I cry out by day, and you answer not;
by night, and there is no relief for me.
Yet you are enthroned in the holy place,
O glory of Israel!

Reader 2: In you our fathers trusted;
they trusted, and you delivered them.
To you they cried, and they escaped;
in you they trusted,
and they were not
put to shame.
All the ends of the earth
shall remember and
turn to the LORD;
All the families of the nations
shall bow down before him.

Reader 3: For dominion is the LORD's,
and he rules the nations.
Let the coming generation be told
of the LORD that they may
proclaim to a people yet
to be born the justice he
has shown.

Psalm 22:2–6, 28–29, 31–32

14 Chapter Review

A Write the name of the person described by each clue.

1. I am the prophet who told the people that God would look after them as a shepherd looks after his sheep. _____

2. I am the prophet who told the people that the ruler of Israel would come forth from Bethlehem. _____

3. I am the prophet who compared his people to sheep who had gone astray. _____

4. I am the prophet who said that the Lord would raise up a descendant of David who would reign as king and do what is right and just. _____

5. I am the Messiah described by the prophets. _____

B Complete the sentences, using words from the box.

1. According to the Scriptures, as Jesus died he called out to God in the words of _____.

2. Christ is the _____, chosen by God to free us from _____.

3. In church on Good Friday, we remember Jesus' _____, or suffering, and remember his Death on the Cross.

4. Many _____ foretold of the coming of a messiah.

sin
Messiah
Psalm 22
Passion
prophets

C Define the following.

Exile: _____

_____

Messiah: _____

_____

Faith in Action

Lectors A trained lector prayerfully prepares to proclaim God's Word at Mass. The Holy Spirit who inspired the writing of Scripture also inspires, or breathes life into, its proclamation. When we prayerfully prepare to hear the Word, we open ourselves to the blessing of growing closer to God. Even when we have heard a Scripture story over and over again, hearing someone new read it can be like hearing it for the very first time. Through his Word, and the ministry of lectors, God speaks to us and reveals himself and his love for us.

In Everyday Life

Activity Put a check mark next to each item that presents a good way for others to know more about you. Then circle the three items that would most accurately reveal your personality to others.

_____ my group of friends

_____ my musical talents

_____ music I listen to

_____ where I like to hang out

_____ the books I read

_____ sports I participate in

_____ Web sites I visit

_____ my neighborhood

_____ my favorite movies

_____ the clothes I wear

In Your Parish

Activity Look up the First Reading from last Sunday's liturgy in your Bible and read the passage. Write the reference to the verses in the space provided. Write in your own words what you think God was trying to say to you in that reading.

Reference: _____

What God is saying to me: _____

_____

_____

Take Home

FAMILY TIME

Hope and Faithfulness

When the people of Judah lived in exile, the prophet Ezekiel helped them realize that, even though they might temporarily turn away from God, God would always be ready to welcome them back. We have this same relationship with God and are called to share it with others.

ACTIVITY

For the Greater Good Look for a neighborhood or community volunteer opportunity in which your family can participate. Check your local newspaper or contact local organizations.

Food Drive

WEEKLY PLANNER

On Sunday
Listen for messages of faith and hope during the readings and the homily.

On the Web
www.blestarewe.com

Visit our Web site for the Saint of the day and the reflection question of the week.

Saint of the Week
Andrew of Phu Yen
(1625–1644)

As a young Catholic Vietnamese, Andrew became a catechist and vowed to serve the Church. He was arrested and advised to renounce his faith, but he refused. At the hour of his execution, Andrew continued to encourage the Christians present to remain firm in their faith. Vietnamese Catholics have a special devotion to Blessed Andrew.
Feast Day: July 27

A Prayer for the Week

Help us appreciate your gift of faith, Lord. Keep us strong in our faith, and let there always be hope in our lives. Amen.

Take Home

FAMILY TIME

✝ Scripture Background

Before the Time of Jesus

Ezekiel's Teachings of Salvation The prophet Ezekiel had a strong influence on the exiled community of Jews. Under his guidance, the Jews came to believe that God was with them wherever they were exiled. Ezekiel told the people that they were like a flock of sheep that had gotten lost, and that God was like a shepherd who would lead them back to safety (Ezekiel 34:11–16). Just as Ezekiel tells the Israelites that God will care for them like a shepherd for his sheep, Jesus reminds us that he is the Good Shepherd who will lay down his life for his sheep (John 10:11–18).

Our Catholic Tradition in Literature

T. S. Eliot T. S. Eliot, who converted to Anglo-Catholicism in 1927, was one of the most renowned literary figures of the twentieth century. Born in the United States in 1888, Eliot gained fame while living in England. He was a prolific writer of poetry, essays, and plays. Eliot's devotion to religion had a profound impact on his work. In his famous poem "The Waste Land," Eliot used the imagery of the dry bones from Ezekiel 37:1–14, which is discussed in this chapter. His well-known play *Murder in the Cathedral* is about the death of Saint Thomas Becket in the twelfth century. Eliot received the Nobel Prize for Literature in 1948. He died in London in 1965.

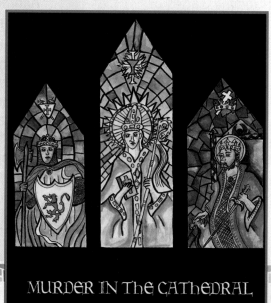

MURDER IN THE CATHEDRAL

A Drama By T.S. Eliot

15 Hope and Faithfulness

LET US PRAY

Do not ask me to leave you!
For wherever you go, I will go.

Based on Ruth 1:16

Share

Do you have friends, cousins, grandparents, or other relatives who live far away? When you are not able to see them very often, you probably begin to miss them and look forward to a visit with them.

Activity

Try to remember the last time you saw a friend or a relative whom you missed very much. Then complete the story by writing in the information and circling the bold words that describe that experience.

I remember the last time I saw my **friend cousin grandmother**

grandfather aunt uncle other: _____, whose

name is _____.

When we first saw each other, we _____

_____.

It was a very happy time. _____ is special to me

because _____

_____.

I missed _____ because **he she**

has always shown love for me by _____

_____.

It has been _____ **months years** since the last time I saw

_____.

I am looking forward to the next visit with lots of hope!

How did God give hope to the Jews in exile?

✝ Scripture Vision of the Dry Bones

The Babylonians conquered Judah, the southern kingdom, and exiled its citizens around 587 B.C. The Babylonians destroyed the Temple. Without their Temple in Jerusalem, the Jews in exile had to find other ways to feel God's presence. Prophets helped them learn that God did not just exist in Jerusalem and in the Temple. God was with them wherever they went. The prophet Ezekiel taught the exiles how to have faith again by telling them of a vision he had.

The hand of the LORD came upon me, and he set me in the center of the plain, which was now filled with bones. Then he said to me, "Prophesy over these bones and say to them, 'Dry bones, hear the word of the LORD! Thus says the Lord GOD: I will bring spirit into you so that you may come to life. I will put sinews upon you, make flesh grow over you, cover you with skin, and put spirit in you so that you may come to life and know that I am the LORD.'" I prophesied as I had been told, and I heard a noise. It was a rattling as the bones came together, bone joining bone. I saw the sinews and the flesh come upon them and the skin cover them, but there was no spirit in them. Then the LORD said to me, "Prophesy to the spirit and say, 'Thus says the Lord GOD: Come, O spirit, and breathe into these so that they may come to life.'" I prophesied as he told me, and the spirit came into them; they came alive and stood upright, a vast army. Then he said, "These bones are the whole house of Israel. They have been saying, 'Our bones are dried up, our hope is lost, and we are cut off.' Therefore, prophesy and say to them, 'Thus says the Lord GOD: I will put my spirit in you so that you may live, and I will bring you back to the land of Israel. I have promised, and I will do it, says the LORD.'"

Based on Ezekiel 37:1, 4–12, 14

Together Again

Ezekiel's vision of the dry bones gave people hope that God would bring them back to their kingdom. The plain scattered with bones represents the Jews scattered across foreign lands during the Exile. The coming together of the bones represents the coming together of God's people after the Exile. Ezekiel said that God told him to prophesy over the bones so that God's spirit would bring life to them. Then the bones became live people, united as an army. This represents God's bringing the exiles home to Israel. Ezekiel's vision came true.

In 539 B.C. Cyrus, leader of the Persians, conquered the Babylonians. He said that the exiles could return home. The Jews who returned had high hopes. They rebuilt the Temple. They also prayed and studied God's Word in synagogues, smaller places of worship. Jerusalem again became the center of worship and government. New prophets led the people in worshiping God. People honored God's Covenant with feasts and celebrations.

The Sabbath was an important occasion for the people then, as it is for us and for Jewish people today. On our Sabbath—Sunday—we recall and celebrate Jesus' Resurrection. For Jews the Sabbath is a memorial of Israel's freedom from Egypt. The Sabbath also recalls the seventh day in the Bible story of Creation, when God rested. During the Exodus, God commanded the Israelites to always keep holy the Sabbath. Honoring the Sabbath is a way of honoring God's Covenant with his chosen people.

Our Church Teaches

We obey God's Commandment to keep holy the Sabbath by attending Mass each Sunday. We must also attend Mass on holy days, confess our sins in Reconciliation at least once a year, receive the Eucharist at least during the Easter season, observe the Church's days of fast and abstinence, and contribute to the Church to provide for its material needs. These are the **precepts of the Church**. They are our obligations as Catholics. Above all, we are required to do good and avoid evil, showing respect for the value of human life.

By living according to the teachings of our Catholic faith, we can hope for everlasting happiness that God promises us. Hope is our trust in God to help us achieve everlasting life. Hope is one of the **Theological Virtues**, three spiritual qualities that come from God and help us become more holy. The other two virtues are faith and charity. Through faith, we believe in God, in everything God has revealed, and in all that the Church teaches us to believe. Faith is necessary for Salvation. Charity is the love we show for others and for God. **Moral Virtues** help us avoid sin, which separates us from God. Temperance is a Moral Virtue. It means not doing too much of any one thing, such as eating too much, driving too fast, or abusing alcohol. Temperance helps prevent danger or sin. For example, speeding and drunk driving can kill or hurt people, and endangerment of human life is a serious sin.

GO TO page 271 to learn more about the virtues.

We Believe

Sin separates us from God and makes us people in exile. We come closer to God by making good moral decisions and following the teachings of our faith.

Faith Words

precepts of the Church
The precepts of the Church are the Church's teachings about our obligations.

Theological Virtues
The Theological Virtues—faith, hope, and charity—come from God and help us become more holy. They connect us with the Trinity.

Moral Virtues
The Moral Virtues are four spiritual qualities—temperance, prudence, justice, and fortitude—that help us avoid sin.

How can you be an example of faith, hope, and charity?

Respond

Faith and Charity

The Book of Ruth in the Old Testament tells this special story about faith and charity.

A Jewish woman named Naomi moved from Bethlehem, in Judah, to Moab with her husband and two sons. But soon after leaving Bethlehem, Naomi's husband died. Naomi's sons married Moabite women, Orpah and Ruth.

For ten years the widow and her family lived peacefully. Then suddenly, both of Naomi's sons died. Now she was in a foreign land without her husband or her sons. And her native people, the Jews, were far away. Naomi decided it was time to return to Bethlehem. Both of her daughters-in-law decided to go with her.

On the road to Bethlehem, Naomi said to Orpah and Ruth, "Go back to your mothers' houses! May the Lord grant each of you a husband and a home in which you will find rest."

Orpah kissed her mother-in-law goodbye and returned to her homeland. But Ruth said, "Do not ask me to leave you! For wherever you go, I will go. Your people shall be my people. Your God shall be my God."

Naomi and Ruth continued their journey and arrived in Bethlehem during the harvest. They were desperately poor and needed food to eat. Ruth went into someone's fields and picked up grain left behind by the harvesters. For many hours she gathered food for Naomi and herself.

Then the owner of the fields, Boaz, approached Ruth. "I have heard what you have done for your mother-in-law," he said. "You have left the land of your birth and have come to a foreign land. May the Lord reward you for what you have done!" Over time, Boaz came to love Ruth. He knew that she was a good woman who lived a life of faith and charity. Boaz and Ruth married. They became the great-grandparents of David, the king.

Based on the Book of Ruth

Activities

1. Complete each sentence with a Theological Virtue.

   Ruth's decisions to stay with Naomi and to gather food for her are examples

   of _____

   When Ruth said, "Your God will be my God,"

   she showed that she had _____ in Naomi's beliefs.

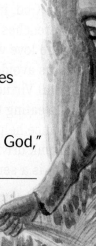

2. Ruth put Naomi's needs above her own. Think about ways you can follow Ruth's example of charity. Complete the diagram below.

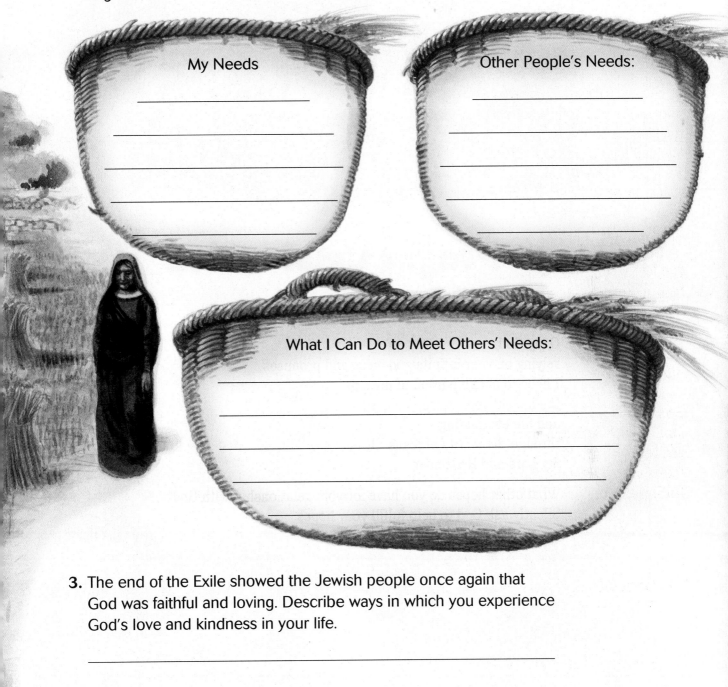

My Needs

_____

_____

_____

_____

Other People's Needs:

_____

_____

_____

_____

What I Can Do to Meet Others' Needs:

_____

_____

_____

_____

_____

3. The end of the Exile showed the Jewish people once again that God was faithful and loving. Describe ways in which you experience God's love and kindness in your life.

_____

_____

_____

_____

_____

What are you hopeful about?

✝ Prayer Celebration

An Act of Hope

O my God,
relying on your infinite goodness and promises,
I hope to obtain pardon of my sins,
the help of your grace,
and life everlasting,
through the merits of Jesus Christ,
my Lord and Redeemer.

What other hopes do you have for your relationship with God?
Silently ask God to help fulfill your hopes.

Chapter Review

A Match Column A with Column B by writing the correct number in the space provided.

A	B
1. Ruth	_____ faith, hope, and charity, which come from God and help us become more holy
2. Book of Ruth	_____ helps us believe in God and what he has revealed, and in the Church's teachings
3. faith	_____ conquered Judah, sent its citizens into exile, and destroyed the Temple
4. Ezekiel	_____ the Church's teachings about our obligations
5. precepts of the Church	_____ had the vision of the dry bones, which gave the exiles hope that God would bring them together again
6. Moral Virtues	_____ remained faithful to her mother-in-law; married Boaz
7. Theological Virtues	_____ tells a special story about faith and charity
8. Sabbath	_____ temperance, prudence, justice, and fortitude, which help us avoid sin
9. Babylonians	_____ the day that recalls the seventh day in the story of creation, when God rested

B Respond to the following.

1. How is being apart from God because of sin like the Israelites' exile from their homeland?

_____

_____

2. Ruth showed charity toward Naomi. In what ways can a young person show charity for family members?

_____

_____

Faith in Action

Apologetics Ministry   Because Catholics and other people often do not fully understand the Catholic faith or the Church's teachings, members of a parish's apologetics ministry study the faith so that they can explain it to others. They strive to lead people of other religions, or even people who may not believe in God at all, to a fuller understanding of the Church's teachings. By defending and sharing the truth of the Church's teachings with others, members of a parish's apologetics ministry serve the parish community and the Church.

In Everyday Life

Activity   Being part of a team or a family means sharing a similar goal and working together to meet that goal. Describe one or two goals of a group that you participate in, who reminds you about those goals and helps keep you focused on the goals, and how you and other participants work together to achieve them.

Goal 1: _____

_____

Goal 2: _____

_____

Motivator: _____

_____

How our team or group works together: _____

_____

In Your Parish

Activity   Describe a person or a group that has had an important influence on your goal to live as a good Catholic.

_____

_____

Take Home

FAMILY TIME

Trust and Prayer

God invites us into a relationship of trust and caring. We sustain that relationship through faith and prayer. The Old Testament story of Esther shows us that we can overcome even extraordinary challenges if we put our faith in God and pray for the strength to carry out his plan for us.

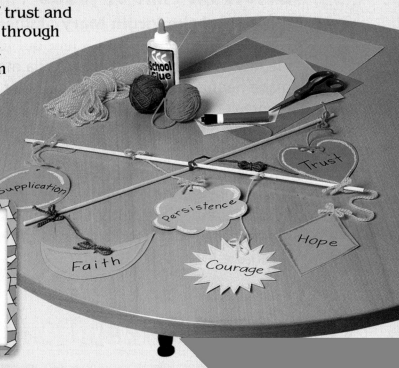

ACTIVITY

What's in a Word? Together, make a mobile that displays some words that exemplify the main ideas of this chapter, such as *faith*, *prayer*, and *trust*. Display the mobile in a prominent place in your home.

WEEKLY PLANNER

On Sunday

As the Universal Prayer (Prayer of the Faithful) is said, pray that you will be a courageous and trustworthy friend.

On the Web

www.blestarewe.com

Visit our Web site for the Saint of the day and the reflection question of the week.

Saint of the Week

Saint Monica
(333–387)

For seventeen years, Saint Monica prayed for her son's conversion to the Christian faith. Her persistence was rewarded. Augustine, later to be known as Saint Augustine, was baptized in 387. Saint Monica died later that same year.

Patron Saint of: wives and mothers
Feast Day: August 27

A Prayer for the Week

Even when we grow weary, Lord, give us the faith to trust in your goodness and compassion and to persist in our prayers. Amen.

Take Home

FAMILY TIME

✚ Scripture Background

Before the Time of Jesus

Esther and the Virgin Mary   Esther's name comes from the Persian word for "star." Esther was a Jew, but for a time she hid her Jewish identity. When King Xerxes of Persia met Esther, he made her his queen. In this role, Esther was able to intercede with the king to save the Jews from death according to a plot devised by the king's adviser, Haman. For Catholics, Esther is a model of virtue and courage. She is even seen as prefiguring the Virgin Mary in her beauty, chastity, and especially in her ability to intercede for others. Read how Esther saved the Jews in the Book of Esther 2—8.

Our Catholic Tradition in World History

Pope Pius XII   During World War II, the Nazis, under the leadership of Adolph Hitler, killed more than 12 million people, including 6 million Jews. In Vatican City in Italy, Pope Pius XII did everything he could to resist and defeat Hitler. He worked to save the Jewish people, concealing many Jews in the Vatican and at Castelgondolfo, the papal summer home. He told bishops, priests, and nuns to help the Jewish people whenever they could and asked that convents and monasteries be opened to Jews. He gave Jewish people Vatican citizenship and helped them escape Europe.

At Pope Pius XII's death in 1958, Golda Meir, Israel's foreign minister, said, "When fearful martyrdom came to our people in the decade of Nazi terror, the voice of the pope was raised for its victims.... We mourn a great servant of peace."

16 Trust and Prayer

O wonder of your humble care for us!

Easter Proclamation (Exsultet), Roman Missal

Share

Think about the people who take care of you, such as your parents or grandparents. Although you may not stop to think about it, every day these people take care of your needs and wants in several ways. What kinds of things do they provide for you daily?

Activity

Needs are things that you require to live a healthy life. Wants are things that make your life more pleasurable. Complete the chart by writing in the needs and wants that people meet for you during each part of the day.

	Needs	Wants
Morning		
Afternoon		
Evening		

How does God take care of us?

Hear & Believe

 **✝ Scripture** A Prayer for Her People

Esther was a beautiful young Jewish woman who lived about 500 years before the birth of Christ. She was adopted by a relative, Mordecai, after her parents died. Mordecai, a Jew, lived in exile in Persia (present-day Iran), where he was appointed to the royal court after saving the king's life.

Soon after Esther went to live with Mordecai, the king decreed that all the young women in his empire move to the royal palace. He planned to choose one of them to be the new queen. Esther then moved to the palace. When the king met Esther, he was struck by her kindness and her great beauty. He made her the queen.

At this time, a man named Haman was the highest official in the royal court. Haman was greedy for fame and power. All the king's servants had to bow down in his presence. Mordecai refused. As a Jew, he would not honor a man in the way he would honor the Lord. Haman was angry about this. He vowed to destroy all the Jews in Persia. He wrote a royal order stating, "All Jews, young and old, including women and children, should be killed in one day."

When Mordecai learned of Haman's plan, he requested that Queen Esther ask the king to save the Jews from death. To plead for the lives of her people, Esther would have to tell the king that she was a Jew. Knowing that this could lead to death, Esther prayed to the Lord for guidance and courage.

"My LORD, our King, you alone are God. Help me, who am alone and have no help but you, for I am taking my life in my hand. Give me courage, King of all. Put in my mouth persuasive words in the presence of the lion and turn his heart to hatred for our enemy. Save us by your power, O LORD."

Then Queen Esther went to the king and enjoyed a great banquet with him. While dining, Esther told the king that she was a Jew. She told him of Haman's plan. She said, "If I have found favor with you, O king, I ask that my life be spared and I beg that you spare the lives of my people. My people and I have been delivered to destruction, slaughter, and extinction."

The king was enraged about Haman's plan. He ordered that Haman be punished and appointed Mordecai to fill Haman's position in court.

Based on Esther A; 2—8

Faith and Prayer

Esther had great faith in the goodness and power of God. In her time of need, she prayed a prayer of **supplication** to the Lord. She humbly and earnestly asked God for help. She asked God to give her the courage to face the king and the wisdom to convince the king to spare her people. Esther prayed with **persistence**. Her prayer arose from her faith that God could really answer her. She trusted that God would meet the needs of his people. Esther's petition, or solemn prayer of request, was granted.

Our Church Teaches

When we pray, we raise our minds and hearts to God and request good things from him. Just as the people who take care of our needs every day, God meets our needs. Our prayers may require persistence. God answers our prayers if we have faith in his power and goodness.

Prayer arises from faith. We pray because we believe that God really hears us. To grow in our relationship with God, we must pray frequently and with patience.

How should we pray if we are in need?

Respond

The Parable of the Persistent Widow

Jesus told a parable about the necessity of praying without becoming weary. He said, "There was a judge in a certain town who neither feared God nor respected any human being. And a widow in that town used to come to him and say, 'Grant a just decision for me against my opponent.' For a long time the judge was unwilling, but eventually he thought, 'While it is true that I neither fear God nor respect any human being, because this widow keeps bothering me I shall make a just decision for her.'" The Lord said, "Pay attention to what the dishonest judge says. Will not God then help his chosen ones who call out to him day and night? Will he be slow to answer them? I tell you, he will see to it that justice is done for them speedily."

Based on Luke 18:1–8

Activities

1. Think about the parable. Imagine you are the widow. Think about how you feel when the judge denies your request. Then think about how you feel when your request is finally granted. Reflect on the message Jesus wants to send you through this story.

What is that message? _____

_____

Name needs that you or other people have. _____

_____

Write a short prayer asking God to fulfill those needs. _____

_____

Quietly and reflectively address your prayer to God.

"That Would Have Been Enough!"

A Jewish custom is to praise God before asking him for something. The *Dayenu* is a Hebrew song that praises God. *Dayenu* means "That would have been enough!" The song celebrates how God delivered the Israelites every time they needed help and then went even further than just meeting each need. It is sung during Passover. Here is a version you can pray.

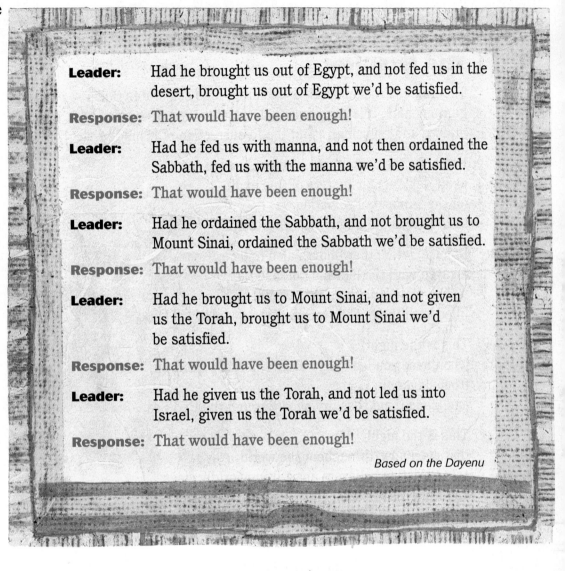

Leader: Had he brought us out of Egypt, and not fed us in the desert, brought us out of Egypt we'd be satisfied.

Response: That would have been enough!

Leader: Had he fed us with manna, and not then ordained the Sabbath, fed us with the manna we'd be satisfied.

Response: That would have been enough!

Leader: Had he ordained the Sabbath, and not brought us to Mount Sinai, ordained the Sabbath we'd be satisfied.

Response: That would have been enough!

Leader: Had he brought us to Mount Sinai, and not given us the Torah, brought us to Mount Sinai we'd be satisfied.

Response: That would have been enough!

Leader: Had he given us the Torah, and not led us into Israel, given us the Torah we'd be satisfied.

Response: That would have been enough!

Based on the Dayenu

2. Think about the ways that God has shown his presence in your group this year. Write some verses for your own group Dayenu.

_____

_____

_____

_____

How is Jesus' Resurrection an answer to our prayers?

 **Prayer Celebration**

The Exsultet

The Easter Proclamation, or Exsultet, also celebrates God's glorious acts. It is sung during the Easter Vigil. It is filled with praises and rejoicings about the Resurrection of Jesus Christ.

Exult, let them exult, the hosts of heaven,
exult, let Angel ministers of God exult,
let the trumpet of salvation
sound aloud our mighty King's triumph!

Rejoice, let Mother Church also rejoice,
arrayed with the lightning of his glory,
let this holy building shake with joy,
filled with the mighty voices of the peoples.

This is the night,
when once you led our forebears, Israel's children,
from slavery in Egypt
and made them pass dry-shod through the Red Sea.

This is the night
that even now, throughout the world,
sets Christian believers apart from worldly vices
and from the gloom of sin,
leading them to grace
and joining them to his holy ones.

O wonder of your humble care for us!
O love, O charity beyond all telling,
to ransom a slave you gave away your Son!

O happy fault,
that earned so great, so glorious a Redeemer!

Exsultet from the Easter Vigil, Roman Missal

A **Complete** the sentences with words from the box.

parable	Dayenu	virtues
supplication	persistence	liturgy
Exsultet	Esther	faith

1. The _____, or Easter Proclamation, is prayed during the Easter Vigil.

2. _____ is humbly and earnestly praying to God.

3. Prayer requires _____ and _____, the act of continually pursuing something in spite of obstacles.

4. Jesus' story of the persistent widow is called a _____.

5. _____ married the king of Persia and convinced him to spare her people.

6. The _____ is a Hebrew song that praises God and means "That would have been enough."

7. The sources of prayer are the Word of God, the _____, and the _____ of faith, hope, and charity.

B **Respond** to the following.

1. Explain Jesus' message about prayer in the story of the persistent widow.

_____

_____

2. How might someone your age apply this message in his or her prayers?

_____

_____

_____

Respect Life Ministries   Helping people to understand and appreciate the Church's teachings about the sanctity, or holiness, of all human life is the most important goal of Respect Life or Pro-Life committees in Catholic parishes. Being "pro-life" means not only protecting the rights of the unborn but also of the elderly, the handicapped, and even people on death row. Through prayer, education, and fundraising, pro-life ministries support activities that demonstrate respect and love for all life as a precious and valuable gift from God—a gift that only God has the right to take away.

In Everyday Life

Activity   For each decision, write an **F** to indicate that it is a decision made out of fear or a **C** to indicate that it is a decision made with courage. Then write about the most courageous decision you've ever known somebody to make.

_____ **Apologize to someone I know I have hurt**

_____ **Audition for the school talent show**

_____ **Visit my grandmother at the hospital**

_____ **Lie to my parents about a test grade**

_____ **Refuse to help a friend cheat on a test**

A most courageous decision: _____

In Your Parish

Activity   List two or three concerns that a young unmarried pregnant woman might have about having a baby. Then tell how your parish might help the woman resolve these concerns. Be sure to identify specific help the parish can provide along with spiritual guidance.

Concerns: _____

_____

How the parish can help: _____

_____

_____

God Promises Us Everlasting Life

John called people to a baptism of repentance. Through our Baptism, we are called to turn our attention always toward the Kingdom of God and to be its witnesses by the way we live.

I am baptizing you with water, for repentance, but the one who is coming after me is mightier than I. He will baptize you with the holy Spirit.

Matthew 3:11, 12

John baptized Jesus in the Jordan River. Early Christians first drew pictures of baptismal scenes in the catacombs of ancient Rome.

Creator of the Stars of Night

Words: Latin, 9th c.
Arranged by Carol Browning

CONDITOR ALME SIDERUM, Chant Mode IV

1. Cre - a - tor of the stars of night,_____
2. In sor - row that the an - cient curse_____
3. When this old world drew on toward night,_____
4. At your great Name, O Je - sus, now_____
5. Come in your ho - ly might, we pray,_____
6. To God Cre - a - tor, God the Son,_____

your peo - ple's ev - er - last - ing light,_____
should doom to death a u - ni - verse,_____
you came; but not in splen - dor bright,_____
all knees must bend, all hearts must bow:_____
re - deem us for e - ter - nal day;_____
and God the Spir - it, Three in One,_____

O Christ, Re - deem - er of us all,_____
you came, O Sav - ior, to set free_____
not as a mon - arch, but the child_____
all things on earth with one ac - cord,_____
de - fend us while we dwell be - low_____
praise, hon - or, might, and glo - ry be_____

we pray you hear us when we call.
your own in glo - rious lib - er - ty.
of Mar - y, blame - less moth - er mild.
like those in heav'n, shall call you Lord.
from all as - saults of our dread foe.
from age to age e - ter - nal - ly.

Take Home

FAMILY TIME

A New Life and a Coming Messiah

Some years after their return from exile, the Jewish people were ruled by nations that tried to prevent them from practicing their faith. The Temple was filled with statues of pagan gods. A group of Jewish warriors led a revolt and reclaimed the Temple. Out of the struggles of God's people grew the hope that God would send a messiah and reward his faithful ones with peace after death.

ACTIVITY

Family Time Capsule The Jewish people drew strength from recalling past experiences of God. Collect items that remind your family of happy times. Store the items in a decorated box. Set a date to open the box.

WEEKLY PLANNER

On Sunday

Light a candle for someone in your family who is struggling, ill, or deceased. Ask God to give that person happiness and peace.

On the Web

www.blestarewe.com

Visit our Web site for the Saint of the day and the reflection question of the week.

Saint of the Week

Saint Lucy
(285–304)

Saint Lucy is honored as a young martyr from the early Church. She was denounced for her faith, and the governor ordered her killed. After torture that included being blinded, she was executed. Legend says her eyesight was restored before her death.

Patron Saint of: people with eye diseases
Saint Feast Day: December 13

A Prayer for the Week

Lord, to believe in you is to believe that even when we walk in darkness, a great light awaits us. Help us to remain firm in our faith. Amen.

Take Home

FAMILY TIME

✛ Scripture Background

Before the Time of Jesus

Reclaiming the Temple   When Antiochus became ruler of the Syrian Empire in 175 B.C., the empire included Palestine. Antiochus wanted to promote Greek culture and suppress Judaism. In 167 B.C., when Antiochus offered a sacrifice to the god Zeus in the Temple, a priest named Mattathias killed the emperor's representative. Mattathias and his sons fled to the hills and gathered an army. By 164 B.C., the Jews again controlled most of Jerusalem, and they cleansed and restored the Temple. The Jewish feast of Hannukah commemorates this event. Read about the purification of the Temple in 1 Maccabees 4:36–56.

OUR CATHOLIC TRADITION in Sacramentals

Lighting Candles   Many Catholic churches feature rows of votive candles in front of statues or sacred images of Jesus and the Saints. A churchgoer can light a candle and pray for a special intention. The burning candle suggests a continual rising of the intention toward Jesus or the Saint who has been asked to intercede.

Burning candles have a long history of religious symbolism. Candles or oil lamps burned outside Saints' tombs in the third century. In the Middle Ages people sometimes lit candles as tall as themselves before they prayed, to signify their coming into the light of faith. Lighting candles in a menorah is also an important part of the Jewish feast of Hanukkah.

+ ST JUDE THADDEUS +
SAINT OF THE IMPOSSIBLE

17 A New Life and a Coming Messiah

The King of the world will raise us up to live again forever.

2 Maccabees 7:9

Share

Can you recall a time when you were very happy? What caused you to be happy—people you were with? a fun activity? a gift you received? No matter what makes us happy, if we had to choose between being happy and being sad, we all know what we would choose.

Now imagine what it would be like to enjoy happiness forever! Jesus promised us everlasting happiness and taught us how to achieve it.

Activity

Circle the things that make you happy, and draw a line through the things that are not important for your happiness.

_____ Winning a game

_____ Giving presents

_____ Having a lot of possessions

_____ Volunteering to help people

_____ Having name-brand clothes

_____ Making fun of people

_____ Being a good friend

_____ Getting away with breaking a rule

_____ Following Jesus

_____ Loving my family

_____ Respecting my parents

_____ Earning good grades in school

_____ People thinking I'm attractive

Now see how close you are to Jesus' idea of happiness. Write the letter *J* on the line next to the things that seem close to Jesus' way to happiness.

How many of your ideas of happiness seem to be the same as those of Jesus?

What would make the Jews of the Old Testament happy?

✝ Scripture The Struggles Under Greek Rule

The period before Christ's birth was difficult for the Jewish people. The Persian rule of Israel ended in 332 B.C., and the Jews came under the control of other foreign rulers, such as the Greeks. The Greeks did not worship the God of Israel. People who worshiped other gods were called pagans or Gentiles.

There sprang a sinful offshoot, Antiochus Epiphanes, son of King Antiochus, once a hostage at Rome. He became king in the year one hundred and thirty-seven of the kingdom of the Greeks.

In those days there appeared in Israel men who were breakers of the law, and they seduced many people, saying: "Let us go and make an alliance with the Gentiles all around us; since we separated from them, many evils have come upon us." The proposal was agreeable; some from among the people promptly went to the king, and he authorized them to introduce the way of living of the Gentiles. Thereupon they built a gymnasium in Jerusalem according to the Gentile custom. They … abandoned the holy covenant; they allied themselves with the Gentiles and sold themselves to wrongdoing.

Then the king wrote to his whole kingdom that all should be one people, each abandoning his particular customs. All the Gentiles conformed to the command of the king, and many Israelites were in favor of his religion; they sacrificed to idols and profaned the sabbath.

In the year one hundred and forty-five, the king erected the horrible abomination upon the altar of holocausts, and in the surrounding cities of Judah they built pagan altars. Whoever was found with a scroll of the covenant, and whoever observed the law, was condemned to death by royal decree.

1 Maccabees 1:10–15, 41–43, 54, 57

A group of devout Jews known as the Maccabees conquered the armies of the king. They took back the Temple, removed the pagan objects, and built a new altar. The Temple was rededicated, and according to tradition a one-day supply of lamp oil for the Temple lasted eight days. The eight-day Jewish feast of Hanukkah celebrates these events.

Everlasting Joy

The belief in **resurrection** is gradually revealed in the Old Testament. The Maccabees believed that God's faithful people would have a rewarding life after death. The Maccabees prayed for the souls of fellow soldiers who were killed.

Catholics, too, pray for the souls of the deceased. We believe we will be resurrected because of Christ's Resurrection. We believe that people who die in God's grace experience everlasting happiness, or **Heaven**. Those who die in God's friendship but in need of purification from venial sins and the temporal punishment due to sin experience **Purgatory**, so as to achieve the holiness necessary to enter Heaven. Praying for the souls in Purgatory helps speed their entry into Heaven. People who die in a state of mortal sin risk eternal separation from God, or **hell**. A mortal sin is a serious act against God's Law done purposely. It separates us from God's grace and normally requires the Sacrament of Penance and Reconciliation to be forgiven.

The community of people in the Church, in Purgatory, and in Heaven is the Communion of Saints.

GO TO page 264 to learn more about the Communion of Saints and everlasting life.

Our Church Teaches

The Jews believed that God would send a messiah to bring peace, justice, mercy, and salvation to all. Jesus Christ is that Messiah. God's promises to people in the Old Testament were completely fulfilled with Jesus Christ. Jesus is both true God and true man, united in one divine person.

Believing in Jesus Christ and in the God who sent him is necessary for Salvation from sin. Jesus said, "No one comes to the Father except through me" (John 14:6). God desires us to come to him through Christ so that we can become more God-like. The Holy Spirit makes this possible. The grace of the Holy Spirit and our desire to be with God cause us to believe in Jesus and say, "You are the Christ, the Son of the living God."

The Holy Spirit inspired the Old Testament writers and is revealed in their writings, including the Creation story, the Exile, and stories about the poor. It is also in the Scriptures that God revealed himself as Father, Son, and Holy Spirit, or the Trinity.

GO TO page 262 to learn more about the Trinity.

We Believe

Jesus Christ is the Son of God and the Savior, as foretold in the Old Testament. Jesus makes everlasting happiness in Heaven possible.

Faith Words

resurrection
Resurrection is the new life given to us when our bodies reunite with our souls at the end of time.

Heaven
Heaven is a life of everlasting happiness with God, and with all people who love him.

Purgatory
Purgatory is a final purification from sin after death.

Hell
Hell is everlasting suffering and separation from God after death.

How does the Holy Spirit lead us?

Saint Lucy

When we have a problem, it is good to talk to someone who understands how we feel. We may also talk to God in prayer. We can ask Saints to pray for our special needs, too.

Because Saints overcame certain difficulties, many Saints are patrons, or helpers, of people with certain needs or characteristics. One of the Saints Catholics honor is Saint Lucy. We celebrate her feast day on December 13. Lucy is the patron Saint of people with eye disease, blindness, or throat ailments. Here is the legend that explains why.

Lucy lived in Sicily—part of what is now Italy—in the third century after Christ's birth. At that time, Christianity was against the law and Christians were often persecuted. When Lucy was a teenager, her mother chose a rich young man for Lucy to marry, even though he wasn't a Christian. Lucy didn't want to marry at all. She had made a vow to live for Christ only. She prayed to God to help her mother accept her decision.

Lucy's mother had been ill for some time. Lucy accompanied her on a pilgrimage to the tomb of Saint Agatha to find healing, and she was miraculously healed. In gratitude to God for his goodness, she accepted Lucy's decision to devote her life to Jesus.

St. Lucy Altarpiece by Francesco Figini Pagani

The rich young man was unhappy with Lucy's decision. To get revenge, he informed the authorities that she was Christian, so she would be persecuted. Soldiers came to arrest Lucy, but she would not leave her house. They tried to pull her out by attaching a herd of oxen to her, but they could not move her. The soldiers decided to torture her. First, they poked out her eyes, then they tried to burn her. But by a miracle she would not burn. Then, one of the soldiers stabbed her in the throat. Before she died, her eyesight was restored. Saint Lucy's feast day is December 13.

Activities

1. On the line, write the name of the patron Saint of your parish, the Saint you are named after, or your favorite Saint. Then draw something you know about the Saint.

Saint _____

2. Name a person you know who is a model of Christ. List three qualities this person has that you would like to imitate.

Person: _____

Qualities I can learn from:

_____

_____

_____

3. Describe an everyday thing you do or can do to be a model of Christ.

_____

_____

_____

How can the
Saints help
us pray?

Prayer Celebration

A Litany Prayer

Here are two litanies, one that requests help from the Saints in Heaven and one for the forgiveness of people who have died. After the leader speaks, pray the response while making the gestures shown.

Leader: Holy Mary,

Response: Pray for us.

Leader:		**All:**	
Mother of God,			(response)
Angels of God,			(response)
Saint Peter and Saint Paul,			(response)
All holy apostles,			(response)
All holy martyrs of Christ,			(response)
Saint Lucy,			(response)
Saint *(name a favorite saint)*,			(response)
All holy men and women,			(response)
Now we will pray to God for other people.			
Lord, show us your kindness.			

Response: Lord, hear our prayer.

Leader:	Save our friends and family.	**All:**	(response)
	For *(name people you know)*		(response)
	Grant eternal rest to all who have died, especially *(name people who have died)*.		(response)
	Bring all people together in trust and peace.		(response)
	Lord Jesus, hear our prayer.		(response)

A **Complete** the sentences, using words from the box.

1. The community of people in the Church, in Purgatory, and in Heaven is the _____.

2. _____ is a final purification from sin after death.

3. The new life given to us when our bodies reunite with our souls at the end of time is called _____.

4. _____ makes everlasting happiness in Heaven possible.

5. _____ is everlasting suffering and separation from God after death.

6. A life of everlasting happiness with God and with all people who love God is called _____.

7. God's promises to people in _____ were completely fulfilled in Jesus.

8. _____ inspired the Old Testament writers and is revealed in their writings.

9. A _____ separates us from God's grace and normally requires the Sacrament of Reconciliation to be forgiven.

> Purgatory
>
> mortal sin
>
> the Old Testament
>
> hell
>
> Communion of Saints
>
> Heaven
>
> Jesus
>
> the Holy Spirit
>
> resurrection

B **Describe** how the example of Saint Lucy might inspire a young person today.

_____

_____

_____

Faith in Action

Confirmation Sponsors   Young people preparing to receive the Sacrament of Confirmation choose a person they know, usually a family member or other relative, to be their Confirmation sponsor. The role of the sponsor is to guide the young person in living a moral life as a committed Catholic. The sponsor does this through his or her words, but especially by serving as a role model of what it means to live as a follower of Christ.

In Everyday Life

Activity   Name two people you know who might be suitable candidates for a Confirmation sponsor for you. Tell what characteristics each person has that would make him or her ideal for this role.

This person...	would be a good Confirmation sponsor because
_____	_____
	_____
_____	_____
	_____

In Your Parish

Activity   Being an involved member of a parish community can help a person be a good Confirmation sponsor. Name a parish ministry (such as being a catechist, being part of a prayer group, and so forth), then tell how being part of this ministry would enrich a person's spiritual life and make him or her a better Confirmation sponsor.

Parish ministry: _____

Benefits: _____

_____

Take Home

FAMILY TIME

Baptism and Repentance

John the Baptist prepared people for the Messiah, Jesus Christ. John preached repentance and the need to wash away one's sins in the waters of Baptism. His story reminds us of the importance of Sacraments and of our need to prepare spiritually for Christ. What helps your family live as people who are ready for God's kingdom?

ACTIVITY

The Spirit of Advent Preparation for Christ is appropiate any time of the year. Create an Advent wreath for next Christmas by inserting three purple taper candles, one pink taper candle, and some artificial greenery into a circular plastic foam base.

WEEKLY PLANNER

On Sunday

As you pray the Lamb of God, think of instances in which you need Christ's mercy.

On the Web

www.blestarewe.com

Visit our Web site for the Saint of the day and the reflection question of the week.

Saint of the Week

Saint Josephine Bakhita (1869–1947)

As a child, Josephine Bakhita was kidnapped from her village in Darfur, Sudan, and sold into slavery. She was rescued about ten years later and taken to Italy. In 1890, Bakhita was baptized—taking the name "Josephine"—confirmed, and received the Eucharist. In 1896, she took religious vows. She went on to live an exemplary life of virtue.

Feast Day: February 8

A Prayer for the Week

God, thank you for the gift of Baptism and for all the Sacraments, as they bring your life and love into our hearts.

Amen.

Take Home

FAMILY TIME

✠ Scripture Background

In the Time of Jesus

John the Baptist   Like the prophets of the Old Testament, John the Baptist warned the Jewish people of their need to repent. Yet John stood apart from the prophets of old in that he proclaimed that God's Kingdom was at hand and announced the coming of the Messiah. Similarly, John's baptisms were based on the Hebrew tradition of ritual washings, but they were performed in expectation of the coming Messiah. When Jesus asked John to baptize him, John was reluctant at first, knowing that Jesus was the Son of God. Read how John the Baptist prepared people for the coming of Jesus in Matthew 3:1–11.

Our Catholic Tradition in Religious Orders

The Benedictines   John the Baptist was called to proclaim to people the news of the coming Messiah. From the Church's early history, there have been Christians with a special vocation to serve and build up the Church. As the Church grew, communities of people sharing this special calling began to develop. One of the earliest of these is the religious order founded by Saint Benedict. In 529, Benedict founded a monastery at Monte Cassino in southern Italy. In the Middle Ages, hundreds of Benedictine monasteries sprang up throughout Europe and played an important role in passing on the Christian faith. Today, Benedictine monasteries can be found in many parts of the world.

Subiaco Abbey, a Benedictine monastery in Subiaco, Arkansas

18 Baptism and Repentance

LET US PRAY The Lord God says: I will give you a new heart and place a new spirit within you.

Based on Ezekiel 36:26

Share

Think about your household when a holiday is coming. Your family will make preparations so that everybody enjoys the holiday. Special meals and activities are planned, especially if guests are visiting. Special occasions are more special when we have time to get ready. God gives us plenty of time to prepare ourselves for his kingdom—a lifetime!

Activity

This calendar shows events that require preparation. In each box with an event, write something you would do to prepare for it.

Sunday	Monday	Tuesday	Wednesday	Thursday	Friday	Saturday
1 Mass	2	3 science test	4	5 piano lesson	6 sleepover party	7
8 cousin's Baptism	9 Mom's birthday	10	11 gymnastics competition	12	13	14 receive Sacrament of Penance and Reconciliation
15 Mass	16 book report due	17	18	19 doctor's appointment	20	21
22 friend's Confirmation	23	24	25	26 sing in school play	27	28 vacation starts
29 Mass	30					

Who prepared people for Jesus' coming?

🕯 Worship Advent Gospel Reading

About 2,000 years passed since Abraham first encountered the Lord. The Jews had survived the Exile and foreign rule. They still believed in Yahweh and the Covenant. In different ways they tried very hard to obey God's laws. The **Pharisees** were Jews who were devoted to the Commandments from the Old Testament. They also followed the spoken teachings of religious leaders. The **Sadducees** followed only the written laws from the Old Testament and valued the Temple rituals. The **Essenes** separated themselves from the rest of the Jewish community. They lived simply in the desert. They may have performed special washing rituals. They also believed in life after death. Some scholars think that John the Baptist was one of them.

During Advent, we prepare to celebrate the birth of Jesus. The following passage is from a Gospel reading for the Second Sunday of Advent. It tells how John the Baptizer prepared people for the coming of Jesus.

A reading from the Gospel according to Matthew.

John the Baptist appeared, preaching in the desert of Judea and saying, "Repent, for the kingdom of heaven is at hand!" It was of him that the prophet Isaiah had spoken when he said:

> *A voice of one crying out in the desert,*
> *Prepare the way of the Lord,*
> *make straight his paths.*

John wore clothing made of camel's hair and had a leather belt around his waist. His food was locusts and wild honey. At that time Jerusalem, all Judea, and the whole region around the Jordan were going out to him and were being baptized by him in the Jordan River as they acknowledged their sins.

When he saw many of the Pharisees and Sadducees coming to his baptism, he said to them, "...Produce good fruit as evidence of your repentance.... Every tree that does not bear good fruit will be cut down and thrown into the fire. I am baptizing you with water, for repentance, but the one who is coming after me is mightier than I. I am not worthy to carry his sandals. He will baptize you with the Holy Spirit and fire."

Matthew 3:1–8, 10–11

The Gospel of the Lord.
Praise to you, Lord Jesus Christ.

The Kingdom Is Coming

John the Baptist prepared people to receive Jesus as the Messiah by telling them to repent, or be sorry for their sins and change their behavior. Some people believed that the coming of the Messiah was a sign of the final judgment of all humans and the resurrection of the dead.

We recognize Jesus as the Messiah. We are baptized in the Holy Spirit. At our Baptisms, water and the words "I baptize you in the name of the Father, and of the Son, and of the Holy Spirit" give us the seal of eternal life and mark us as belonging to Christ. Confirmation deepens our baptismal commitment. It seals us with the gift of the Holy Spirit in oil and gives us grace to witness to our faith in word and deed. Baptism and Confirmation are called Sacraments of Initiation. They strengthen us to live as members of the Church and to spread Jesus' Word.

Our Church Teaches

The Sacraments of Baptism and Confirmation affect our souls permanently, so we celebrate them only once. On the other hand, we should celebrate the Sacrament of Penance and Reconciliation, frequently—at least once a year. This sacrament helps us spiritually in many ways. It reconciles us with God if we have committed a mortal sin, giving us God's grace again. It also reconciles us with the Church. It excuses us from eternal punishment for mortal sins and from some of the punishment due for all sin after death. Finally, it brings us peace of mind, comfort, and the strength to avoid temptation. Through this Sacrament, we prepare for the Final Judgment at the Second Coming of Christ.

Before confessing our sins to the priest, we carefully examine our consciences, reflecting upon how we have sinned. The Church teaches that we should confess to the priest all unconfessed grave sins. The Church does not require that venial, or less serious, faults be confessed. However, it strongly recommends it. After we confess our sins and express our sorrow, the priest will absolve us, saying, "God, the Father of mercies, through the death and resurrection of his Son has reconciled the world to himself and sent the Holy Spirit among us for the forgiveness of sins; through the ministry of the Church may God give you pardon and peace, and I absolve you from your sins in the name of the Father, and of the Son, and of the Holy Spirit" *(Rite of Penance)*.

We Believe

To obtain reconciliation with God and with the Church, we must confess grave sins to a priest.

Faith Words

Pharisees
Pharisees were Jewish people who accepted both the written law of the Old Testament and spoken teachings and tradition.

Sadducees
Sadducees were Jewish people who accepted only the written law of the Old Testament and rejected spoken teachings and tradition.

Essenes
Essenes were devout Jewish people who lived simply in the desert.

How do the Sacraments lead us to holiness?

Respond

Activities

1. Fill in the missing information about the Sacraments.

Type of Sacrament	Sacrament	What is it?	Who may receive it?
Healing	Penance and Reconciliation		
	Anointing of the Sick	an anointing of people suffering from serious illness or old age, giving special graces, including forgiveness of sin	people who are sick or dying
Initiation	Baptism		babies or adults who have not been baptized
	Confirmation	the receiving of the Gifts of the Holy Spirit	people who are ready to carry on the mission of the Church
	Eucharist		
Service of Communion	Matrimony	a lifelong covenant between a husband and wife to love and serve one another and to raise and love children, teaching them to follow Christ	
	Holy Orders	a commitment to serve the Church as bishop, priest, or deacon	

GO TO pages 265–267 if you need help with this activity.

2. Fill in the blanks with names of the Sacraments to complete the story of one young person's experience with the Sacraments.

When Arthur was a baby, he was welcomed into the Catholic

Church through the Sacrament of _____.
When he was seven, he experienced the Sacrament of

_____ for the first time, in which he celebrated God's forgiveness. Soon after, Arthur celebrated the Sacrament of

_____ and received the Body and Blood of Christ.
At thirteen, he received the Gifts of the Holy Spirit in

_____. As an adult, instead of celebrating

_____ and having a family, Arthur chose to

receive the Sacrament of _____ and become
a priest. He was then able to administer the Sacraments, including

the _____, in which elderly and ill
people receive special grace from God to help them in their suffering.

3. Write a prayer asking God to help you choose the vocation that is

right for you when you are older. _____

_____

_____

How does prayer renew us?

Prayer Celebration

A Prayer of Renewal

What images from nature remind you of birth? The prophet Ezekiel told the Jewish people that God would make Israel "born again" after the Exile. At Baptism the following passage from the Book of Ezekiel may be read. The reading reminds us that Baptism gives us new life. Close your eyes and quietly listen to the passage. The leader will pause after each sentence and ask you to imagine a beautiful flower or plant growing step by step.

Leader: A reading from Ezekiel, chapter 36, verses 24 to 28. "For I will take you away from among the nations, gather you from all the foreign lands, and bring you back to your own land." *Imagine hands planting seeds in soil.*

"I will sprinkle clean water upon you to cleanse you from all your impurities, and from all your idols I will cleanse you." *Imagine a watering can over the soil and water sprinkling out.*

"I will give you a new heart and place a new spirit within you, taking from your bodies your stony hearts and giving you natural hearts." *Imagine tiny green sprouts shooting up from the soil.*

"I will put my spirit within you and make you live by my statutes, careful to observe my decrees." *Imagine a green stem beginning to grow, with buds and leaves slowly appearing.*

"You shall live in the land I gave your fathers; you shall be my people, and I will be your God." *Imagine the stem growing into a beautiful plant or a flower in full bloom, with sunlight shining on it. Imagine a meadow of flowers around it.*

All: Thank you, God, for the new life you gave us in Baptism. Help us grow in faith and love. Amen.

18 Chapter Review

A **Match** Column A with Column B by writing the correct number in the space provided.

A

1. Reconciliation
2. Confirmation
3. Pharisees
4. John the Baptist
5. Matrimony
6. Sadducees
7. Holy Orders
8. Essenes
9. Ezekiel
10. Anointing of the Sick

B

_____ Jewish people who accepted only the written law of the Old Testament

_____ a lifelong covenant between a baptized man and a woman

_____ a commitment to serve the Church as a bishop, priest, or deacon

_____ the receiving of the Gifts of the Holy Spirit

_____ devout Jewish people who lived simply in the desert

_____ Sacrament administered to the elderly or those who are suffering from serious illness

_____ told the Jewish people that God would make Israel "born again" after the Exile

_____ Jewish people who accepted both the written law and tradition

_____ preached in the desert and baptized in the Jordan River

_____ reconciles us with God if we have committed a mortal sin; should be celebrated at least once a year

B **Explain** how the following Scripture verse relates to Baptism: "I will give you a new heart and place a new spirit within you" (Ezekiel 36:26).

_____

_____

Faith in Action

Godparents   When a Catholic child is baptized, godparents are chosen to support the child as he or she grows in faith and understanding of Jesus' love. Godparents share openly about their own faith and help guide and encourage new and growing Catholics to be committed to Jesus and to the Catholic Church. They pray for their godchildren and support them as they prepare to receive and celebrate other Sacraments as well. God gives godparents special graces to help them make a positive difference in the lives of their godchildren.

In Everyday Life

Activity   Identify a "team" that you participate in. In addition to attending practices or meetings, list five important things you can do to show you are committed to meeting your responsibilities on that team.

1. _____
2. _____
3. _____
4. _____
5. _____

In Your Parish

Activity   Write three questions about your personal faith, the Catholic Church, the Sacraments, or the Scriptures. See how your classmates would respond to them. Then discuss them with a parent or godparent.

1. _____
2. _____
3. _____

Take Home

FAMILY TIME

Christians and the Reign of God

The New Testament story about the boy Jesus in wise conversation with Temple priests inspires us to reflect upon the great love of God, who let us share in his own divinity through a seemingly ordinary boy. When we value our dignity as Christians and as God's children, we are able to understand that all people deserve our love and that we can become holy people and Saints ourselves.

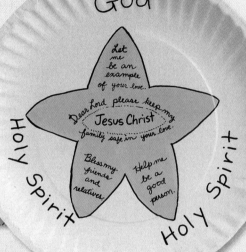

God

Holy Spirit

Holy Spirit

Let me be an example of your love.

Dear Lord please keep my family safe in your love.

Jesus Christ

Bless my friends and relatives.

Help me be a good person.

ACTIVITY

The Star Prayer Have each family member draw an outline of a star and write *Holy Spirit* on the left and right of it, *Jesus Christ* in the center, and *God* above its top point. Inside the star, each person should jot down anything for which he or she would like to pray. With the help of the Holy Spirit, the "beams" of your prayers rise up to God through Jesus Christ.

WEEKLY PLANNER

On Sunday

Live the message of the Sign of Peace at Mass by doing something special for a member of your family.

On the Web

www.blestarewe.com

Visit our Web site for the Saint of the day and the reflection question of the week.

Saint of the Week

Blessed Teresa of Calcutta (1910–1997)

Mother Teresa of Calcutta worked among the "untouchables" of India's society. With the sisters of the religious order she founded, she cared for the most neglected people of Calcutta. She founded orphanages for unwanted children and homes for the sick and dying, and cared for them physically, emotionally, and spiritually. Mother Teresa died in 1997 and was beatified in 2003.

A Prayer for the Week

Lord Jesus, you became one of us and taught us how to live. Help us learn from your example and from the example of the holy people who live lives of goodness and virtue. Amen.

Take Home

FAMILY TIME

✠ Scripture Background

In the Time of Jesus

Jesus Before His Ministry Jesus' life is known almost solely from the Gospels, and although the Gospels provide details about Jesus' birth and early infancy, they provide little other information about Jesus before his public ministry. The exception is the story of Jesus in the Temple when he was twelve, where we see him speaking with the teachers. In Luke's story of Jesus in the Temple, we see that even before he began his public ministry, and even as a boy, Jesus was aware of his unique relationship with God. Read about Jesus in the Temple in Luke 2:41–51.

Our Catholic Tradition in Ireland

Celtic Monks A well-known path called Saints' Road winds through the Dingle Peninsula in County Kerry, Ireland. Beginning in the sixth century, monks traveled such paths to convert Christians to the monastic life. Christians lived, studied, and worshiped on the Dingle Peninsula between the sixth and tenth centuries. Ruins of early Christian settlements are abundant on the coast, from oratories to holy wells to Celtic crosses to small stone huts once belonging to the monks. Some sites remain remarkably intact from the time they were abandoned in the twelfth century. Saints' Road connects the holy site of Mount Brandon to Gallarus Oratory, a stone church more than 1,100 years old (shown below).

19 Christians and the Reign of God

"Blessed are they who hunger and thirst for righteousness, for they will be satisfied."

Matthew 5:6

Share

Have you ever made something out of clay? From a lump of clay you can form something beautiful in any shape you want.

God lovingly shaped us in his own image, giving us his goodness and love within us. God gave each person beautiful gifts and talents. God sees beauty in all of us— inside and out. When we recognize the beauty within ourselves, we are better able to respect the inner beauty of others.

Activity

This photograph shows a situation in which God's image is not respected. In the space provided draw an opposite situation, in which God's image is honored.

How do we show that we are all created in God's image?

✝ Scripture   The Boy Jesus in the Temple

In keeping with Jewish custom, each year Jesus and his parents went to Jerusalem for the feast of Passover. When Jesus was twelve years old, he was separated from Mary and Joseph, having stayed behind in the Temple.

After they had completed the celebration, as they were returning, Jesus remained behind in Jerusalem. But his parents did not know it, and thought that he was in the caravan. They journeyed for a day and looked for him among their relatives and acquaintances. When they did not find him, they returned to Jerusalem to look for him.

After three days they found Jesus in the Temple, sitting in the middle of the teachers, listening to them and asking them questions. All who heard him were astounded at his understanding and his answers.

When his parents saw him, they were astonished, and his mother said to him, "Son, why have you done this to us? Your father and I have been looking for you with great anxiety." Jesus said to them, "Why were you looking for me? Did you not know that I must be in my Father's house?" But they did not understand what he meant. He went with them to Nazareth, and was obedient to them. His mother kept all these things in her heart. And Jesus advanced in wisdom, age, and favor before God and man.

Based on Luke 2:41–52

Jesus: Son of God, Son of Man

On the journey back to Nazareth, Mary would have traveled with the women, and Joseph with the men. Each parent probably thought Jesus was with the other one. They were relieved to find Jesus but did not understand what he was doing in the Temple. The teachers in the Temple were amazed at Jesus' answers to their difficult questions.

Jesus was the Son of God, the Messiah. He was also a missing twelve-year-old Jewish boy with worried parents. He was both man and divine. We are created in God's image and share in God's divine nature through Jesus Christ. How special we are that God would make this possible!

All people have dignity as God's children. Human dignity gives people certain rights. People have a right to make moral choices, to have religious freedom, and to express belief in God. People have a right to govern their families, which are formed by married men and women and their children, without interference from other institutions.

Our Church Teaches

We respect people's dignity by treating them with love and kindness. We can do this by practicing the **Spiritual Works of Mercy** and the **Corporal Works of Mercy**, loving deeds that fulfill the needs of other people. The Spiritual Works of Mercy include helping others do what is right, praying for others, comforting the suffering, forgiving people, and being patient with others. The Corporal Works of Mercy fulfill the physical needs of others. They include feeding the hungry, sheltering the homeless, visiting the sick, and burying the dead.

 page 276 to learn about the Corporal and Spiritual Works of Mercy.

Saint Paul said, "Do you not know that you are the temple of God, and that the Spirit of God dwells in you?" (1 Corinthians 3:16). Each Christian is a **temple of the Holy Spirit**. As temples of the Holy Spirit, we are called to respect our bodies. For example, God's gift of sex is noble and honorable and should be shared only by a husband and wife, for the creation of children and as an expression of love and commitment.

As temples of the Holy Spirit, we are also called to be Saints, holy people who follow the example of Jesus. Holiness comes from living simply, as the Saints did. The Saints denied themselves possessions and avoided distractions from serving God. Holiness comes from the struggle of overcoming temptation and trying to imitate Christ.

Faith Words

Spiritual Works of Mercy
The Spiritual Works of Mercy are loving deeds to meet the spiritual needs of others.

Corporal Works of Mercy
The Corporal Works of Mercy are loving deeds that relieve the physical suffering of others.

temple of the Holy Spirit
Each of us is a temple of the Holy Spirit because the Holy Spirit dwells within us. As temples of the Holy Spirit, we are called to imitate Jesus.

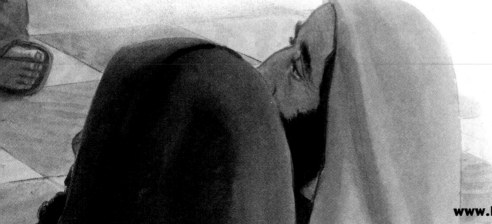

How can we use our gifts to help others?

Respond

Blessed Mother Teresa

Mother Teresa of Calcutta understood that every human being has dignity, and dedicated her life to working with the weakest members of society—the poor, the orphaned, and the sick and dying.

Mother Teresa was born Agnes Bojaxhiu in Yugoslavia in 1910. When she was fourteen years old, she read about the missionary work of the Loreto sisters working in Calcutta, India. She knew with certainty that this was work she wanted to do. A few years later, she made her final profession as a Loreto sister and took the name Teresa, after Saint Thérèse of Lisieux (Saint Teresa of the Child Jesus). As a Loreto nun she went to India, where she first worked as a teacher. But as she saw the less fortunate members of the city, Teresa longed to help them. Feeling called by God, Teresa left the convent and traveled to Calcutta, to live and work among the poor. Encouraged by the archbishop of Calcutta, Teresa started her own order of sisters, who came to be called the Missionaries of Charity. Their habit was a white sari trimmed with a blue border. Led by Mother Teresa, the Missionaries of Charity cared for the "poorest of the poor" in India. They founded homes where they could bring the dying people that lay on the streets of the city, so that they may spend their last hours in the company of people who treated them with love and compassion. The sisters then established a home for children, a place where orphaned and unwanted children could be nurtured and loved.

Mother Teresa and her sisters worked tirelessly among the "untouchables" of India's society. They cared for the poor, the sick, those afflicted with leprosy, AIDS, tuberculosis or any illness, and the neglected and unloved. Following the example of Jesus, Mother Teresa sought out the lowliest members of society and brought them comfort, love, and the joy of knowing God's infinite love for them.

Mother Teresa died on September 5, 1997. Today the Missionaries of Charity number in the thousands and carry out their ministry in countries around the world. Mother Teresa was beatified on October 19, 2003.

Activities

1. Jesus said, "You are the light of the world. Your light must shine before others, that they may see your good deeds and glorify your heavenly Father" (Matthew 5:14, 16). Imagine that you are the lighthouse in the picture. Each boat is named with a difficulty it must overcome. On each light beam, write a gift you have that will guide each boat to shore unharmed.

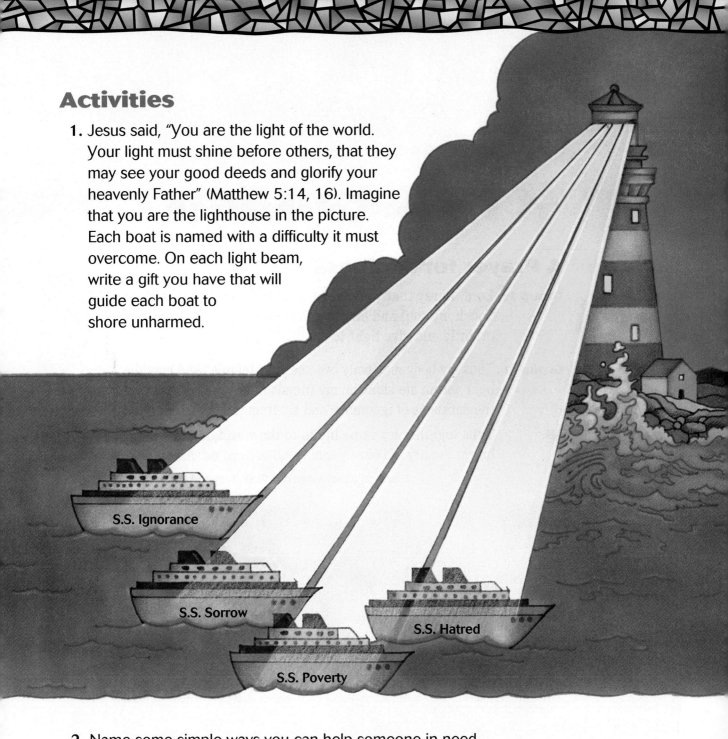

S.S. Ignorance

S.S. Sorrow

S.S. Poverty

S.S. Hatred

2. Name some simple ways you can help someone in need, following the example of Mother Teresa.

_____

_____

_____

_____

What is a good prayer for holiness?

✟ Prayer Celebration

A Prayer for Holiness

Group 1: Lord, I pray that you may be a lamp for me in the darkness. Touch my soul and kindle a fire within it, that it may burn brightly and give light to my life.

Group 2: Thus my body may truly become your temple. And may the light within me shine on my friends that it may drive away the darkness of ignorance and sin from them also.

All: Thus together let us be lights to the world, manifesting the bright beauty of your Gospel to all around us. Amen.

Based on a prayer by Saint Columbanus, A.D. 540–615

19 Chapter Review

A Circle the letter of the best answer.

1. Each year Jesus went to Jerusalem with Mary and Joseph for the feast of ____.
   a. Hanukkah
   b. Purim
   c. Passover
   d. Yom Kippur

2. When Mary and Joseph were looking for Jesus, they found him in the ____ talking to the ____.
   a. market, high priest
   b. Temple, teachers
   c. Temple, Pharisees
   d. caravan, elders

3. Deeds that relieve the physical suffering of others are the ____.
   a. Corporal Works of Mercy
   b. Theological Virtues
   c. Moral Virtues
   d. Spiritual Works of Mercy

4. Loving deeds to meet the spiritual needs of others are the ____.
   a. Corporal Works of Mercy
   b. Theological Virtues
   c. Moral Virtues
   d. Spiritual Works of Mercy

B Complete the following sentences.

1. Each of us is a _____ of the Holy Spirit because the Holy Spirit dwells in us.

2. All people are made in God's _____.

3. _____ comes from living simply, as the saints did.

4. Human _____ gives people certain rights, including the right to make moral choices and to express belief in God.

C Label each of the following actions with either an S for Spiritual Works of Mercy or a C for Corporal Works of Mercy.

____ forgiving someone who hurt us

____ helping a friend avoid a sin

____ praying for others

____ visiting a sick relative

____ donating food to a soup kitchen

____ being patient with a younger sibling

____ consoling someone who is suffering

____ sharing possessions with the needy

Faith in Action

Ministries of Comfort One of the Spiritual Works of Mercy is comforting the sorrowful. A parish's bereavement ministry offers comfort to people who have experienced the death of a loved one. Often, people who have experienced the pain of a similar loss come together and offer comfort and support to one another, with the guidance of a counselor trained to help people through these experiences. Other ministries of comfort in a parish might be for cancer patients and for children of divorced parents. By sharing faith and encouragement, members of these groups support and care for one another.

In Everyday Life

Activity Before we can offer comfort to others, it helps to stop and think about how we ourselves get through difficult situations and what we have learned from our experiences. Fill in the blanks below so that you can be ready to help someone the next time a need arises.

The hardest thing I ever had to get through was _____.

Talking to _____ really helped a lot. Other resources I found

helpful were _____.

One thing I learned about myself was _____.

One thing I learned about God was _____.

The most important thing I learned was _____

_____.

In Your Parish

Activity Every parish provides comfort ministries. What are some questions you have about your parish's comfort ministries, such as the bereavement group? Be prepared to discuss your questions with your group.

_____

_____

Take Home

FAMILY TIME

Hope for the Ages

Jesus, the hope of the ages, not only taught us how to pray in words but through his actions. Jesus ordinarily prayed alone in silence. He depended on prayer to help him through the most difficult moments in his life. Periods of silence and prayer may be rare in our lives, but Jesus' example shows us how to achieve a richer life of prayer.

ACTIVITY

A Family Prayer Write each line of the Lord's Prayer (see page 280) on a separate slip of paper. Have each family member read a line out loud, and discuss its meaning together.

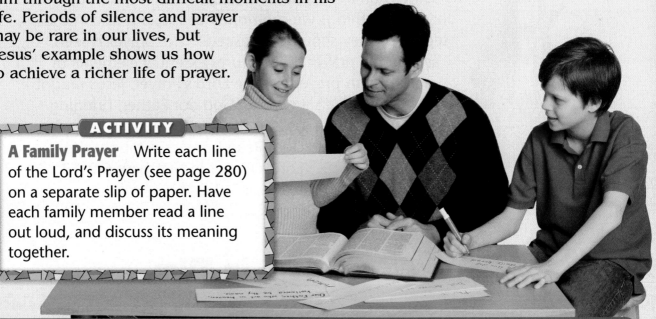

WEEKLY PLANNER

On Sunday

Listen to what the priest says just after the Lord's Prayer. What should you do when you are worried and why?

On the Web

www.blestarewe.com

Visit our Web site for the Saint of the day and the reflection question of the week.

Saint of the Week

Our Lady of Czestochowa

The image of Our Lady of Czestochowa is sometimes called Our Lady of Jasna Góra, after the monastery in Poland in which it has been kept for six centuries. Many miracles have been attributed to the image, including the halt of an impending Russian invasion of Poland in 1920. Polish Catholics have a special devotion to Our Lady of Czestochowa.

A Prayer for the Week

Lord, through the intercession of the Blessed Mother, we come to you in prayer for all our needs. Hear and answer us. Amen.

Take Home

FAMILY TIME

✠ Scripture Background

In the Time of Jesus

The Lord's Prayer The prayer that Jesus taught, the Lord's Prayer, was called "the most perfect of prayers" by Saint Thomas Aquinas. He said, "In it we ask not only for the things we can rightly desire, but also in the sequence they should be desired." The prayer is seen as a model prayer that features essential elements of all Christian prayers. In the Lord's Prayer, Jesus taught us to call God our Father, bringing us into the relationship he had with God. Read how Jesus taught the Lord's Prayer in Matthew 6:9–13 and Luke 11:2–4.

OUR CATHOLIC TRADITION in Film

Alfred Hitchcock The films of late director Alfred Hitchcock often betray his Catholic roots. Educated at St. Ignatius College in London, Hitchcock often relied on Catholic imagery and plots about suffering for other people's crimes. In the 1953 film *I Confess*, his most overtly "Catholic" film, a parishioner confesses a murder to a priest. When the police learn that the murder victim had been trying to blackmail the priest, the priest becomes the main suspect. The sacred seal of confession, however, prevents the priest from revealing the truth. The priest is subjected to a trial and public humiliation. One scene depicts the priest walking past statues of Christ carrying the Cross.

20 Hope for the Ages

"The spirit of the Lord GOD is upon me,
because the LORD has anointed me;
He has sent me to bring glad tidings to the lowly."

Isaiah 61:1

Share

Parents or other adults who care for us love us and want us to be happy. They do much more than meet our material needs. They are also there to guide us when we need help making decisions. Like Jesus, we have earthly caregivers and our heavenly one, God. Mary and Joseph were Jesus' earthly parents, who guided him on Earth. God was Jesus' heavenly Father, who guided him spiritually. Jesus often talked to God when he had a problem, and Jesus was obedient to God.

Activity

Fill out this certificate of achievement for an adult you love. List three ways in which the person has done much more than meet your material needs.

*This Certificate of Achievement
for an Outstanding Caregiver*

Is Awarded to

_____

IN HONOR OF LOVING ACCOMPLISHMENTS,
ESPECIALLY...

1. _____

2. _____

3. _____

This Award Is Granted with Love on _____
DATE

Signed _____
YOUR NAME

How did
Jesus teach
us to pray?

Hear & Believe

† Scripture Jesus' Ministry

Throughout his ministry, Jesus often spoke to large crowds, teaching about the Kingdom of God.

Jesus came to Nazareth, where he had grown up, and went to the synagogue on the Sabbath day. He stood up to read a scroll of the prophet Isaiah. He read,

> "The Spirit of the Lord is upon me,
>   because he has anointed me
>   to bring glad tidings to the poor.
> He has sent me to proclaim liberty to captives
>   and recovery of sight to the blind,
>   to let the oppressed go free,
> and to proclaim a year acceptable to the Lord."

The eyes of all in the synagogue stared at him. He said to them, "Today this Scripture passage is fulfilled in your hearing." And all spoke highly of him and were amazed at his words. But soon people in the synagogue became angry. They could not accept Jesus' claims that he fulfilled the prophecies from their Scriptures and that God's saving message was not just for themselves.

Jesus then went around all of Galilee, teaching in their synagogues, proclaiming the gospel of the kingdom, and curing every disease and illness among the people. Great crowds followed him. When he saw the crowds, he went up a mountain.

Jesus taught the crowds, saying, "When you pray, do not be like the hyprocrites, who love to stand and pray in the synagogues and on street corners so that others may see them. When you pray, close your door, and pray to your Father in secret. And your Father who sees in secret will repay you. This is how you are to pray:

> Our Father in heaven,
>   hallowed be your name,
>   your kingdom come,
> your will be done,
>   on earth as in heaven.
> Give us today our daily bread;
> and forgive us our debts,
>   as we forgive our debtors;
> and do not subject us to the final test,
>   but deliver us from the evil one."

Based on Luke 4:16–29 and Matthew 4:23, 25; 5:1–2; 6:5–6, 9–13

Jesus Taught Us How to Pray

The scroll of Isaiah referred to Jesus. Jesus was the one who had come to help the poor, heal people, teach people about God, and free people from sin. People flocked to hear Jesus preach. Jesus announced that God wanted *everyone* to know his love and forgiveness! Jesus taught people how to pray.

In the Lord's Prayer, Jesus called God "Father." He actually used the word *Abba*, which means "Father" in Aramaic. Calling God "Father" would have seemed unusual to people. Jewish people would not even speak God's name. But Jesus taught people that God is a loving Father who looks after his children. Jesus said, "Your Father knows what you need before you ask him" (Matthew 6:8).

Jesus taught that we should pray in secret, or in private. Jesus said it was important to focus on God alone. He said that people who wanted everyone to see how well they prayed and how much they gave to the poor were hypocrites, or people who are not sincere.

Our Church Teaches

When Jesus taught the Lord's Prayer, he wanted people to know and understand its meaning. He sent the Holy Spirit to teach us to pray to God as "our Father." In the Lord's Prayer and every prayer, the Holy Spirit, through the Word of God, moves us to pray to God as our Father.

Prayers to God should be sincere. One way to pray quietly and sincerely is through **meditation**. This is a type of prayer in which we are silent and concentrate on our feelings, our imagination, and our thoughts of God.

Faith Word
meditation
Meditation is a type of prayer in which we are silent and concentrate on listening to God through our feelings, imagination, and thoughts. We can meditate by thinking about a Scripture story, art, and music.

How did Jesus pray for help?

Your Will Be Done, Father

As more people began to follow Jesus, his opponents became angry. Eventually this led to his suffering and Death on the Cross, a death he endured for the Salvation of all people. Before Jesus died, he called on God in prayer. His final prayers are perfect examples of his obedience to and love for God.

Activity

Follow the trail of Jesus' prayers below. On the lines beneath each prayer, write what you think it means.

Jesus stopped to pray in a garden. He knew he was about to be led to his death. He prayed, "Abba, Father, all things are possible to you. Take this cup away from me, but not what I will but what you will" (based on Mark 14:32–36).

_____

_____

_____

After Jesus was condemned to death, he carried the Cross up to the place where he would be crucified. He prayed, "Forgive them, Father, for they know not what they do" (based on Luke 23:26–34).

_____

_____

_____

Even though it was daytime, darkness came over the land. Jesus was dying on the Cross. He cried out, "My God, my God, why have you abandoned me?" (based on Mark 15:33–34)

_____

_____

_____

As Jesus breathed his last breath, he cried out in a loud voice, "Father, into your hands I entrust my spirit" (based on Luke 23:46).

_____

_____

_____

Women who followed Jesus came to his tomb on the third day after he died. But the tomb was empty. The stone in front of it had been rolled away. Jesus was risen! (based on Luke 24:1–7)

How does the Holy Spirit guide our prayers?

Prayer Celebration

A Meditation Prayer

After Jesus rose from the dead and ascended to Heaven, the Holy Spirit gave Jesus' disciples the strength and wisdom to carry on Jesus' message. The Holy Spirit fills us with the desire to pray to our Father. We can ask the Holy Spirit to give us strength, wisdom, and the ability to pray.

Come, Holy Spirit, fill the hearts of your faithful
and kindle in them the fire of your love.
Send forth your Spirit, and they shall be created:
And you will renew the face of the earth.

Meditation:

Look at the painting on this page. It shows the Pentecost. On Pentecost, the Holy Spirit came to the disciples of Jesus to give them strength to carry out Jesus' mission. How do you think the disciples felt? What symbols for the Holy Spirit are in the painting? What do those symbols tell you about God's power?

20 Chapter Review

A Match Column A with Column B by writing the correct number in the space provided.

A

Jesus

1. Forgive them, Father, for they know not what they do (based on Luke 23:34).

2. Take this cup away from me, but not what I will but what you will (Mark 14:36).

3. My God, my God, why have you abandoned me? (Mark 15:34)

4. Father, into your hands I entrust my spirit (based on Luke 23:46).

B

Meaning

_____ God, I give myself to you completely.

_____ Oh, God, why have you allowed me to suffer like this?

_____ Let me avoid this suffering, but only if it is your will.

_____ Please forgive the people who are persecuting me. They are not aware of their sin.

B Complete the following sentences.

1. _____ is a type of prayer in which we are silent and concentrate on listening to God.

2. Come, _____, fill the hearts of your faithful and kindle in them the fire of your love.

3. On _____, the Holy Spirit came to Jesus' disciples to give them strength to carry out his mission.

C Describe what Jesus wanted us to know when he taught the Lord's Prayer.

_____

_____

_____

Prayer Intercessor Groups   Praying to God with confidence and hope that he will respond is what members of a prayer group do. These people make themselves available to pray in groups or as individuals during special times each week. Specific prayer requests can be given to the intercessors so that they can pray for those expressed needs. The intercessors also talk to God in prayer and ask him to act powerfully in situations they may not even know about. Their prayer recognizes that God is in control and asks that we trust him in all things, even when our prayers are not answered the way we would like.

In Everyday Life

Activity   Sometimes we are afraid to do something because we do not think we can do it perfectly. In the space provided, list one or two things you are good at that you were afraid to try at first. Then describe how good you are at praying and what you can do to be better at it.

I am good at: _____

How well I pray: _____

_____

_____

In Your Parish

Activity   Write some needs or prayer requests that you are aware of from your parish community or elsewhere. Be sure to take some time this week to bring these needs to God in prayer.

_____

_____

_____

FEASTS AND SEASONS

The Liturgical Year

The Church calendar is called the liturgical year. Throughout the liturgical year, the Church leads us through a cycle of specially chosen prayers and readings to help us recall various mysteries of Jesus, from his birth, to his suffering, Death, Resurrection, and Ascension. We also celebrate feasts honoring Mary and the Saints.

ORDINARY TIME

Holy Week begins on Passion Sunday, also called Palm Sunday, when we remember Jesus' triumphant entry into Jerusalem, and ends with the celebration of the Triduum. The events we recall during Holy Week are at the center of our lives as Christians.

HOLY WEEK

Advent is the four-week season that precedes Christmas. During this time, we joyfully await the coming of the Messiah, the long-awaited Savior who will save us from sin and bring us eternal life.

ADVENT

The liturgical year begins.

The **Triduum** begins on Holy Thursday evening and ends on Easter Sunday evening. During these days, we recall the Last Supper when Jesus gave us the Eucharist, Jesus' Death on the Cross to save us from sin, and his Resurrection from the dead.

The **Easter** season begins on Easter Sunday evening and continues until Pentecost. During the Easter season, we rejoice in the Resurrection of our Savior, Jesus Christ.

EASTER

Lent begins on Ash Wednesday and lasts until the evening of Holy Thursday. The Church sets aside these forty days to help us prepare to celebrate Christ's Resurrection. Lent is a season of prayer, almsgiving, and repentance.

Ordinary Time is celebrated in two segments: between the Baptism of Our Lord and Ash Wednesday, and between Pentecost Sunday and the first Sunday of Advent. During Ordinary Time we reflect on Jesus' life and message.

LENT   **ORDINARY TIME**

The **Christmas** season begins with the Solemnity of Christmas, when we celebrate the birth of Jesus, the Son of God. The Christmas season ends with the Feast of the Baptism of the Lord.

CHRISTMAS

Holy Days of Obligation

Our Catholic Church guides us in celebrating the great events and people of our faith through the seasons and feasts of the liturgical year. The special feasts of the liturgical year include Sundays and the holy days of obligation. The holy days of obligation are special days when we honor Jesus, Mary, and the Saints. Like Sunday, these holy days are so important that the Church requires us to attend Mass. In the United States, the Church observes the following holy days of obligation.

Sunday

On Sunday, also called the Lord's Day, we celebrate the Resurrection of Jesus. We gather with our family and our parish community to give thanks to God for sending his Son, Jesus, to save us from sin and death and give us eternal life. We are required to attend Mass every Sunday.

The Immaculate Conception of the Blessed Virgin Mary December 8	We celebrate that Mary, the Mother of Jesus, was conceived without Original Sin.
The Nativity of the Lord (Christmas Day) December 25	We celebrate the birth of Jesus, our Savior.
Mary, the Holy Mother of God January 1	We celebrate that Mary is the Mother of God's Son, Jesus Christ.
The Ascension of the Lord 40 days after Easter (or the Seventh Sunday of Easter)	We celebrate the moment when Jesus, in his resurrected body, returned to his Father in Heaven.
The Assumption of the Blessed Virgin Mary August 15	We celebrate that Mary was taken body and soul into the glory of Heaven and fully shares in the Resurrection of Jesus.
All Saints November 1	We celebrate all those people who lived holy lives while on Earth and now live with God forever in Heaven.

Advent

 More than sentinels wait for the dawn,
let Israel wait for the LORD.

Psalm 130:6–7

Making and Keeping Promises

Making and keeping promises is a familiar part of our lives. We often make promises to our families that we will do our best in school and will do our share of the household chores. We make promises to our friends to always be there for them when they need us. And we make promises to our teachers and coaches to play by the rules, finish our assignments on time, and cooperate with them and with our classmates and teammates.

It's easy to make promises, but keeping them can sometimes be very difficult.

Activity

Think about one promise you made to someone and kept and another promise you broke. Tell about those promises here. Then tell how God treats the promises he makes.

A Promise Kept

_____

_____

A Promise Kept

_____

_____

_____

God's Promises

_____

_____

_____

God Keeps His Promises

God made many promises to his chosen people. He promised never to destroy the Earth again by water, and then he set a rainbow in the sky as a sign of his promise. God promised Abraham and Sarah that he would make of them a mighty nation and their descendants would be as many as the stars in the sky. Then Sarah, who was childless, became pregnant in her old age. God promised to deliver his people from slavery in Egypt, and he led them into a land overflowing with milk and honey. In the Bible these examples show God's generosity in keeping his promises.

Christians believe that Jesus is the fulfillment of God's promise to us. We believe that when the time was right, God sent his only Son to be our Messiah and to save all people from sin. Advent is the time in the liturgical year when we recall God's promise kept and await with joy Jesus' promise to return to us in glory at the end of time.

One way the Church recalls and awaits Jesus' Second Coming is by chanting the "O Antiphons" during Advent. During the liturgies of the last days of Advent, beginning on December 17, an antiphon—or short hymn verse—beginning with "O" is prayed and chanted. The "O Antiphons" come from Old Testament prophecies. Each antiphon calls for the coming of the Messiah. The popular hymn "O Come, O Come, Emmanuel" is based on the O Antiphons.

Here is the first of the O Antiphons.

O Wisdom,

> you came forth from the mouth of the Most High,
> and reaching from beginning to end,
> you ordered all things mightily and sweetly.
> Come, and teach us the way of prudence.

Based on Sunday Vespers at Advent

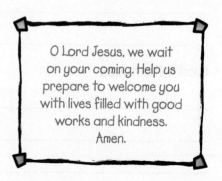

O Lord Jesus, we wait on your coming. Help us prepare to welcome you with lives filled with good works and kindness. Amen.

The Immaculate Conception

I will give thanks to you, O LORD, with all my heart, . . .
in the presence of the angels I will sing your praise.

Psalm 138:1

Unexpected Blessings

Unexpected blessings come into our lives every day. Sometimes these are routine events, such as a visit from a special friend or fun time with our family. At other times, they are life-changing, such as recovery from a life-threatening illness or the birth of a new baby.

A great blessing in our lives is the gift of God's grace within us. Because we share in God's grace, we have the ability to accept God's will for our lives and to say yes to God's plan for our lives.

Activity

Create some headlines that tell about God's grace working in the lives of people, and the blessings it leads to. You can take the headlines from recent news reports you've heard or read or from your own experience. The first one has been done for you.

Gift from Mystery Donor Saves Homeless Shelter

Mary, Full of Grace

On December 8, 1854, Pope Pius IX declared the dogma, or infallible teaching, of the Immaculate Conception. This doctrine states that the Blessed Virgin Mary was free from Original Sin from the first moment of her existence. Since that declaration, Catholics have celebrated the Solemnity of the Immaculate Conception of the Blessed Virgin Mary on December 8.

In 1847, even before Pope Pius IX's declaration, the bishops of the United States had asked Rome that the Blessed Mother, under the title of the Immaculate Conception, be declared the patroness of the country. At that time they made plans to build a national shrine to the Immaculate Conception in Washington, D.C. The cornerstone was laid in 1920. The church was dedicated in 1959—more than a hundred years after the plans were made! In the United States the Solemnity of the Immaculate Conception is a holy day of obligation. Holy days of obligation are feasts that are considered so important to the Catholic Church that Catholics are required to go to Mass.

From its earliest days the Church saw Mary as a very special person. Over the centuries, as Christians thought about Mary and reflected on the Scriptures, they realized that there was a unique holiness about Mary. In Luke's Gospel, the angel Gabriel addressed Mary with these words, "Hail, Mary, full of grace" (based on Luke 1:28). Mary's cousin Elizabeth greeted her with the words, "Mary, you are blessed among all women" (based on Luke 1:42). These Scripture quotes tell us that Mary was very close to God. After all, she was the one chosen to be the Mother of his Son.

The Immaculate Conception
by Guido Reni

Father, you let Mary share in the Salvation Christ would bring by his death, and kept her sinless from the first moment of her conception. Help us by her prayers to live in your presence without sin. We ask this through Jesus Christ, our Lord. Amen.

Nativity of the Lord (Christmas)

God is a saving God for us;
Blessed be God!

Psalm 68:21, 36

A Happy Season

For most people, Christmas isn't just a one-day celebration. Our families decorate, attend Christmas parties, prepare special meals, and exchange gifts with relatives and friends. Activities and preparations for Christmas often begin long before December 25! In the same way, the Christmas season doesn't end on that day either.

Activity

On the calendar grid below, write in some of the events you will take part in during the Christmas season. Be sure not to forget events that will be happening in your parish church.

17 December	24	31
18	25	1 January
19	26	2
20	27	3
21	28	4
22	29	5
23	30	6

A Holy Season

In the early days of the Church, Christmas was not a regular feast on the calendar. All Christians celebrated Easter from the very beginning, but it wasn't until around the fourth century that the Church established a date for celebrating the Nativity, or birth of Christ. At first the date for Christmas was January 6, and later December 25. The Solemnity of Epiphany (celebrating the coming of the Magi) was then assigned to January 6.

Today the Christmas season begins with a Vigil Mass (celebrated in the evening) on December 24. Christmas Day is, of course, on December 25. The Feast of the Holy Family of Jesus, Mary and Joseph is celebrated on the Sunday between Christmas Day and January 1. If there is no Sunday on these days, the feast is celebrated on December 30. The Solemnity of Mary, the Holy Mother of God, is celebrated on New Year's Day. The next Sunday is the Solemnity of the Epiphany of the Lord, an ancient celebration that recalls the Magi's visit to the Christ child. The Christmas season ends with the Feast of the Baptism of the Lord, usually celebrated on the Sunday after Epiphany.

Jesus, may your Spirit be reborn in our hearts and in the hearts of others. Teach us to see you in ourselves and in all people and to welcome you always. You are our Savior and our Lord, today and forever. Amen.

The Presentation of the Lord

The couple brought him to Jerusalem so that he could be presented to the Lord.

Based on Luke 2:22

Baptism

In Luke's Gospel, the story of Jesus' birth is followed by the story of the presentation of the infant Jesus in the Temple. When Jesus was forty days old, Mary and Joseph presented him to God. In the same way, Catholic parents bring their newborn babies to be baptized and welcomed into the Catholic Church. As Catholics, we are called to be disciples of Christ and to continue his mission on Earth.

Activity

1. As a Catholic, you are called to live as a disciple of Christ. Circle the actions in the list below that show that you are Jesus' disciple.

   being honest

   showing compassion

   being thankful for
   God's gifts

   gossiping

   celebrating the
   Sacrament of Penance
   and Reconciliation

   not sharing

   praying

   using my talents
   to do good

   respecting my parents

   attending Mass on Sunday

2. What good habits can you take up to live a more committed life as a baptized follower of Christ?

   _____

   _____

   _____

   _____

The Promised Messiah

Jesus was born into a family that cherished its Jewish traditions and practices. The Jewish people cherished new babies because they saw all children as blessings from God. Male babies were especially welcomed. In the time and culture of Jesus, sons were necessary to every family. It was a grown son's responsibility to care for his aging parents. And only male children could inherit property or land.

According to custom, when Jesus was forty days old Mary and Joseph took him to the Temple in Jerusalem and presented him to God. The Jewish people believed that the firstborn son belonged to God.

When the child was presented, an offering of a pair of turtledoves or two young pigeons would be made at the Temple. On the day that Jesus was presented in the Temple, God revealed to an old priest named Simeon that this baby was the promised Messiah. Simeon held the baby in his arms and blessed God, saying, "Now, Master, you may let your servant go in peace, according to your word, for my eyes have seen your salvation" (Luke 2:29–30). Simeon had waited all his life to see the Messiah. He knew now that God had fulfilled his promise.

The Church celebrates the Feast of the Presentation of the Lord on February 2.

> Loving God, we present our lives to you this day. May you find them acceptable, and may your holy name be praised forever! Amen.

Lent: A Time of Preparation

 The Lord is the Spirit, and where the Spirit of the Lord is, there is freedom.

2 Corinthians 3:17

Getting Ready

Everyone has experienced a time when something important is about to happen, such as moving to a new home, entering a new school, taking final exams, or playing in a championship sports match. Before the event happens, we know that we have to take time to prepare if the event is to be successful. We have to concentrate on our goal, whether it is to pass an exam, make new friends, or contribute to a winning team. We can't allow ourselves to be distracted.

Activity

Write about an event that you found difficult to prepare for.

What was the event?

_____

How did you choose to prepare for it?

_____

_____

What was the most difficult part of your preparation?

_____

_____

How did you keep from being distracted?

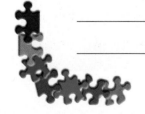

_____

_____

Striving to Live a Christian Life

The number forty is important in both the Old Testament and the New Testament. The Book of Exodus tells us that the Israelites, our ancestors in faith, wandered for forty years in the desert before they arrived in the promised land. Having been the slaves of the Egyptians, the Israelites trusted God to lead them into freedom, so they endured many hardships to reach their goal.

In the Gospels we read about Jesus and his stay in the desert. For forty days, Jesus prayed, fasted, and wrestled with temptation. And for forty days, God was with him, assuring him of his presence and faithfulness. When Jesus returned home from the desert, he knew that he had been with God and that God had made clear to him who he was and what he was to do so all people might know what it means to live as the children of God.

The Church sets aside the forty days of Lent to remind us of our goals as Christians. During Lent, we prepare for Easter. We do this by considering how we can follow the Gospel message better and by reflecting on the challenges we experience in our lives. We try to become better Christians. We may try to follow the example of the heroes of our faith, such as Saints or people of the Old Testament, who lived their faith in times of challenge and struggle.

Jesus, be our strength. Help us follow your example to prepare for your Resurrection and for the Kingdom of God. We ask this through the Holy Spirit. Amen.

Lent: The Gift of Forgiveness

 Then the peace of God that surpasses all understanding will guard your hearts and minds.

Philippians 4:7

Seeking and Offering Forgiveness

During the six weeks before Easter, a season we call Lent, the Church asks us to look into our lives and repent of our sins. Lent is a special time of repentance for our sins. We are called to turn back to God and to seek forgiveness. We must also set goals for ourselves for what we can do to live more as God wants us to.

One of the ways we can live according to God's will is by seeking and offering forgiveness. We can ask forgiveness of those whom we have hurt by our words or actions, and we can forgive those who have hurt us. Just as God is loving and forgives us when we repent, we too must be willing to offer forgiveness to others.

Activity

To me, forgiveness means _____

_____ .

Forgiving those who have hurt us is better than

remaining angry with them because _____

_____

_____ .

Asking forgiveness can be hard, but it is important because

_____

_____

_____ .

One way I can grow to be a more forgiving person is by

_____

_____

_____ .

The Sacrament of Penance and Reconciliation

Jesus knew that one of the gifts we would need most in our lives is the gift of forgiveness. Whenever we sin, either by doing something wrong or by failing to do the right thing, our relationship with God is weakened. Jesus knew that we would need a way to turn back to God and ask for forgiveness.

The **Sacrament of Penance and Reconciliation** is our celebration of God's forgiveness in our lives. This Sacrament is called a Sacrament of Healing because when we celebrate it, we heal our relationship with God and one another. It also heals us of the pain and guilt caused by our sins. When we confess our sins and express our sorrow, we are *reconciled*, or brought back together, with God and the Church.

In order to experience God's gift of healing in the Sacrament of Penance and Reconciliation, we need to do several things. We need to feel sorrow for our sins, to want to change the way we are living, and to confess our sins to a priest. In the Sacrament, the priest will pray a prayer of absolution over us, which asks for God's mercy. The priest will also suggest a penance, an action or prayer to help us change our lives and avoid sin in the future.

The gift of forgiveness that we receive in the Sacrament of Penance and Reconciliation is so powerful that Catholics have many different ways of describing this Sacrament. It is described as a Sacrament of *conversion*, a word that means "being changed." This name is fitting because this Sacrament helps us change our lives and become united with God again. It is also called the Sacrament of Penance, because in it we admit our wrongdoing and express our wish to make up for what we have done or failed to do. And it is called the Sacrament of forgiveness, because through this Sacrament we receive God's forgiveness.

> Jesus, thank you for your gift of mercy and forgiveness. Help us forgive others as you have forgiven us. Guide us in making moral choices and avoiding sin. Amen.

Holy Week

 It is in Christ and through his Blood that we have been redeemed and our sins forgiven.

Based on Ephesians 1:7

A Walk Through Holy Week

We call Holy Week "holy" because for Christians it is the holiest week of the year. During Holy Week we recall and celebrate God's great love for us, as demonstrated in the suffering and Death of his Son, Jesus, for our Salvation.

Activity

After the name of each day in Holy Week, write something you remember about that particular day.

Passion Sunday (Palm Sunday)

_____

_____

Holy Thursday

_____

_____

Good Friday

_____

_____

Holy Saturday

_____

_____

Easter Sunday

_____

_____

Celebrating Our Salvation

Holy Week begins on Passion Sunday, also called Palm Sunday, and ends with the celebration of the **Easter Triduum**. The events we recall during Holy Week are at the center of our lives as Christians. We believe that God loves us so much that he sent his only Son to suffer, die, and rise to new life that we may be free of sin and live with him forever.

Passion Sunday

Most Catholics refer to this day as Palm Sunday. On Palm Sunday we recall Jesus' entry into Jerusalem by waving palm branches and singing "Hosanna."

Holy Thursday

Holy Thursday evening is when we celebrate the Mass of the Lord's Supper. On the night before he died, Jesus gave us the gift of himself in the Eucharist.

Good Friday

The day we recall Jesus' suffering and Death on the Cross is called "good" not because Jesus suffered and died but because his suffering and Death brought about God's gift of resurrection and new life.

Holy Saturday

The morning and afternoon of this day in Holy Week is filled with silence and waiting. We recall Jesus' time spent in the tomb and God's promise of resurrection. The evening of the Easter Vigil is considered the holiest night of the year. At the Easter Vigil Mass, we praise and thank God for raising Jesus from death to new life. It is also the time when we welcome new members into the Church.

Jesus, help us to walk by your side through Holy Week. May we keep our eyes and hearts focused on you and recognize you as King, Messiah, and Lord. Amen.

Easter

Blessed are they who have not seen and have believed.

Based on John 20:29

A Fresh Start

Our lives are full of new beginnings. Every birthday can seem like a new beginning, just like every new school year or every summer vacation. We see ourselves growing, changing, and becoming stronger, smarter, and more capable. Easter is a new beginning for us, too. It is a chance to live our new life in Christ.

Activity

1. Recall an event in your life that was a new beginning for you, such as the start of a new school year or a move to a new home. Then describe some changes you experienced because of that event.

   Event: _____

   Changes it brought into my life: _____

   _____

2. How is Easter a new beginning in your life? _____

   _____

   _____

3. What steps can you take so you can get the most out of this new beginning? _____

   _____

   _____

God Raises Jesus to New Life

On Easter Sunday and throughout the Easter season, we rejoice in the Resurrection of Jesus. God the Father raised Jesus to new life. Jesus did not return to his old life after the Resurrection. Instead, God gave him new life that would last forever.

Jesus shares that new life with us. No longer are we our old selves, returning to the same habits and sins of our old lives. We are now alive in Jesus, through his Passion, Death, and Resurrection. We live in him, and he lives in us.

Believing in Jesus' Resurrection requires faith. Jesus' first disciples struggled to understand the Resurrection and what it meant for them. They had locked themselves in a room out of fear, but Jesus came and stood before them. Wishing them the gift of peace, Jesus showed his friends the wounds in his hands and his side so that they would believe that it was he, risen from the dead.

Easter is the time of the church year when we rejoice that God raised Jesus from death to new life. The Easter season lasts for fifty days. During that time we also celebrate Jesus' Ascension into Heaven and the sending of the Holy Spirit on Pentecost. We praise and thank God for giving us his Son and for bringing us to new life in him.

> Risen Jesus, help us believe with certainty that all who fall asleep in death will rise to new life with you, the Father, and the Holy Spirit forever. Amen.

Saint Teresa Benedicta of the Cross

 O God, you are my God whom I seek;
For your kindness is a greater good than life.

Psalm 63:2, 4

Coming to Know God

Most people of faith come to know God at a very early age. Others learn about God later in life.

Activity

Complete the survey below to record how and when you came to know God.

Faith Survey

1. How old were you when you first learned about God? _____

2. Who first introduced you to God? _____

3. How would you have described God when you were a young child?

_____

4. How would you describe God now? _____

_____

5. If you didn't believe in Jesus, how might your life be different?

_____

_____

6. How would you describe who Jesus is to someone who has never

been introduced to him? _____

_____

_____

Discovering Faith

Born in 1891 in eastern Germany, Edith Stein was one of eleven children. Edith's family was Jewish. She and her brothers and sisters were raised in a faith-filled and loving home. Edith went to college, worked on her doctorate degree on and off, and finally finished it in 1913.

At this time, discrimination against Jews was spreading rapidly in Edith's part of the world. It was almost impossible for a Jewish woman to obtain a teaching position at a college or university. Edith was very discouraged. She longed to share her knowledge with young students.

For a while Edith struggled with questions about the meaning of life. At one point, she even questioned the idea of God. Then, while staying with some friends, Edith came across a copy of the autobiography of Saint Teresa of Ávila (Saint Teresa of Jesus). Edith's search for meaning in her life had ended. She met Jesus in Teresa's writings and wanted to become a Catholic. Edith was baptized and soon began teaching in a convent school. Many years later, Edith joined the Carmelites and took the religious name of Sister Teresa Benedicta of the Cross.

In 1938, Sister Teresa moved to Holland. There she eventually lived in a local convent with her sister, Rosa, who had also become a Catholic and joined the Carmelite community.

Holland was now occupied by the Nazis who began to persecute the Jews. When the Dutch bishops denounced the Nazis' actions, the Nazis were angered. In turn they rounded up all the Jews who had become Catholic.

Edith and Rosa were taken to Westerbork concentration camp. While there Edith spent her time helping and consoling the other women. Eventually, Edith and Rosa were taken to Auschwitz, another concentration camp, where both sisters died in the gas chambers in 1942.

Pope John Paul II canonized Sister Teresa Benedicta of the Cross on October 11, 1998.

> Saint Teresa Benedicta of the Cross, pray for us that we may remain faithful to the God who calls each of us to follow him. Amen.

Venerable Solanus Casey

Rejoice in hope, be patient under trial, persevere in prayer. Be generous in offering hospitality.

Based on Romans 12:12–13

Selfless Giving

Making a difference in someone else's life doesn't have to involve dramatic or life-altering acts. Sometimes even a simple gesture of kindness can make a great difference for the person receiving the kindness. We are not all called to be missionaries or to sacrifice all our comforts to help others. But we are all called to treat all people with love and consideration, and to offer comfort and hospitality to others in whatever ways we are able.

Activity

Even though sometimes it is easier to worry only about ourselves and to do what makes us comfortable, being generous toward others and selfless in our treatment of others has its own rewards.

Write about a time when you acted in a selfless way toward another person or group of people. _____

_____

_____

What did this experience teach you about how being selfless can be much more rewarding than being selfish?

_____

_____

A Life of Simple Holiness

Almost from the day he was born, Barney Casey was known for his cheerfulness, kindness, and gentleness. Barney was a natural leader, with a strong personality, whom everyone liked.

Barney's family was Irish-American. His parents practiced their Catholic faith and passed on the faith to their children. When Barney was an older teenager, he felt that God was calling him to the priesthood. Barney was accepted into the seminary, but because he was not a good student, he was asked to leave after only his first year in college.

In time Barney decided to enter a Franciscan order called the Capuchins. Barney struggled through his schooling in the monastery but was eventually ordained a Capuchin priest. The leaders of the Capuchin Franciscans were impressed with Barney's holiness, but they still felt it best not to allow Barney to hear confessions or give homilies. Father Solanus, as he was now known, accepted these limitations with great patience and humility. He felt that God had other ways for him to serve his people.

And Father Solanus was right. His order sent him to a parish in New York City, where he was put on doorbell duty. Whenever anyone rang the bell, Father Solanus would answer. He was kind, patient, helpful, and hospitable. Beggars would be asked to come in for a large cup of coffee and a huge slice of bread with butter. Some people would come and ask for Father Solanus to pray for them or someone they loved. Soon many people heard of Father Solanus's gift of healing through his prayers. Often Father Solanus would spend the entire day at the front door, welcoming people, without taking time to eat his meals or rest. Hospitality was Father Solanus's gift to the people who rang the rectory doorbell.

Father Solanus died in 1957. The Church has begun the process of recognizing this simple man of great holiness as an official saint of the Church. He is presently recognized as Venerable Solanus Casey.

Venerable Solanus Casey, you give us a perfect example of how to welcome others. Pray for us that, like you, we may see in each person the face of Jesus, and welcome that person into our lives. Amen.

Our Lady of Fatima

My being proclaims the greatness of the Lord. My spirit finds joy in God my Savior.

Based on Luke 1:46–48

The Power of Mary

When we wander away from God, he sometimes gives us reminders of how we are to live. Sometimes the Blessed Mother appears in visions, called apparitions, to bring us God's message. Marian apparitions, such as the one in Fatima, Portugal, bring many people back to their faith.

Activity

1. If Mary appeared in a vision today, what might be some specific requests she would make of people about how to live in the modern world? Name at least three requests you think Mary would make.

   _____

   _____

   _____

2. Choose one of those requests and tell how you would fulfill it in

   your own life. _____

   _____

3. How would your faith be strengthened by hearing a message from

   Mary? _____

   _____

Mary Calls Us to God

On May 13, 1917, the Blessed Mother appeared to ten-year-old Lucia dos Santos and her two young cousins, Francisco and Jacinta Marto. As the children were busy tending their sheep in their village of Fatima, Portugal, Mary, dressed all in white, appeared to them in a dazzling light. She asked the children to make sacrifices and pray for sinners, and to pray the Rosary every day to obtain peace in the world.

On June 13, Mary appeared to the children again. She was holding a heart with thorns around it. The children realized this was the Immaculate Heart of Mary. The thorns represented sins for which people had to repent. Mary appeared to the children four more times. On the day of Mary's last apparition, October 13, 1917, a crowd of about 70,000 had gathered. When Mary appeared, she told Lucia that people must repent for their sins, ask God for pardon, and change their lives. Then, as Mary ascended into heaven, the children saw in the sky a number of visions, including Saint Joseph holding the Christ Child. The crowd, however, saw the sun begin to whirl rapidly and move around the sky. As the crowd watched in amazement, able to look directly at the sun unhurt, the sun seemed to fall to the earth before returning to its normal position in the sky. This occurrence became known as the miracle of the sun.

In her appearances at Fatima, Mary called for people to change their lives. She also asked Catholics to attend Mass and receive the Eucharist on the first Saturday of five consecutive months. This is called the Devotion to the Immaculate Heart of Mary. She promised that the whole world would be in peace and that many souls would be saved if her requests were obeyed.

Today, the Fatima shrine in Portugal is one of the most visited Catholic pilgrimage sites in the world.

> Pray for us, O holy Mother of God, that we may be made worth of the promises of Christ. Amen.
>
> *From the Angelus*

OUR CATHOLIC HERITAGE

WHAT CATHOLICS BELIEVE

We share a common faith based on Sacred Scripture as found in the Bible and on the Sacred Tradition of the Church founded by Jesus Christ.

ABOUT
THE BIBLE

The Bible is the Word of God. It contains the story of God and his people. God is truly the author of the Bible because the Holy Spirit inspired the people who wrote it.

Although we usually see the Bible as one volume, it is actually a collection, or a library, of 73 books. The Bible is divided into two parts. The first is called the Old Testament. There are 46 books in the Old Testament, which includes stories, laws, history, poetry, and prayers. The Old Testament tells the story of our Salvation before the birth of Christ. In it we can read the words of the prophets, such as Isaiah and Ezekiel, that foretold of the new Covenant and of Jesus' birth.

The Old Testament books are usually listed in four sections: the Pentateuch, the Historical Books, the Wisdom Books, and the Prophetic Books. When we see them referenced, their titles are often abbreviated.

The second part of the Bible is the New Testament, which contains 27 books. The New Testament begins with the four Gospels, the accounts of Jesus' life and ministry according to Matthew, Mark, Luke, and John. These are followed by the Acts of the Apostles, then by the letters of Paul, James, Peter, John, and Jude, which were written to the early Christians. After Jesus ascended into Heaven, the Apostles and early Christians naturally talked about him and all that had happened since the start of his ministry. The Apostles wrote the Gospels and letters to share many of the important teachings and events of Jesus' life and instruct new converts. The New Testament ends with the Book of Revelation.

You can learn more about the Bible in the section "A Great Bible Expedition" on pages 15–21 of your book.

One way that Jesus is present to us is in God's Word, the Bible. Catholics are encouraged to read the Bible daily. Every chapter in your religion book contains information from the Bible.

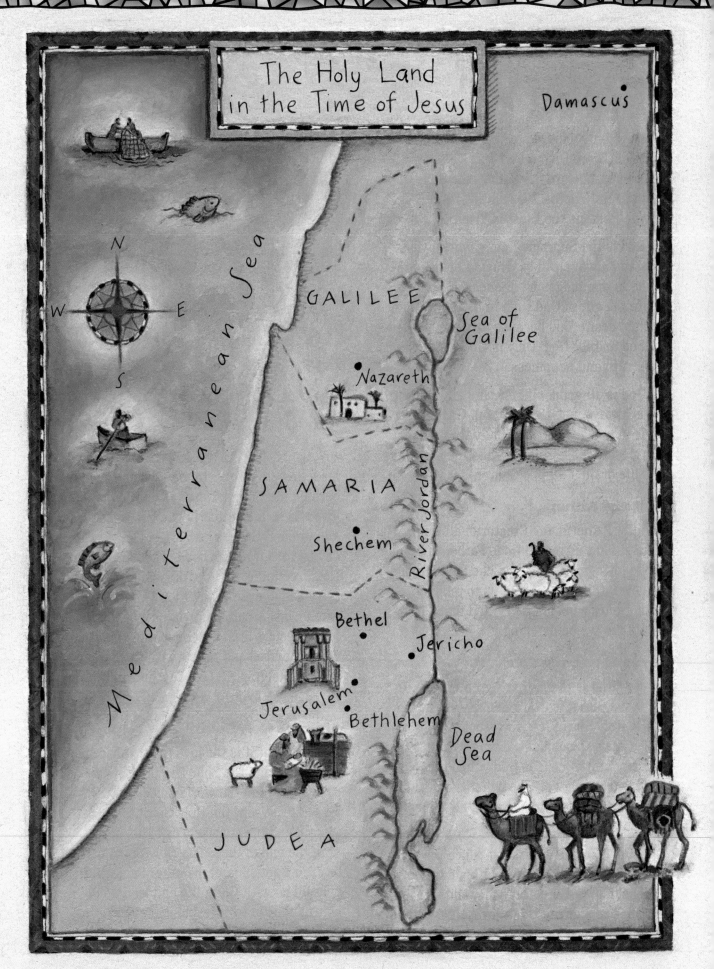

The Holy Land in the Time of Jesus

Damascus

GALILEE

Sea of Galilee

Mediterranean Sea

Nazareth

SAMARIA

River Jordan

Shechem

Bethel

Jericho

Jerusalem

Bethlehem

Dead Sea

JUDEA

ABOUT THE TRINITY

There is only one God, who is revealed to us as Three Divine Persons. The Three Persons are the Father, the Son, and the Holy Spirit. We call the Three Divine Persons the Blessed Trinity.

God is the Supreme Being, who always was and always will be. Human beings are made in the image and likeness of God. We share the gift of God's life in us. All men and women desire God because they are created by God and for God. Only in God will we find real truth and happiness.

God is all-good, all-holy, and all-knowing. He is always just and merciful. God speaks to us in many ways, especially through his Son, Jesus, the Scriptures, and the teachings and life of the Catholic Church.

God, the Father

God the Father is the Creator of all things. Jesus taught us to call God "Father," because of the loving care that God has for everyone and everything. Jesus told us to tell our Father our needs in prayer, and that God would always be listening.

Jesus Christ, the Son

Jesus Christ is the Father's greatest gift to us. Jesus Christ is God's Son. By the power of the Holy Spirit, Jesus was born of the Virgin Mary. Jesus has a divine nature and a human nature. Jesus is God who became man and lived among us. This belief is called the **Incarnation**. Jesus is like us in all things but sin.

Jesus' mission was to announce the Good News. Jesus carried out his mission by teaching, healing, forgiving, and working miracles as signs of God's love. He gathered his followers into a group of disciples who became the Church. Jesus is our Savior. Jesus loved us so much that he died on the Cross for all our sins. He was buried, and on the third day he rose from the dead. The truth of the Resurrection is that death is not an ending but leads to everlasting life. We receive grace when we share in the divine life of the Risen Jesus. Jesus Christ ascended into Heaven, where he lives and reigns with the Father and the Holy Spirit. One day, he will return to judge the living and the dead.

God, the Holy Spirit

The Holy Spirit is the love that is shared by the Father and the Son. The Holy Spirit has been at work in the world since creation. Jesus Christ sent the Holy Spirit to guide his Church and the consciences of his people until the end of time. The Holy Spirit comes to us in Baptism and the other Sacraments to help fill us with God's life and lead us to be true followers of Jesus.

ABOUT THE CATHOLIC CHURCH

The Church is **one, holy, catholic,** and **apostolic**. We call these the four Marks, or qualities, of the Church. They distinguish the Catholic Church and show its truth and origin in God.

The Church is one. We believe in one God—Father, Son, and Holy Spirit; one faith; and one Baptism. The Catholic Church is one because we are united in Jesus Christ. We are also one in our celebration of the same sacramental life. We pray to the Holy Spirit to strengthen our unity as one Body of Christ.

The Catholic Church is holy because Jesus Christ, together with the Father and the Holy Spirit, is holy, and because of God's grace we too are holy. Our holiness will increase through our participation in the sacramental life of the Church.

The Church is catholic, or universal, because Christ is present in the Church and because we welcome all people as Jesus does. Membership in the Catholic Church is open to all, regardless of race, nationality, or culture. We especially welcome those who are poor and disadvantaged into our community of hope.

The Church is apostolic because it is founded on the teachings of Jesus Christ and the Apostles. The chief teacher of the Church is the Pope. The Pope is the successor of Peter, the Apostle Christ chose to lead the Church. Peter was the first bishop of Rome. The Pope is the Vicar of Christ. As Jesus' representative in the world, he leads and serves God's people on Earth.

The Pope, with the bishops, priests, and deacons, helps us understand God's Word, celebrate the Sacraments, and serve others.

When the Pope speaks officially for the Church to define a matter of faith or morals, he speaks without error. This is called the doctrine of papal infallibility. This doctrine assures us that the Pope teaches with the guidance of the Holy Spirit.

THE VIRGIN MARY AND THE SAINTS

Mary, the mother of Jesus, is our greatest Saint. Mary was filled with grace from the first moment of her life. She was conceived without Original Sin. This mystery is called the Immaculate Conception. Mary lived a sinless life on Earth. She remained a virgin in giving birth to Jesus, throughout her life, and for all time. Catholics honor her as the Mother of Jesus and the Mother of the Church.

Because she always followed God's plan, supported Jesus in his ministry, and offered her strength and holiness to the early Church, Mary is our most important model of faith.

Mary was taken body and soul into Heaven. This belief is called the Assumption.

Saints are holy people whose example shows us how to live as Jesus taught us. We honor the Saints and ask them to pray to God for us. We believe that one day we will live with Mary and all the Saints forever with God.

LIFE EVERLASTING

The Kingdom of God will be completed at the end of time. The Catholic Church teaches that at the end of time, Jesus Christ will come again to restore all things in peace, love, and justice.

Jesus teaches us that if we live as he taught us, we will have life everlasting. This means that we will live forever with God in Heaven. Jesus told us that Heaven is unending happiness with God and all who love God.

All who die in God's grace and friendship but still have faults and imperfect love will be united with God forever in Heaven, but first they must undergo a purification. The Church has given the name *Purgatory* to this purification.

We believe that we are united with all those who believe in Jesus Christ in this world and the next. All those who have gone before us into everlasting life and who share in God's wonderful grace and all those who are being purified in purgatory are joined with us in the Communion of Saints. Together we make up the membership of the Church.

We have always included those who are in Purgatory as part of the Communion of Saints. We pray regularly for those who are in Purgatory that they will soon enjoy the happiness of Heaven. Our prayers and good works can gain for us and for the souls in Purgatory indulgences, which remove some of the punishments we must suffer in Purgatory for the effects of the sins we have commited.

Those who deliberately refuse to love God and their neighbor freely choose to separate themselves from God for all eternity. We call this separation *hell*.

HOW CATHOLICS WORSHIP

We celebrate our faith in worship when we give honor and praise to God. Worship is so important for us that the Church calls it the first "work" of God's people. The official public worship of the Church is called "liturgy."

ABOUT
THE SACRAMENTS

We place the Sacraments into three groups to better understand their purpose. The first group is called the *Sacraments of Initiation*.

ABOUT
THE SACRAMENTS OF INITIATION

We become full members of the Catholic Church through the *Sacraments of Initiation*: Baptism, Confirmation, and Eucharist. These three Sacraments are most often received at different times, as a person grows from infancy to maturity. Before being received into the Catholic community, older children and adults go through a period of formation called the catechumenate to prepare for Baptism, Confirmation, and Eucharist.

Baptism

In the Sacrament of Baptism, we receive the Holy Spirit and are anointed with the Sign of the Cross. Through the waters of Baptism, which represent life and death, all sin, including Original Sin, is washed away and we rise with Christ to new life. The grace of Baptism makes us conscious of our faith and ready to accept God's call.

Confirmation

In the Sacrament of Confirmation we stand with a sponsor before the church community and proclaim our faith and our readiness to respond to God's call to discipleship. We should be in a state of grace and old enough to understand the commitment we are making.

When we are confirmed, the bishop or priest says, "Be sealed with the Gift of the Holy Spirit" (*Rite of Confirmation*). The bishop or priest places his hand on our head and anoints our forehead with the Oil of Chrism. Our baptismal faith is strengthened through the coming of the Holy Spirit.

The grace of Confirmation gives us the courage to live our faith and to be committed to the work of the Catholic Church.

Eucharist

The Eucharist is the Sacrament of the real presence of Jesus Christ with us under the appearances of bread and wine. The changing of bread and wine into the Body and Blood of Jesus Christ is called **transubstantiation**. When we worship together at Mass, we celebrate the Eucharist. The word *Eucharist* means "thanksgiving." During the Mass we praise and thank God for all our gifts, especially the gift of his Son, Jesus Christ.

At Mass, Jesus is present in the bread and wine, in his Word, in the people gathered, and in the priest who celebrates the Mass.

ABOUT
THE SACRAMENTS OF HEALING

The second group of sacraments is the *Sacraments of Healing*.

Penance and Reconciliation and Anointing of the Sick are Sacraments of Healing because they celebrate God's healing and forgiveness.

Penance and Reconciliation

Penance and Reconciliation is the Sacrament that celebrates God's loving forgiveness. God always loves us and is ready to forgive our sins. When we sin, we freely choose to turn away from God and one another. The Sacrament of Penance and Reconciliation reunites us with God and the church community. We may celebrate Reconciliation whenever we need God's mercy and peace and are sorry for our sins. We may celebrate the Sacrament individually or with others.

We prepare for the celebration of Reconciliation by examining our consciences.

When we meet the priest, he welcomes us in the name of Jesus and the Church. He may read a story or lesson from the Bible. Then we confess, or tell the priest our sins. The priest may suggest ways we can improve and grow closer to God. He then asks us to do some act of service or to pray a particular prayer or prayers. This is called an act of penance. The priest then asks us to tell God we are sorry for our sins by praying the Act of Contrition.

Then, on behalf of the Church, the priest extends his hands over us and prays, "I absolve you from your sins in the name of the Father, and of the Son, and of the Holy Spirit" *(Rite of Penance)*. This action is called "absolution." Then, with the priest, we praise God for his mercy. The priest tells us to go in peace and that our sins are forgiven. We respond, "Amen."

Anointing of the Sick

In the Sacrament of Anointing of the Sick, we follow the custom of the early Church described in the Letter of James. The Church prays for the healing and forgiveness of the person who is ill, and the priest anoints him or her with holy oil as a sign of the healing power of the Holy Spirit.

The grace of Anointing of the Sick is the comfort brought about by the prayer of the Church, which can ease the suffering of mind and body.

THE SACRAMENTS AT THE SERVICE OF COMMUNION

The third group of Sacraments is the *Sacraments at the Service of Communion*. These Sacraments are Holy Orders and Matrimony. Those who receive these Sacraments have a special mission to serve and work for the Salvation of others and to build up the People of God.

Holy Orders

Holy Orders is the Sacrament that celebrates the ordination of bishops, priests, and deacons to serve the Church in a special way. The word *ordain* means "to set aside or to empower a person to carry on the work of the Apostles." Bishops carry on the work of the Apostles and serve the Church by leading a diocese. Priests are ordained by the bishop to assist him by celebrating the Sacraments, proclaiming God's Word, and guiding the parish community. Deacons, also ordained by the bishop, assist with the work of the parish. They may read the Gospel and give the homily at Mass, baptize, witness marriages, and preside at funerals. Transitional deacons are men who have been ordained deacons as the final step before becoming priests. Permanent deacons have the same ministries as those of transitional deacons but can be married.

At the celebration of Holy Orders the bishop lays his hands on the head of the man being ordained. He prays a special prayer asking God to bless the man being ordained and to help him preach the Gospel, celebrate the Sacraments, and serve others.

Matrimony

The Sacrament of Matrimony celebrates the commitment of a man and a woman to each

other for as long as they live. In the sacrament of Matrimony, the man and woman's love for each other is a sign of Christ's love for the Church. In the Sacrament, God gives them special grace to sustain them and to help them grow in their love for each other. Through their physical love, which is the complete giving of themselves to each other and a sharing in God's creative power, they become one. This is why Catholics believe that sexual love is reserved for married couples only.

Catholic parents accept the responsibility of sharing their faith with their children. The love and care that parents give to their children are a reflection of God's love.

In the celebration of the Sacrament of Matrimony, the man says to the woman, "I take you to be my wife." The woman says to the man, "I take you to be my husband." The couple confer the Sacrament on each other in the presence of a priest or deacon and the church community.

ABOUT
THE MASS

The greatest and most important prayer of the Catholic Church is the Mass. At Mass, we come together to worship God with our parish community. Jesus is present with us at Mass in the priest who leads our worship, in the Word of God that is read, in the bread and wine that have become his Body and Blood, and in the community that gathers in his name.

The Introductory Rites

The Entrance Procession and Opening Hymn

The priest and those assisting him in the Mass enter the church. As the procession begins, we sing the opening hymn.

The Greeting

The procession pauses before the altar to show reverence, and the priest, deacon, and servers move to their places. The priest kisses the altar to show reverence for the table on which the bread and wine will be offered.

As we begin our worship. The priest welcomes us by saying, "The Lord be with you." We answer, "And with your spirit."

The Penitential Act

As a community, we confess that we have sinned. We ask for God's forgiveness and the prayers of the church community. Then we say or sing, "Lord, have mercy."

The Gloria

We sing or pray the Gloria, which is a hymn of praise to God. Then we pray an opening prayer.

The Collect

The priest prays a prayer that helps us focus on the theme of the Mass for that day.

The Liturgy of the Word

The First Reading

The lector reads a story about God's love for us. The first reading is usually from the Old Testament. We sit quietly and listen to God's word.

The Responsorial Psalm

The cantor sings a psalm, and we sing the response.

The Second Reading

The lector reads from one of the books of the New Testament, other than the Gospels. The second reading is usually from one of Saint Paul's letters. We sit quietly and listen to God's Word.

The Gospel Acclamation

Before the Gospel is proclaimed, we praise God by singing the "Alleluia" or another acclamation.

The Gospel

We stand in reverence as the priest or deacon reads the Gospel.

The Homily

The priest or deacon explains the meaning of the Gospel and the other Scripture readings. We sit quietly and pay attention as the homily is given.

The Profession of Faith

We recite the Nicene Creed as a community of faith to affirm our belief in what the Catholic Church teaches.

Prayer of the Faithful

We pray for the Church, our country, and the needs of God's people. We also pray for those who are sick and those who have died.

The Liturgy of the Eucharist

The Preparation of the Altar and the Gifts

As the altar is prepared, members of the community bring the gifts of bread and wine in procession to the priest.

The Eucharistic Prayer

In this prayer of praise and thanksgiving, the priest praises God our Father and invites us to lift up our hearts to the Lord in prayer. We join with the angels and say or sing the "Holy, Holy, Holy."

The priest prays to the Holy Spirit, asking that the bread and wine become the Body and Blood of Jesus. Then in the words of Jesus himself at the Last Supper, the priest says the prayers of consecration, and Jesus Christ becomes truly present in the bread and wine.

Memorial Acclamation

After the consecration, we proclaim the mystery of our faith by singing or saying these or similar words of joy and promise: "We proclaim your Death, O Lord, and profess your Resurrection until you come again."

The Great Amen

At the conclusion of the Eucharistic Prayer, we sing or pray "Amen."

The Communion Rite

The Lord's Prayer

We pray the prayer that Jesus taught us.

The Sign of Peace

We offer each other a sign of peace to show that we wish goodness for our brothers and sisters in Jesus.

The Breaking of the Bread

As the priest and deacon prepare for the distribution of Holy Communion, we say or sing, "Lamb of God, you take away the sins of the world, have mercy on us."

Communion

We reverently walk up to receive the Body and Blood of Jesus in the Eucharist. When we receive the eucharistic bread, the priest, deacon, or extraordinary minister of Holy Communion says, "The Body of Christ." We respond, "Amen." When we receive the cup, the priest, deacon, or extraordinary minister of Holy Communion says, "The Blood of Christ." We respond, "Amen." We return to our places and spend time in quiet prayer and thanksgiving.

Concluding Rites

Blessing

The priest blesses us in the name of the Father, and of the Son, and of the Holy Spirit. We answer, "Amen." Our celebration ends when the priest or deacon tells us to go in peace. We respond, "Thanks be to God."

Dismissal

The priest, deacon, altar servers, and lector leave the altar in procession as we sing a song of praise and thanksgiving.

ABOUT
RECONCILIATION

In the Sacrament of Penance and Reconciliation, we celebrate God's forgiveness. We ask the Holy Spirit to help us better live as Jesus taught us.

Preparation

I examine my conscience by thinking of things I might have done or said on purpose that were harmful to myself or others. I remember that I may have sinned by not doing something good when I should have.

Rite of Reconciliation of Individuals

Priest's Welcome

The priest welcomes me in the name of Jesus and the Church.

Reading from Scripture

The priest may read a part of the Bible or tell me a story from the Gospels. He talks to me about the importance of living as Jesus taught and caring for others as God wants.

Confession

I tell the priest my sins. The priest asks me to do a kind act or to say a prayer, to show that I am sorry for my sins and to remind me to be more loving.

Prayer of Sorrow

I tell the priest that I am sorry for all my sins. The priest asks me to say the Act of Contrition. I say aloud a prayer of sorrow for sin.

Absolution

On behalf of the Church, the priest extends his hands over me and asks God to forgive me. The priest gives me absolution in the name of the Father, Son, and Holy Spirit.

Prayer of Praise and Dismissal

With the priest, I say a prayer of praise. The priest tells me to go in peace. I answer, "Amen."

HOW CATHOLICS LIVE

Living as Jesus taught us is not easy, but God gives us lots of help. Our conscience and other special gifts help us. When we turn away from sin and make good choices, we live as children of God.

ABOUT
CONSCIENCE

Our conscience is a gift from God. Our conscience helps us know what is right and what is wrong. We must learn ways to form a good conscience. The Beatitudes, the Ten Commandments, the teachings of Jesus, and the guidance of the Church help us develop a good conscience.

One of our greatest blessings is free will. Free will is our freedom to choose to do what is right or what is wrong. We can pray to the Holy Spirit to guide our choices, but we must always take responsibility for our actions.

ABOUT
THE THEOLOGICAL AND MORAL VIRTUES

The Holy Spirit gives us gifts that are so wonderful they help us become more like God. These gifts include the Theological and Moral Virtues.

Virtues are often called habits. The more we practice virtues, the more natural they seem to us and the easier they are to live out.

The Theological Virtues are faith, hope, and charity. Faith helps us believe in God. Hope allows us to trust in God's promises. Charity prompts us to show our love for God and others.

The Moral Virtues are prudence, justice, fortitude, and temperance. Prudence is the habit of making good judgments and decisions. Justice is the practice of treating others fairly. Fortitude is the courage to do what is right. Temperance is the habit of living in moderation and controlling desires.

ABOUT SIN AND MERCY

The Bible tells us that Jesus came to show mercy to sinners. Before Jesus was born, an angel told Joseph, Mary's husband, "You are to name him Jesus, because he will save his people from their sins" (Matthew 1:21).

Sin

Sin is a free choice to turn away from God's love. We sin by doing what we know is wrong. Sin keeps us from living as Jesus taught us. Sin turns our hearts away from God.

Mortal sin is a very serious refusal to love God. A sin is mortal when:

1. The action is seriously wrong;

2. We know that the action is seriously wrong; and

3. We make a free choice to commit the sin.

Less serious sins are called venial sins. Venial sins weaken but do not completely destroy our relationship with God and the church community.

Mortal and venial sins committed by individuals are called personal sins. Our personal sins are always our choices. But some of our personal sins may tempt others to sin. We have a responsibility for the sins committed by others when we cooperate in them.

Social sins are those that reflect the unjust and oppressive wrongs in our society. Some examples of social sins are racism, failure to pay just wages, abortion, unjust wars, sexism, ignoring the poor, and prejudice in any form. As Catholics, we must work to put an end to these sins wherever they exist.

Mercy

Even when we sin seriously, we can remember that God's mercy never leaves us. Mortal sins must be confessed in the Sacrament of Penance and Reconciliation. Through Christ we receive God's forgiveness, and we are reunited with the church community.

God loves us so much and wants to forgive us even more than we want to be forgiven. When we share in God's life of love, we receive the grace to live good and holy lives. The Holy Spirit helps us turn away from sin. The Holy Spirit helps us form our conscience so that we know when something is right or wrong.

ABOUT
THE BEATITUDES

Jesus gave us the Beatitudes to teach us how to love God and others. The Beatitudes are Jesus' way of telling us what life will be like in the Kingdom of Heaven. When we live the Beatitudes, we can be truly happy.

The Beatitudes	Living the Beatitudes
Blessed are the poor in spirit, for theirs is the kingdom of heaven.	We know that we need God more than anything else. We obey God and trust in his goodness.
Blessed are they who mourn, for they will be comforted.	We try to help those who are in sorrow or those who are hurting. In turn, we know the Holy Spirit is with us and will comfort us when we are in sorrow.
Blessed are the meek, for they will inherit the land.	We try to be gentle and patient with others. We try to please God more than anyone else so we will share in his promises.
Blessed are they who hunger and thirst for righteousness, for they will be satisfied.	We try to be fair and just toward all people everywhere. We share what we have with those in need.
Blessed are the merciful, for they will be shown mercy.	We forgive those who are unkind to us. We know that God will forgive us.
Blessed are the clean of heart, for they will see God.	We try to keep God first in our lives. We show our love for God by loving our neighbor. By doing this we will live forever with God.
Blessed are the peacemakers, for they will be called children of God.	We try to bring God's peace to the world. When we live peacefully, we are known as God's children.
Blessed are they who are persecuted for the sake of righteousness, for theirs is the kingdom of heaven.	We try to do what is right even when we are made fun of or insulted. By doing this we will be with God forever.

Matthew 5:3–10

ABOUT THE COMMANDMENTS

The Ten Commandments are God's law of love. God gave the Ten Commandments as a gift to help people live in peace with one another. The Ten Commandments are a guide to help us live as children of God. Jesus told us that it is important to obey the Commandments.

The Ten Commandments	Living the Ten Commandments
1. I am the Lord your God. You shall not have other gods besides me.	We believe in God. We only worship God. We love him more than anyone and anything else. We offer God prayers of adoration and of thanksgiving.
2. You shall not take the name of the Lord, your God, in vain.	We never use the name of God or Jesus in an angry way. We use the names of God, Jesus, Mary, and the Saints with respect at all times.
3. Remember to keep holy the Sabbath day.	On Sunday we honor God in a special way. We worship him by attending Mass with our family.
4. Honor your father and mother.	We love, honor, respect, and obey our parents and all adults who care for us.
5. You shall not kill.	God gives us the gift of life. We must protect the lives of children not yet born, the sick, and the elderly. We must respect the life and health of others. We must live peacefully and prevent harm from coming to ourselves and others.
6. You shall not commit adultery.	God created man and woman in his image. He calls each to accept his or her identity and to practice the virtue of chastity. We must respect our bodies and the bodies of others. We honor the lifelong marriage covenant.
7. You shall not steal.	We share with others the gifts God has given us. We do not waste the Earth's resources so others who come after us will have them, too. We do not cheat.
8. You shall not bear false witness against your neighbor.	We must not lie, or mislead others on purpose. We must not hurt others by what we say. If we have misled somebody, then we must correct what we have said.
9. You shall not covet your neighbor's wife.	We respect the promises married people have made to each other. We must always dress and act in a decent way.
10. You shall not covet anything that belongs to your neighbor.	We are satisfied with what we have. We are not jealous, envious, or greedy. We place God first in our lives.

Based on Exodus 20:2–17

274

The Great Commandment

Jesus told us that all of God's Laws can really be summed up in the Great Commandment: "Love God with all your heart, with all your soul, with all your mind, and with all your strength, and love your neighbor as yourself" (based on Mark 12:30–31). The Great Commandment teaches us that God's Laws are based on love of God and love of neighbor.

The New Commandment

Jesus told us that besides wanting us to keep the Great Commandment, he also wanted us to keep a New Commandment. The New Commandment Jesus gave us is, "Love one another as I have loved you" (based on John 13:34). We are called to live as followers of Jesus. When we love others and treat them as Jesus taught us, we live in happiness and freedom.

ABOUT THE GIFTS OF THE HOLY SPIRIT

The seven Gifts of the Holy Spirit help and guide us. Below is a list of the Gifts of the Holy Spirit and what they do for us.

1. Wisdom helps us know how God wants us to live.

2. Understanding helps us know what God teaches through Jesus, the Bible, and the Church.

3. Knowledge helps us know and appreciate that God is more important than anything else in life.

4. Right judgment helps us make good decisions in our everyday lives.

5. Courage helps us be strong when we face problems.

6. Reverence helps us love God more than anything else.

7. Wonder and awe help us to be thankful for all that God creates.

THE WORKS OF MERCY

Jesus expects us to care for the poor and those who are in need. Jesus wants us to live in peace and to be just. Jesus even wants us to love our enemies. Catholics call these ways to show love for others the Spiritual Works of Mercy and the Corporal Works of Mercy. The Corporal Works of Mercy are described in Matthew 25:31–46.

The Spiritual Works of Mercy
Help others do what is right.
Teach the ignorant.
Give advice to the doubtful.
Comfort those who suffer.
Be patient with others.
Forgive injuries.
Pray for the living and the dead.

The Corporal Works of Mercy
Feed the hungry.
Give drink to the thirsty.
Clothe the naked.
Visit those in prison.
Shelter the homeless.
Visit the sick.
Bury the dead.

THE PRECEPTS OF THE CHURCH

The Catholic Church also gives us some very specific duties and responsibilities. These are called the precepts of the Church. They are:

- Celebrate Mass on all Sundays and holy days of obligation.
- Confess your sins at least once a year.
- Receive the Eucharist at least during the Easter season.
- Fast and abstain on the days appointed by the Church.
- Contribute to the Church to provide for its material needs.

ABOUT VOCATIONS

Many of us were baptized when we were infants. Our parents and godparents wanted to give us the opportunity to grow in faith, hope, and love within the Catholic community. They knew that we would need strong values and guidelines in order to live a full and happy life.

As we get older, we begin to think about what choices we will make in the future. Because of our life in the Church, we know that those choices will include devoting time to service in the Catholic community. We call the choices we make about our place in the Church our vocation—what we feel the Gospel message of Jesus calls us to do.

All Christians have a vocation. Although people can choose to be single, married, or part of a religious community, all of us are called to hear and respond to the same Gospel message.

Many Ways of Serving

Many people devote some of their time to service within the church community. They choose a particular ministry in their parish or diocese, such as caring for the poor, teaching, planning and leading the liturgy, helping with parish management, or inviting others to join the Catholic Church.

Some women and men choose to devote their lives completely to the work of the Catholic Church. Many decide to join religious communities of sisters or brothers who take vows of poverty, chastity, and obedience. The vows help them be completely devoted to their ministries. Each religious community chooses to concentrate its efforts on a particular ministry, such as teaching, working with the sick and the poor, preaching, prayer and contemplation, or parish work.

In the Catholic Church there are also ordained ministers—bishops, priests, and deacons. Men who feel that they are called to the priesthood have the special vocation of leading the community in worship as well as serving in other ways. There are diocesan priests who serve as pastors of parishes, as educators, and as counselors or in other capacities. There are priests who, like sisters and brothers, belong to religious communities. They may also be assigned as pastors or as teachers or to lead a particular ministry of their community.

There are also men who are ordained as permanent deacons—or deacons who are not going to become priests. They can assist the pastor by leading the celebrations of Baptism and Marriage, giving the homily at Sunday Mass, and helping with parish management. Permanent deacons can be married and live with their families.

Discernment

In what ways are we being called to serve? Answering this question is called **discernment**, which means determining, with God's help, God's will for our lives. We should pray that God will help us understand what the Gospel is calling us to do. We should also try to know more about the possibilities for us in the Catholic community. Talk to a priest, teacher, parish minister, or religious brother or sister to find out more about how God's invitation can be answered.

ABOUT
PRIESTS

Priests are men who have been ordained, or set apart. They have received the Sacrament of Holy Orders. Priests may or may not be members of religious orders. Priests do not marry. Rather, they devote their lives to serving the People of God, the Catholic community.

Religious Order Priests and Diocesan Priests

Father Tom is a priest at St. Peter's parish. He is a member of the Salesians, a religious order founded in the 1800s.

Father Pat is a priest at Our Lady of Mercy parish. He has been there since he was assigned to the parish right after being ordained seven years ago. Father Pat does not belong to a religious order; he is a diocesan priest.

Father Tom and Father Pat explain why they chose their particular styles of priesthood.

Father Tom: When I was growing up, the priests at my parish church made a strong impression on me. They were very prayerful, but they also had a great rapport with the parishioners and were well liked. They lived in a rectory called a friary and belonged to a religious order called the Salesians.

As I learned more about this order, I discovered that these religious had parishes all over the country as well as other parts of the world. They were also very active in missionary work. I also learned that the Salesian priests took vows of poverty, chastity, and obedience. Those vows put an even greater emphasis on the community, and I found that appealing. When I felt called to the priesthood, I knew this religious order was right for me.

Father Pat: I grew up in a large parish in a big city, and every night something was happening in the parish. The mornings and weekends were just as busy. Between the many Masses, funerals, and meetings—not to mention the weekend weddings and marriage preparations—those priests were constantly on the go. They knew people all over the diocese, as well as many of the priests from the neighboring parishes.

That's what appealed to me—staying in one area or diocese and getting to know it well by working within it.

Father Tom and Father Pat are involved in the same ministry, yet their lives are not identical. Father Tom gets support from his fellow priests in the friary and is able to minister in different parts of the world. Father Pat finds strength and support from the priests and people of the diocese in which he lives and works. It is wonderful that the Church offers these two possibilities of priesthood for young men to consider.

HOW CATHOLICS PRAY

When we pray, we are expressing our faith in God. We can pray privately. We can also pray with others in the church community when we gather to worship.

ABOUT
PRAYER

Prayer is talking and listening to God. We pray to praise the goodness and love of God, to thank him for the many gifts we have received, and to ask him for special blessings for ourselves and others. Sometimes we ask Mary or one of the saints to pray to God for us.

God always hears our prayers and answers them in the way that is best for us.

It is important to set aside a special time or place to pray each day, so that we can form a habit of daily prayer.

We also learn and pray the prayers that are part of our Catholic heritage, such as the Lord's Prayer, the Hail Mary, the Glory Be, and the Act of Contrition.

As Catholics, we begin our prayers with the Sign of the Cross, to remind us that we offer our prayers in the name of the Father, the Son, and the Holy Spirit. We end our prayers with "Amen," which means "I believe."

ABOUT
KINDS OF PRAYER

Praying is not always asking God for something. Our prayers should include praise and thanksgiving, too.

Quiet Prayer

It is always possible to pray. We can pray without saying words. When we are quiet and think about God, we are praying. In this way, the Holy Spirit speaks to our hearts.

We can pray quietly and think about a Bible story. When beautiful sights in nature remind us of God's wonderful gifts we can pray a quiet prayer of thanks to God.

Prayers with Words

Sometimes we pray by talking to God using our own words.

ABOUT
MEDITATIVE PRAYER

Meditation is praying without words so that God can speak to us in our minds and hearts. Meditative prayer begins with thinking about a single subject. We may begin by reading a Bible story or by thinking about a holy person whom we admire. All the while we concentrate on God's relationship to this single subject. Another way to meditate is to call upon the Holy Spirit to help us think about whether we are followers of Jesus. We can think about how we can better our relationship with God.

Then, we sort out our thoughts and feelings and think about what God wants us to do. Our prayer leads us to a better understanding of what God wants us to do as followers of Jesus.

THE LORD'S PRAYER

Jesus gave us the Lord's Prayer to teach us how God wants us to live and so that we can honor God and remember his love for us.

The Lord's Prayer

Our Father, who art in heaven, hallowed be thy name;

God is our Father. We praise and thank him for all the wonderful gifts he has given us. We pray that God's name will be spoken with respect and reverence at all times.

thy kingdom come,

Jesus told us about God's kingdom in Heaven. We pray that everyone will live as Jesus teaches us to live. We look forward to the day when God's kingdom will finally come about.

thy will be done on earth as it is in heaven.

We pray that everyone will obey God's Laws. We know that Jesus has taught us how to live as his followers. We wish to show others how to live as Christians.

Give us this day our daily bread,

God cares for us. We know that we can pray for our needs. We know that we must pray for the needs of the poor. We ask God for the good things we can share with others.

and forgive us our trespasses,

as we forgive those who trespass against us;

We ask God for forgiveness when we have done something wrong. We forgive those who have hurt us.

and lead us not into temptation,

We pray that God will help us make good choices and do what is right.

but deliver us from evil.

We pray that God will protect us from what is harmful. We know that we should care for our own health and the well-being of others.

Amen.

When we say "Amen," it means "I believe."

Glossary

altar An altar is a raised place where sacrifices are offered. The altar used for the center of worship during the Mass is also a table, where we gather to share the Eucharistic meal. *(page 39)*

amen *Amen* is a word we usually say at the end of our prayers. It means "I believe" or "So it is." *(page 143)*

Ark of the Covenant The Ark of the Covenant was a special box that held the stone tablets of the Ten Commandments. *(page 91)*

catholic The word *catholic* means "universal." With a capital *C*, it describes the Church founded by Christ's Apostles. *(page 113)*

chosen people In the Old Testament the chosen people were Abraham and his descendants, whom God had selected to receive his Word. People who choose to follow God's will today are also chosen people. *(page 101)*

conscience Our conscience is our ability to judge what is right and what is wrong. *(page 133)*

Corporal Works of Mercy The Corporal Works of Mercy are loving deeds that relieve the physical suffering of others. *(page 217)*

covenant A covenant is a sacred agreement or relationship, sometimes sealed by a ritual or ceremony. Isaac honored the Covenant the Lord made with his father, Abraham. *(page 49)*

discernment Discernment is discovering, with God's help, God's will for our lives. *(page 101)*

Essenes Essenes were devout Jewish people who lived simply in the desert. *(page 207)*

exile Exile is the forced removal of people from their homeland to another land. The Israelites captured by the Assyrians were living in exile. *(page 165)*

Exodus The Exodus is the Old Testament story of how God freed the Hebrews in Egypt. Exodus is the second book of the Old Testament. *(page 71)*

faith Faith is the assurance of things hoped for, the conviction of things not seen. *(page 29)*

fidelity Fidelity is faithfulness and loyalty to something or someone. Joseph is a model of fidelity to God. *(page 59)*

guidance Guidance is help in making the right choices. God gives us guidance to help us develop our conscience. *(page 133)*

Heaven Heaven is a life of everlasting happiness with God, and with all people who love him. *(page 197)*

hell Hell is everlasting suffering and separation from God after death. *(page 197)*

Incarnation The Incarnation is God's Son becoming man, one like us, Jesus Christ, who is both man and divine. *(page 262)*

laity The laity are people who are part of the Church and are not clergy or religious brothers and sisters. *(page 113)*

liturgical year The liturgical year is the Church's yearly calendar of celebrations and seasons. *(page 81)*

manna Manna is the breadlike food that God gave the Israelites in the desert. *(page 91)*

meditation Meditation is a type of prayer in which we are silent and concentrate on listening to God through our feelings, imagination, and thoughts. We can meditate by thinking about a Scripture story, art, and music. *(page 227)*

messiah A messiah is a person chosen to save people from a particular fate. The word means "annointed." Jesus Christ is our Messiah, chosen by God to free us from sin and death. *(page 165)*

ministry A ministry is a way of serving and caring for others in Christ's name. *(page 113)*

Moral Virtues The Moral Virtues are four spiritual qualities—temperance, prudence, justice, and fortitude—that help us avoid sin. *(page 175)*

Original Sin Original Sin is the sin of the first man and woman, passed on to all human beings. Because of it, we are weakened in our ability to resist sin and do good. *(page 155)*

Paschal Mystery The Paschal Mystery is the way that Jesus' Passion, Death, Resurrection, and Ascension saved us from sin and gave us life after death. *(page 81)*

Passover Passover is the Jewish celebration of the Israelites' exodus from Egypt. *(page 81)*

patriarch A patriarch, a term meaning "father," is a great leader of the Hebrews from early Scripture times. A patriarch is also the male leader of a family or clan. *(page 29)*

persistence Persistence is the act of continually pursuing something in spite of obstacles. Prayer often requires persistence. *(page 185)*

Pharisees Pharisees were Jewish people who accepted both the written law of the Old Testament and spoken teachings and tradition. *(page 207)*

piety Piety is putting God above everything else. *(page 59)*

precepts of the Church The precepts of the Church are the Church's teachings about our obligations. *(page 175)*

promised land The promised land is Canaan, the sacred place God promised to Abraham, Isaac, Jacob, and the Israelites in Egypt. *(page 71)*

prophet A prophet is a person sent by God to speak out against behavior that does not follow God's will. *(page 155)*

psalms Psalms are religious songs and prayers from the Old Testament. Psalms often express praise, thanksgiving, or sorrow. *(page 143)*

purgatory Purgatory is a final purification from sin after death. *(page 197)*

resurrection Resurrection is the new life given to us when our bodies reunite with our souls at the end of time. *(page 197)*

Revelation Revelation is God's act of revealing himself and inviting us to respond with faith. *(page 29)*

reverence Reverence is honor and respect. We can show reverence for God through our prayers. *(page 143)*

Sacrament A Sacrament is a sacred sign and cause of grace instituted by Christ in the Church to continue his saving action through the Holy Spirit. *(page 123)*

sacramental A sacramental is a symbolic prayer, blessing, object, or action instituted by the Church that can lead us to a fuller participation in the grace of the Sacraments. *(page 123)*

sacramental grace Sacramental grace is the unique gift of God's love that we receive in each Sacrament. *(page 133)*

sacrifice A sacrifice is an act of unselfish giving. It is also a ritual offering made to God by a priest on behalf of the people. *(page 39)*

Sadducees Sadducees were Jewish people who accepted only the written law of the Old Testament and rejected spoken teachings and tradition. *(page 207)*

Salvation Salvation is freedom from the pain of sin. *(page 155)*

Spiritual Works of Mercy The Spiritual Works of Mercy are loving deeds to meet the spiritual needs of others. *(page 217)*

supplication Supplication is humbly and earnestly asking for help. Like Esther, we address prayers of supplication to God. *(page 185)*

Temple The Temple was the Jewish place of worship in Jerusalem that contained the Ark of the Covenant. *(page 123)*

temple of the Holy Spirit Each of us is a temple of the Holy Spirit because the Holy Spirit dwells within us. As temples of the Holy Spirit, we are called to imitate Jesus. *(page 217)*

Theological Virtues The Theological Virtues—faith, hope, and charity—come from God and help us become more holy. They connect us with the Trinity. *(page 175)*

transubstantiation Transubstantiation is the sacred mystery in which bread and wine are changed into the Real Presence of Jesus Christ. *(page 265)*

Yahweh Yahweh is the most sacred name of God, spoken to Moses. It means "I am who I am." *(page 71)*

Index

Persecution of early Christians, 50, 198, 254

Persians, 175

Persistence, 185, 186

Personal sin, 272

Petition, 185

Pharisees, 206, 207

Piety, 59

Pius IX, Pope, 240

Plague, 70
  of death, 70, 79, 80, 81

Pope, 82, 111, 124, 254, 262
  Francis, 82, 83
  John Paul II, Blessed, 82, 254

Potiphar, 58

Prayer, 101, 200, 226–230. *See also* names of individual prayers.
  kinds of, 61, 62, 104, 158, 185, 227, 279

Precepts of the Church, 175, 276

Presentation of the Lord, Feast of, 243–244

Priests, 113, 124, 208, 256, 263, 267, 277, 278

Promised land, 71, 122
  conquest of, 100–101

Prophet, 155
  Elijah, 154
  Ezekiel, 174–175, 210
  Hosea, 154, 155
  Isaiah, 155, 164, 197
  Jesus Christ as, 155
  Micah, 154, 155
  Samuel, 112, 113
  Second Isaiah, 164, 165

Proverbs, 154

Prudence, 175, 271

Psalms, 142, 143, 144, 145

Purgatory, 197, 264

R

Rachel, 58

Rahab, 100, 101

Rebecca, 48, 49

Reconciliation, Sacrament of, 133, 175, 197, 207, 208, 266, 270

Red Sea, 70–71, 73, 74, 100, 122

Rehoboam, 154

Religious orders, 92, 113, 256, 277, 278

Repentance, 206, 207

Resurrection, 197, 252, 262

Revelation, 29, 51, 71, 175, 197

Reverence, 143

Rosary, The, 13

Ruth, 176, 177

S

Sabbath, 42, 52, 175, 187, 196, 225, 226

Sacramental grace, 122, 133

Sacramentals, 123, 126

Sacraments, 123, 133, 208, 265–267
  of Healing, 133, 175, 197, 207, 208, 266, 270. *See also* Anointing of the Sick, Penance and Reconciliation.
  of Initiation, 39, 49, 51, 122, 123, 165, 207, 208, 210, 265. *See also* Baptism, Confirmation, Eucharist.
  at the Service of Communion, 124, 208, 267, 278. *See also* Holy Orders, Matrimony.

Sacrifice, 38, 39, 40, 111

Sadducees, 206, 207

Saints and holy people
  André Bessette, 55
  Andrew Kim Taegon, 35
  Andrew of Phu Yen, Blessed, 171
  Benedict, 82
  Frances Xavier Cabrini, 97
  Francis of Assisi, 109, 114
  Francis Xavier, 151, 156, 157
  Franciscans, 114
  Pope Gregory the Great, 139
  Jerome, 20
  John Paul II, Pope, Saint, 82, 254
  John Vianney, 119
  Joseph, 25, 216, 244
  Josephine Bakhita, 203
  Laura Vicuña, Blessed, 129
  Lucy, 193, 198
  Martin de Porres, 67
  Mary, 29, 30, 49, 62, 81, 166, 216, 217, 223, 225, 236, 240, 242, 244, 257, 258, 262, 264
  Maximilian Kolbe, 161, 166, 167
  Missionaries of Charity, 218
  Monica, 181
  Paul, Saint, 29, 45, 50, 51, 217, 260, 268

Peter Claver, 68
Sharbel Makhlouf, 77
Solanus Casey, Venerable, 230
Teresa of Ávila, 87, 92, 94, 254
Teresa Benedicta of the Cross (Edith Stein), 254
Teresa of Calcutta, Blessed, 213, 218
  patron, 198

Salvation, 71, 155, 165, 175, 197, 260

Samuel (prophet), 112, 113

Sarah, 28, 29, 30, 238

Saul, 50. *See also* Paul.

Saul, King, 112, 113, 123, 132, 133

Scripture, 16–21, 29, 94, 101, 197, 219, 226, 260. *See also* Bible, Old Testament, New Testament.

Scripture stories,
  God's promise to Abraham, 28
  the near-sacrifice of Isaac, 38
  Jacob takes Esau's birthright, 48
  Joseph saves his brothers, 58–59
  Moses leads the Israelites out of Egypt, 70–71
  the Passover, 80–81
  Moses receives the Ten Commandments, 90–91
  the fall of Jericho, 100–101
  God calls Samuel, 112
  King David and Bathsheba, 132
  Adam and Eve disobey God, 132
  David praises God, 142
  the rule of King Solomon, 154–155
  Isaiah's prophecy, 164–165
  Ezekiel's vision of the dry bones, 174
  Esther saves her people, 184
  the Jews under Greek rule, 196
  John the Baptist preaches in the desert, 206
  the Boy Jesus in the Temple, 216
  Jesus teaches us how to pray, 226

Second Isaiah, 164, 165

Seder, 79, 83, 84

Shofar (ram's horn), 102

Sign of the Cross, The, 126, 265, 279

Sign of Peace, 269

Simeon, 244